Competitive Freedom versus National Security Regulation

COMPETITIVE FREEDOM VERSUS NATIONAL SECURITY REGULATION

Manley Rutherford Irwin

Q

QUORUM BOOKS
New York • Westport, Connecticut • London

Library of Congress Cataloging-in-Publication Data

Irwin, Manley Rutherford.
 Competitive freedom versus national security regulation / Manley
Rutherford Irwin.
  p. cm.
 Includes index.
 ISBN 0-89930-233-5 (lib. bdg. : alk. paper)
 1. Industrial laws and legislation—United States. 2. Trade
regulation—United States. 3. United States—National security—Law
and legislation. I. Title.
KF1600.I79 1989
343.73'08—dc19
[347.3038]   88-18254

British Library Cataloguing in Publication Data is available.

Library of Congress Catalog Card Number: 88-18254
ISBN: 0-89930-233-5

First published in 1989 by Quorum Books

Greenwood Press, Inc.
88 Post Road West, Westport, Connecticut 06881

Printed in the United States of America

The paper used in this book complies with the
Permanent Paper Standard issued by the National
Information Standards Organization (Z39.48-1984).

10 9 8 7 6 5 4 3 2 1

to Doris

Contents

Abbreviations

AT&T	American Telephone and Telegraph
BSPPD	Bell Systems Purchase Product Division
BTL	Bell Telephone Laboratories
CCEP	Commercial Communications Endorsement Program
CEO	Chief Executive Officer
CGCT	Compagnie Générale d'Electricité
COCOM	Coordinating Committee for Multilateral Export Control
CWA	Communications Workers of America
DEC	Digital Equipment Corporation
DES	Data Encryption Standard
DOD	Department of Defense
DRE	Office of Defense Research and Engineering
DTIS	Defense Technical Information Service
EDI	Electronic Data Interexchange
ELV	Expendable Launch Vehicles
EOSAT	Earth Observation Satellite Co.
FCC	Federal Communications Commission
GAO	General Accounting Office
GM	General Motors, Inc.
GNP	Gross National Product

HUD	Housing and Urban Development
IC	Integrated Circuit
ISDN	Integrated Services Digital Network
ISP	International Security Policy (Department of Defense)
ITAR	International Trade and Arms Regulation
MCTL	Military Critical Technologies List
NASA	National Aeronautics and Space Administration
NOAA	National Oceanic and Atmospheric Administration
NSA	National Security Agency
NSC	National Security Council
NSDD	National Security Decision Directive
NTIA	National Telecommunications and Information Agency
NTIS	National Technical Information Service
OTA	Office of Technology Assessment
PPG	Pittsburgh Plate and Glass
PTTs	Postal, Telephone, and Telegraph Agencies
RBOCs	Regional Bell Operating Companies
R&D	Research and Development
RTDNA	Radio/Television News Directors Association
VANS	Value-added Network Services
VSATs	very small aperture terminals

Preface

Every study has its roots in the past and this one is no exception. In 1972, the Federal Communications Commission (FCC) found itself engaged in a formal investigation of the American Telephone and Telegraph Company (AT&T) otherwise known as the Bell System. Some twenty-three affiliated Bell operating companies purchased the bulk of their telephone equipment from Western Electric, AT&T's manufacturing subsidiary. AT&T justified those purchases on economic grounds; Western Electric prices were low, its product quality unsurpassed, its technology without rival. According to Bell, the Manufacturing monopoly insured the telephone user of the best equipment and the best service at the lowest possible price.

To examine the premise and validity of Western Electric's performance, the Commission formed an AT&T Trial Staff. As Chief of the Western Electric Group, AT&T Trial Staff, I participated in that endeavor. The trial staff engaged in discovery, assembled evidence, and presented recommendations of fact and findings to an FCC administrative law judge. I testified on behalf of the trial staff and I recommended that the FCC adopt a policy of divestiture and competition in telecommunications manufacturing. All testimony is subject to vigorous cross-examination and my testimony was no exception. All told, I was on the stand for a week.

AT&T opposed a policy of competitive entry, a position that was both long-standing and predictable. But the Bell System was not alone in defending the monopoly. AT&T was joined by the Department of Defense. Defense not only rejected competition in the manufacturing sector of the economy, the department recommended that the FCC regulate the profits of Western Electric. As a policy option, the Department of Defense embraced commission regulation and rejected market competition.

That position provided the genesis of this book—national security as a new rationale for economic regulation. As this study suggests, national security as a justification for government intervention in the private sector is now generic—no longer confined to the Department of Defense alone. Other federal agencies have invoked national security as a policy rationale.

The draft of the manuscript was completed during a sabbatical from the University of New Hampshire in 1986-87. During that period and after, I received support from both Dean Carole Aldrich and Dean Kenneth Rothwell of the Whittemore School of Business and Economics. To them I express my appreciation. Nor would this study have been possible without the typing, editing, and patience of Maddy Piper, who was assisted by Sinthy Khounrasaphiphak. To both, my thanks and gratitude. Through it all, my wife stood by my side. To her, the book is dedicated.

Competitive Freedom
versus
National Security
Regulation

1

Introduction

The central policy issue of U.S. national security regulation is control versus freedom. Can national security be achieved through a policy of government control over private products? Or can national security be attained through a policy of competitive freedom?

This study attempts to grapple with two opposing forces confronting the U.S. economy today. On one hand, information technology is softening industry boundaries, diffusing across national borders, multiplying the number of competitive players, accelerating the rate of product introduction, contracting the rate of development cycles, and increasing the pace of product obsolescence.

On the other hand, the national security argument is regulating more and more private firms, commercial products, and international competitors. The national security argument regulates U.S. export of products and services, and U.S. imports of goods and resources. The rationale for such regulation is that technology transfer aids and abets our adversaries, the Soviet bloc. Consider recent competitive trends.

Technology is migrating and diffusing across more and more industries within the United States. The explosion of knowledge is such that no one industry possesses the exclusive hold of technology whether in genetic engineering, semiconductors, robotics, or fiber optics.

In addition, the market entry process introduces more competitors and more players into a given market or industry. Market entry is driven by a coalescence of telecommunications and computer industries as market boundaries intersect and overlap—pitting distant rivals into direct competitors.

Furthermore, the intensity of competition impels more firms to seize the corporate network as a competitive response—a strategy that proceeds in incremental steps. The firm may secure the components of a telecommunications network as a cost-saving exercise. Next, the firm resells excess capacity on its network to outside users and clients. Finally, the firm leverages the network to introduce value-added services to both existing customers as a means to tap new markets. In doing so, the firm crosses industry boundary lines and subtly redefines itself, its markets, its customers, and its rivals. The corporate network today represents still another dimension of the entry process.

Moreover, as technology integrates markets globally an internationalization of the entry process takes place. Geography no longer serves to protect or insulate the firm. A global constituency of players thus multiplies and increases, and places a premium on competitive flexibility, efficiency, and innovation. Whether measured by domestic or international standards, corporate performance assumes a new dimension of market assessment.

And finally, international rivalry activates and hastens product and service development. Today product life cycles of twenty to thirty years are an anachronism. Rather, global competition has expedited the rate of product introduction and the pace of product obsolescence. As one observer put it, "If you celebrate a new product announcement, you fall fifteen minutes behind your rival."

In sum, today's U.S. firm encounters global technological diffusion, global market entry, global market softening, spatial erosion, a multiplication of rivals and competitors, a quickening of product development, a contraction of product life cycles, and an acceleration of product obsolescence. It is in this global environment that we expect U.S. firms to not only compete, but to acquit themselves effectively on both price and nonprice dimensions of corporate conduct.

NATIONAL SECURITY REGULATION

Against this trend stands national security regulation. The invocation of unilateral federal oversight of private products in a world of competitive substitutes proceeds on the premise of static rather than dynamic change. Consequently, regulation ignores the fact that market entry is an ongoing process, both at home and abroad.

Regulation also tends to ignore the coalescence of markets, an environment of dissolving market distinctions between products, services, and industries. Market coalescence constitutes another form of market entry.

In addition, national security regulation often misperceives the global pervasiveness of technical know-how and expertise—from West to East, from developed to lesser developed nations. Brazil manufactures telephones, South Korea exports IC chips, India sells software, Peru manufactures personal computers, and China hoists satellites.

Also consider that security oversight usually prefers the monopoly solution to the competitive solution in U.S. telecommunications. The national security argument defends the incentives of cost-plus, monopoly in research, monopoly in manufacturing, and monopoly in service. In doing so, the national security argument opposes market diversity, market innovation, and market efficiency.

Furthermore, national security regulation has erupted as internecine warfare within the federal establishment over jurisdictional control of private corporations. The struggle over turf broke out first within the Department of Defense; it then proceeded between Defense and Commerce, Commerce and Customs, State and Defense, Commerce and State, the National Security Agency and the National Bureau of Standards, and so forth. In the world of integrated global markets, turbulent domestic restructuring, and international rivalry, Washington D.C. leisurely indulged in a civil war as each federal agency sought to out Pentagon the Pentagon. To a GS-15, time is a free good.

U.S. firms also witnessed more and more federal agencies demanding control, sanction, clearance, and enforcement over management's decisions to buy, sell, invest, or innovate. U.S. corporations found themselves attempting to resist micromanaging by the Department of Defense, the Department of State, the Department of Commerce, the National Technical Information Services, the National Oceanic and Aerospace Agency, and the Federal Communications Commission with little success.

In addition, export regulations continued to mount and pile up unilaterally. U.S. firms were told to monitor the sales of their overseas customers, the Department of Commerce was told to audit private firms and commercial sales, the Department of Defense was instructed to audit the Department of Commerce—all participants encircling one another as the U.S. high technology trade moved from surplus to deficit.

Recognizing that unilateral national security regulation penalized the competitive stature of U.S. firms, the federal government is nevertheless reluctant to abolish export or import controls. Rather, in the name of national security, the U.S. government elects to extend regulation to America's competitors—NATO countries; free world non-NATO nations; and now the newly industrialized nations of Taiwan, Singapore, South Korea, and Hong Kong. The United States is in the unseemly position of sponsoring, running, and policing an internationalized technological cartel among rivals and competitors.

As the government gained control over the managerial prerogatives or the private firm, corporations became subject to cost-price squeeze. Firms found that regulation diminished their exports as free-world customers "de-Americanized" their products. Firms found that the compliance cost of regulation privatized government regulation and put upward pressures on total costs. Dampened total revenues, inflated total costs, and squeezed earning threatened to curtail resources for future product development. As federal regulation of private products increased, European rivals marveled over what they perceived as the second coming of the Marshall Plan.

Moreover, federal agencies, witnessing the erosion of U.S. global positions in key products, elected to help U.S. firms through subsidies, consortiums, and the largess of the federal establishment. In the name of national security, major industries are invited to become wards of a beneficent state.

Finally, a policy that rewards our competitors at the expense of U.S. firms is grounded on political consensus. The political right favors export control, whereas the political left supports import control. The United States has fashioned a national security policy that serves to punish the U.S. firm in an environment of increased global risk, competition, and rivalry.

And what commercial products qualify as endowed with a national security component? Telephone equipment, telecommunications software, IC circuits, kidney dialysis equipment, rodent laboratory devices, and butcher gloves. In the future, a U.S. auto embedded with one thousand dollars worth of electronic equipment may very well qualify as a sensitive export product.

And what services merit national security oversight? The FBI recently interviewed public librarians in New York City and found that commercial on-line data bases of magazines apparently qualify as sensitive information. All of these policies proceed on the premise that national security interests of the United States can be found in control, audit, surveillance, enforcement, punishment, fines, and sanctions of private sector business.

A mixture of economics and armaments in public policy tends to be incompatible. Any policy that conditions export trade with Soviet conduct—linkage—is self-defeating and counterproductive. Better to have sent Stinger missiles to the Afghans in December 1979 than reward Komatsu pipelaying tractors at the expense of Caterpillar.

It is the thesis of this book that, in the long run, the answer to national security is economic freedom. Freedom of the firm to buy, sell, invest, embrace risk and entrepreneurship, develop new products, to be innovative, and to be accountable to the vicissitudes of the marketplace at home and abroad. Any policy of regulation that handicaps and punishes the firm in a global marketplace constitutes a self-inflicted handicap.

The contrast between global competition and national security regulation has not invited discussion or debate in the United States. Rather, a political consensus has evolved that mandates more control, less freedom, more oversight, and less vitality as the nation's resources are drained and atrophied by the police power of the federal government. In the long run, the opportunity cost of national security regulation will be a diminution of competitive vitality in the private sector. Ultimately, that diminution will compromise the national security of this nation.

2

Telecommunications Services

PREDIVESTITURE

The divestiture of the Bell System marked a watershed in U.S. telecommunications history. The break up of AT&T signalled the end of regulation in the traditional sense and unleashed markets, services, and networks of unprecedented dimension. Divestiture overturned decades of economic incentives that drove the industry. Before divestiture, cost-plus served as the guiding force in setting telecommunications prices and tariffs. Postdivestitute, cost reduction, and efficiency now dominate the players in U.S. telecommunications.

Divestiture has clearly altered the pace of product and service introduction. Prior to the breakup of AT&T, monopolies established the pace of new service offerings to the subscribing public. Today, market forces drive both the rate and direction of technological innovation. Before examining the environment of postdivestiture, it is instructive to look at the salient traits of U.S. telecommunications under regulation.

Before the breakup of AT&T, the Bell System provided most of the U.S. interstate toll services and the bulk of U.S. local exchange services. The so-called independent telephone carriers, which were largely rural carriers, provided the remaining local service. The Long Lines division of AT&T supplied both domestic and international telephone services; and AT&T's operating telephone subsidiaries, the twenty-three local Bell companies, operated in separate geographic areas throughout the country.

Under regulation markets were segregated between long distance and toll, business and residential, switched and dedicated, rural and city. Service classes were long understood and well-established, even though such demarcations were less than clear-cut. The telephone companies perceived toll rates as essentially price elastic, and over time, as rates were reduced, revenue flows expanded and grew. Local exchange rates, by contrast, were defined as insensitive to price changes. Over time, upward cost pressure on basic telephone service increased. But prices did not rise proportionately. Price adjustments were minimized by a complex division of revenues from toll users to local users. Under an assumed mandate of universal telephone service, state and FCC regulators encouraged the transfer of revenues from the long distance market to the local exchange market to minimize any rise of the latter. Thus the economies of toll service underwrote the capital intensity of local exchange equipment, whether central office or local loop plant. Flat rate local service was supported by time measured long distance service.

Given the absence of alternatives, telephone companies enjoyed an exclusive franchise. Naturally, they perceived marketing activities as a relatively passive exercise. AT&T or Bell organization charts did not include marketing at the vice-presidential level until the 1970s. Entry into long distance markets began to redefine marketing and, by the mid-1970s, identifying and responding to user changes became an explicit industry mandate.[1]

This is not to say that in an era of monopoly carriers do not solicit customers or market telephone use. But inasmuch as the telephone subscriber, business or residential, was devoid of any real choice, carriers were under little external pressure or penalty to anticipate corporate needs in the private sector. The telephone industry insisted that a homogeneous end-to-end network embodied sufficient flexibility to match the requirements of banking, retail, manufacturing, and distribution industries.

By definition, a monopoly franchise insures that carriers generate a reasonable return on their capital. To be sure, regulators monitored telephone service and facility quality with concern, dedication, and commitment. The problem was that any service benchmark established by the FCC resisted any external market test. Corporate standards for service were largely company-derived. Regulators thus assessed telephone company progress. Any question as to the quality of U.S. telecommunciations was met by the rejoinder: "Have you made a call in Paris?" One could only say that U.S. telephone service would be better today than yesterday, but probably less satisfactory than tomorrow.

Local exchange carriers were assigned geographic pockets of exclusive operation. State commissions, created to stand between a monopoly firm on one side and the subscribing public on the other, monitored the prices, service, investment, and budget allocations of the local franchise. Market forces in telecommunications were thought to be unworkable, inefficient, duplicative, and wasteful. Regulation, serving as a proxy for a competitive market, stood between the subscriber on one side and the carrier on the other side, insuring the user adequate telephone service at reasonable prices.

Commission regulation imposed a limit on corporate earnings; that is, a return on the company's investment, which is measured by an opportunity cost of capital. An ever vigilant Commission monitored telephone company earnings. Lower profits or high costs were compensated by higher rates imposed on the subscriber. Higher profits and low costs precipitated rate cuts. Whether costs were high or low, however, the carrier's return tended to be fixed and guaranteed. The result was predictable. Regulation anesthetized the carrot and stick of profit and loss. How, with assured profits, could a regulatory agent insure that a monopoly's performance was both progressive and innovative? The answer was never reassuring. What was perceived as a brilliant institutional solution to the natural monopoly problem in the long run proved to be elusive and frustrating to carrier and commission alike. But all agreed that private ownership was superior to government monopoly.

Under commission rule, telephone pricing became an exercise in cost-plus. The carrier summed its operating expenses, added up its outlays to supplies, legal fees, depreciation, maintenance, wages, salaries, and taxes—then passed operating costs forward as an allowable expense. Carriers expected to be compensated dollar for dollar for such expenditures.

Telecommunications constituted a capital intensive industry. The firm added up its capital outlays in customer equipment, central office hardware, transmission, equipment, and microwave as an investment base upon which the firm's owners were entitled to earn a return on that investment. The higher the investment, the higher the absolute earnings. Over time, regulation tended to sever or mute any connection between economic profit and corporate performance.

Rate cases took place to establish the reasonableness of operating expenses and to secure a proxy for the firm's cost of capital. Eventually, this exercise took on the order of a ritual. The carrier would file for a rate increase based on rising costs, equity and debt, operating expenses, depreciation, and taxes. (If revenues failed to cover expenses, the carrier risked loss of property without due process.) On the other hand, the commission's staff saw its mandate as refuting the assumptions of the carriers. Invariably, the commission's staff argued for a rate decrease.

By definition, rate setting constituted an adversarial process. Commission staff personnel challenged the carriers' proposals through the administrative hearings, dockets, briefs, testimony, cross-examination, final decisions, eventually spilling into judicial review. Then a subsequent rate case would begin anew.

In some instances, commissions concluded that the administration hearing process was exorbitant in time, resources, and costs. As an alternative, commissions elected to negotiate an appropriate rate with the carrier. A telephone company, for example, might request a $150 million rate increase. The commission's staff would seek rate reduction, whereas the commission would conclude that a $75 million rate increase was appropriate. Once the regulatory game became codified, the outcome held few surprises. In the end, parties, agency, and carrier achieved their goal. The carrier's financial integrity was protected and the commission (either FCC or state) informed the public it had forestalled extortionate rates. Due process replaced the marketplace. Thus was defined the public interest.

Service offerings to telephone customers were determined in large measure by the carrier's capital expenditures. User choices were obviously constrained and limited by hardware and software features of carrier equipment. In an environment insulated from market entry, equipment choice was defined as a prerogative of management. Telephone company management determined the introduciton of products and, ultimately, the retirement of equipment. Just as the carrier controlled the rate of product innovation, to a large degree the industry determined the rate of product obsolescence. Billions of dollars of investment decisions were committed under the aegis of federal and state oversight.

Yet commissions did influence and condition the pace of technological change. In a capital intensive industry, annual cost depreciation constituted a large percentage of the carrier's operating expense. Commissions found the conclusion irresistible that depressed depreciation expenses would hold down the revenue requirements of the telephone company and, as a result, reduce the prices to telephone subscribers. Accordingly, commissions insisted that equipment life and annual depreciation expense be stretched over as many years as possible—in some cases forty years. During that depreciation cycle, the carrier would generate sufficient revenues to compensate for the original capital investment. Then the capital investment cycle would begin again.

The premise of capital recovery was not totally invalid in an era of regulated monopoly. Clearly, the carriers exercised management discretion over the introduction and retirement of plant and equipment. Indeed, a central office switch installed in the 1920s in New York remained in service until the 1970s. Although technically and economically obsolete, the equipment worked mechanically. Subscribers lifting the handset still received a dial tone.

Not only did the carriers determine the technical change of product and hardware, telephone companies established the priority of plant introduction and installation. When, for example, should a new generation of central office hardware be installed? Within AT&T, which particular Bell operating company should receive a new digital multiplexing system, a new toll switcher, or a new PBX? With a plant investment of some $140 billion (1980s) it was incumbent that AT&T exercise some rationing process in order to determine the place and the time of plant introduction. Not every company would receive a new central office machine simultaneously.

Production capacity clearly forestalled such action. Accordingly, the Bell System strategy elected to place the development of digital switching hardware in large metropolitan toll centers. Eventually rural exchange subscribers would be able to secure comparable hardware. Investment installation thus approached a trickle down theory. By contrast, independent telephone industries, operating in the end office or rural areas, introduced digital switching equipment into their exchanges before many Bell operating companies.

The regulator's assumption of technological preeminence and exclusivity of the industry was not without merit. The research effort by Bell Laboratory, AT&T's research arm, was world renown. Its personnel, honored by Nobel awards, was at the cutting edge of virtually every facet of telecommunications technology. Bell Telephone Laboratories (BTL) personnel generated a patent a day. AT&T insisted that centralized, coordinated research was the optimum model to technological proficiency. The beneficiaries of that research productivity rebounded to Bell's local operating companies and ultimately the general subscriber.[2]

But what acted to spur research and innovation in a monopoly industry? The answer is that firms were self-sufficient, self-directed, and self-motivated. Market control, not market entry, best guaranteed economic efficiency. Monopoly, not competition, best insured technological progress. When, in the late 1960s and 1970s the FCC attempted to solicit entry in customer premise equipment, specialized and satellite carriers, an AT&T sponsored study cast doubt on any connection between competition and economic performance. Arthur D. Little observed that "competitive entry in the intercity microwave communications should not be justified on the expectation that a large increase in innovation shall result."[3]

POSTDIVESTITURE

The breakup of the Bell System separated AT&T from the ownership of its regional twenty-three Bell operating companies.[4] Regional Bell operating companies (RBOCs) have now recast the incentive systems of each operation. Postdivestiture AT&T retains its manufacturing affiliate, its research laboratory, and competes with satellite, microwave, and fiber optic carriers in a $50 billion long distance interexchange market. AT&T continues to operate its international telephone service, and is diversifying equipment production into both Europe and the Far East.

Today, intercity telecommunications is populated by MCI, Allnet, Sprint, satellite carriers, Contel/ACS, regional and national fiber optic networks, regional and national value-added companies, intelligent buildings, and private corporate networks. To be sure, AT&T remains the dominant player in the intercity market. Nevertheless, a postdivestiture world is no longer a monolithic, unified market in terms of facilities, features, or investment. At the same time, market entry has resulted in corporate consolidation, mergers, and even exit as players in the telecommunications industry undergo continual adjustment.

This churning of entry and exit has been accompanied by rate adjustments between toll rates and local exchange service. Since divestiture, toll rates are estimated to have declined by some 34 percent, local rates are said to have risen by over 40 percent. Entry has challenged and exposed long traditions of rate cross-subsidy. On the other hand, there is some dispute as to whether rate alignment is caused by divestiture or merely reflects inflationary costs.[5]

Market entry has impelled AT&T to reexamine the nature of its costs, prices, and marketing effectiveness. Through layoffs and early retirements, the company has reduced its three hundred and seventy thousand personnel to just under three hundred thousand. On several occasions, plant product equipment writedowns have been announced. Management tiers have been shrunk as AT&T endeavors to expedite its management decision-making process.

Today no single company in telecommunications exercises total exclusivity as to product and service innovation. Although AT&T remains the central player in intercity services, the company nevertheless has been under pressure to reevaluate the cost of its technology and operations. The company has quickened the pace of its plant investment. A company official observed that AT&T "just about completely rebuilt our network since divestiture almost three years ago."[6]

Accelerated innovation is also evident in subscriber terminal equipment, transmission apparatus, and central office systems. New entrants have challenged Bell's definition of basic telephone hardware, key telephone systems, PBXs, and automatic call directors. IBM's acquisition of Rolm and MCI has injected a competitive element in both service facilities and equipment. Clearly, the boundary lines between computers and telecommunications are overlapping. Today the telecommunications industry is pushing new generations of equipment, lower costs, more features, and lower prices while cutting maintenance and installation time.

The choices open to the business subscriber have necessarily expanded and multiplied under a competitive environment. Corporate customers now possess the opportunity to operate private digital transmission with ISDN (Integrated Services Digital Network) capability and features. In response, AT&T has introduced Megacom 800 software-defined networks as an alternative to corporate network ownership. Other carriers in intercity service have introduced comparable competitive services.

Some corporate users have elected to employ fiber optics and very small aperture systems (VSATs satellite dishes) as an alternative to carrier supplied toll switching and transmission services. AT&T has responded with T-1 links, dedicated subscriber access through the formation of their own subscriber networks. And as noted, AT&T's fiber optic network is two years ahead of schedule.

Corporate users can also elect to buy central office equipment with embedded and enhanced features. This investment permits users to bypass telephone facilities and directly links the corporate parent with subsidiary and remote locations. The carriers have responded by expediting the rate of digital service introductions under pressure to retain customers and maintain market share.

It was inevitable that innovation would spill into the international arena. Private fiber optic cable and satellite plants have been announced across the Pacific, Atlantic, and Caribbean basin. AT&T is not only in the process of installing an Atlantic fiber optic cable, but has also announced plans to construct a second cable.

What is the result of this point-counterpoint of product, service, and facility innovation? The answer, acknowledged by participants and observers alike, is that market entry yields more investment, new services, lower price, faster innovation, and accelerates responses to customer needs. Old depreciation schedules no longer suffice. Competition has precipitated a faster write-off of plant and equipment.

Recently, AT&T requested relief from traditional FCC rate base regulation. The FCC accommodated that request by proposing a price or rate cap on AT&T's services. Now efficiency can be rewarded with higher earnings rather than a guaranteed profit irrespective of corporate performance. Another area of regulation is replaced by market incentives. Competition has so revitalized telecommunications plant and equipment that *U.S. Business Week* was prompted to observe that "only three years ago (1984) advanced voice and data transmission made possible by fiber optic and digital switching seemed a decade away. Now it looks as if the majors will convert by 1988."[7]

THE REGIONAL BELL OPERATING COMPANIES (RBOCs)

A similar redefinition has visited the now divested regional Bell operating companies (RBOCs). True, the regional operating companies enjoy what many regard as a local loop monopoly. And interexchange carriers must pay in order to access local distribution facilities. Nevertheless, the regional Bell operating companies have felt it necessary to reorganize, cut costs, reduce personnel, contract decision cycles, or diversify into markets both within and outside the United States. Although the Modified Final Judgement, the settlement that governs the Bell operating diversification, precludes the companies from moving into toll service, equipment manufacturing and enhanced or information products, the regional companies seek relief from these restraints. And the regional Bell operating companies are not alone. "Freeing the BOCs" has generated support from the Department of Justice, the Communication Workers of America, the Department of Commerce, state public utility commissions, and the FCC.[8] Thus far, Judge Greene, the presiding judge, has relaxed information service as a source of RBOC diversification only.

A similar point-counterpoint of innovation is manifest at the Bell regional level as well. AT&T must pay the operating companies for local loop access, both at the origination and termination point; an expenditure that accounts for some 50 percent of AT&T's overall outlay. AT&T's customers, seeking ways to reduce costs, may circumvent AT&T in order to build their own terminal systems, whether digital termination operations, T-1 carrier, digital microwave, or fiber optics. To retain its customers, AT&T is offering its customers network-switched systems embedded with greater cost efficiencies. At the same time, AT&T is pressing the operating companies to reduce their access charges.

AT&T may choose to bypass RBOC's analog switches because of high cost, insufficient quality, and limited features. The operating companies must now find ways of retaining the patronage of their former parent. The result is predictable. The regional Bell operating companies are themselves pushing fiber optic networks, improving their plant efficiency, introducing ISDN capability, regenerating Centrex telephone services, reaching for lower costs, modifying pricing schedules in response to competition from both corporate users as well as intercity carriers.

At the same time, the regional Bell operating companies are vulnerable to rivals at the interconnect or the subscriber equipment market—PBXs with digital capability, new features, lower cost, located on the user's premises. And this equipment competes with the Centrex switching services of the Bell operating companies.

In the 1970s AT&T elected to deemphasize Centrex service as it pushed new generations of customer premise in PBXs. In a postdivestiture requirement, the Bell operating companies have rejuvenated Centrex investment in order to retain their business subscribers. In response to PBX rivalry, the regional operating companies have injected vitality into Centrex with enhanced features and least cost route capability.[9] The result has expedited innovation in customer premise equipment and has led to lower prices and new features as subscribers witness new options and choice.

Beyond the pressure for productivity, the Bell operating companies have introduced cellular radio systems and, through joint ventures, have diversified internationally. NYNEX (New York, New England Telephone Co.), for example, has applied to build a private fiber optic cable in the Atlantic basin to compete with AT&T's facilities; and Pacific Telesis is seeking to build a private fiber optic cable in the Pacific basin. Innovation point-counterpoint facilities and services have thus spilled over into the global markets and services as well.

In this counterpoint, each regional company is developing its own corporate identity, product definition, and market strategy. A growing diversity and pluralism in telecommunications research, investment, facilities, services, and marketing is now apparent. The RBOCs are no longer monolithic in attitude or response. Bellcore, established by the regional operating companies to secure a common reference case in terms of standards, engages in joint research and development for the regionals. Today the Bell regionals regard Bellcore as only one source of telecommunications R&D. Some Bell operating companies are establishing in-house research facilities.[10] Other corporations are securing proprietary research contracts to Bellcore. Still other RBOCs are buying research and development from the software industry, the computer industry, and the equipment industry.[121] Bellcore acknowledges the explosion of diversity in technology with the observation: "Technology is moving so quickly that we can't cover it all."[12]

At the same time, entry and competition have mandated that regional operating companies not only reassess their plant cost, but telephone buying practices as well. Before divestiture, as part of an integrated holding company, the Bell carriers took most of their hardware from their affiliate, Western Electric. Today, the regional Bell operating companies solicit, indeed demand, competitive bidding and choices in hardware. Ironically, the operating companies seek to engage in equipment manufacturing on grounds that there is insufficient rivalry and choice in large switching hardware and systems.

Some of the regional operating companies seek to approach total deregulation of their operations, specifically freedom from rate base economics, freedom to price according to market, and freedom to diversify, and generate earnings on the basis of market performance. True, not all regional Bell operating companies are willing to cash in their franchises. But there is evidence that more and more regionals are moving away from the public utility principle of cost-plus. Falling market boundaries, new customers, and revenues appear ever attractive and inviting.

Finally, the United States has unwittingly exported its model of telecommunications competition, deregulation, and market entry. Telecommunications systems are being privatized throughout the world—Britain, the Netherlands, Canada, Switzerland, Hong Kong.[13] Even France and West Germany are reevaluating telecommunications policy—and the European community has advocated outright deregulation. The process is discernible in newly industrialized countries as well. And with denationalization, a global trend toward relaxed restrictions, expanded service options, and a diversity in switching and transaction technology is now taking place.

U.S. telecommunications policy is being emulated in Europe, North America, and the Far East. The notion that a telecommunications monopoly, self-sufficient and alone, can perform effectively in price, cost, and innovation is now questioned on an international scale. As market entry sweeps the world, public and private telecommunications networks multiply and proliferate. With that proliferation, we witness a less inhibited flow of data, knowledge, and information.

SUMMARY

How can one summarize the postdivestiture era in U.S. telecommunications? Consider that market entry has realigned the pricing, costing, capital depreciation, and rate of return of U.S. telephone carriers. Toll rates have declined, local rates have risen, and the validity of tacit cross-subsidies is now in question.

In addition, the telephone companies have responded vigorously to an environment of competitive entry. Carriers have scrutinized their expenses, reduced their costs, and reevaluated organizational structure in order to achieve higher levels of efficiency, productivity, and responsiveness.

Also, the regional operating companies and AT&T, though still possessing elements of market power, are entering into a competitive arena. The regional operating companies are examining their investment, costs, and innovation record with an eye to improvement. Telecommunications innovation no longer resides within the confines of a single firm. Today, more and more carriers are pushing new hardware, features, and apparatus as the regional operating companies scramble to retain their corporate customers and sales revenues.

The regional operating companies are quickening plant introduction and modernization, prompting the carriers to reexamine traditional depreciation schedules and capital retirement plans. At the same time competition has enlarged the choices open to the subscriber, whether in PBXs, transmission, multiplexing, or software packages. The regional operating companies have both enlarged their access to research and development and broadened their buying options of equipment.

Furthermore, AT&T and some of the regional Bell operating companies have moved toward the status of total telecommunications deregulation. For AT&T, such a strategy may have been predictable if not inevitable. But some state commissions have been surprised to witness Bell operating companies insist that, in return for freedom from regulation and rate base constraint, they will forfeit their local exchange franchise.

Finally, the results of U.S. telecommunications deregulation have served as a policy model of emulation. Foreign nations are separating postal operations from telecommunications, privatizing telecommunications, and then introducing competitive market entry. International deregulation is being driven by the confluence of telecommunications and computers as market boundaries and industry demarcations soften and erode. If AT&T and the Department of Justice had not concluded the breakup of the Bell System in 1982, surely the imperatives of information technology would have mandated the demise of the private monopoly, public regulation model.

NOTES

1. Malcolm Gladwell, "By Passing Ma Bell's Orphans," *Insight* (September 15, 1986):10.

2. David Fishlock, "Mission Control for the New Wave," *Financial Times,* February 9, 1987, p. 10.

3. Dean Gillete, "Commentary on Innovation," *Bell Telephone Magazine* (January/February 1977):5.

4. See *United States vs. Western Elective Inc.* et al., *Order,* U.S. District Court, District of Columbia, September 10, 1987, Harold Greene, Judge.

5. James L. Lande and Peyton L. Wynns, *Primer and Source Book on Telephone Price Indexes and Rate Levels,* Industry Analysis Division, Common Carrier Bureau, Federal Communications Commission, April 1987; Robert W. Crandall, "Local Phone Rates Catch up with Costs," *Wall Street Journal,* February 27, 1987, p. 14.

6. Janet Guyon, "AT&T Plans to Defend its Long-Distance Turf," *Wall Street Journal,* November 21, 1986, p. 7.

7. "The Long Distance Wars Get Hotter," *Business Week* (March 22, 1987):151.

8. Leonard Heymann, "Greens Gets Pros, Cons of Freeing the BOC's," *Communications Week* (March 16, 1987):1.

9. Courtney A. Klinck, "Just When you Thought it Made Sense to Get Rid of Centrex. . . ," *Data Communications* (March 1986):118.

10. Dave Rounan and Leonard Heymann, "U.S. West Dislikes Policies, Threatens to Lease Bell Core," *Communications Week* (January 12, 1987):1.

11. Johnnies L. Roberts, "Growing Competition Among Regionals is Changing for Whom the Bell Toils," *Wall Street Journal,* April 8, 1987, p. 6.

12. "Why Regulate: A Global Survey," *Intermedia* (July/September 1987): 24-76.

13. Guy De Junguieres, "More Telecom Freedom Urged within Europe," *Financial Times,* May 29, 1986, p. 8; "Switzerland to Ease Monopoly on Telecoms," *Financial Times,* July 3, 1986, p.2.

3

Telecommunications Equipment

The contrast between a world of equipment regulation and a postdivestiture world is striking. Prior to the breakup of the Bell System, AT&T and the Bell operating companies were integrated into manufacturing through their subsidiary Western Electric. The vertical integration of telephone equipment manufacturing foreclosed the Bell market from competitive access and attenuated measures of corporate efficiency or innovation. A closed market constructed boundaries between telecommunications manufacturing and computer manufacturing; between the U.S. equipment market and overseas supply markets. Holding company control of telephone service and manufacturing invited regulatory surveillance over the latter, however indirect.

The postdivestiture world of telecommunications stands in sharp contrast. Vertical integration of local operating companies and the equipment manufacturing has now ended. The regional Bell operating companies can purchase hardware, equipment, and apparatus on the open market; equipment cost, price, and innovation are now measured by market standards. The boundary line between telecommunications manufacturing and computer products has coalesced and fused, global industry rivalry of equipment manufacturing and hardware has intensified, and market competition is now replacing regulation as a standard and measure for industry performance.

PREDIVESTITURE

Before 1984 AT&T, through the ownership of the twenty-three Bell operating companies and its manufacturing affiliate, Western Electric, was integrated into telephone service and telephone manufacturing. That ownership conditioned the buying practices of the Bell operating companies. Rather than solicit bids from outside or non-Western Electric suppliers, the operating companies took the bulk of their equipment, plant, products, and hardware from their in-house manufacturer.

Within this industry structure, Western Electric enjoyed a captive market for its supply and output. As part of the Bell System, Western was accorded exclusive access to the buying practices of the operating company, their plant and equipment forecasts. Western's plant tooled up and manufactured products to proprietary specifications established by Bell Laboratory, cleared by AT&T. Nonintegrated suppliers resided essentially as observers outside the holding company Bell family; no access to specs, plans, budgets, or Bell operating company product needs. Independent manufacturers viewed the Bell Western market as a closed market for all intents and purposes.

How did an integrated system perform within such a closed environment? Was Western Electric economically efficient? Was Western responsive and innovative? The answer was difficult to reach in an industry immune from any external market benchmark. AT&T's own studies concluded that Western enjoyed economies of scale, cost, and low price and that its equipment quality remained the standard of the telecommunications industry.[1]

Regulatory commissions requested that AT&T submit price studies comparing Western Electric's prices against that of other suppliers. Invariably these studies concluded that through a variety of products, telephone sets, PBXs, cable wireless, central office hardware, and transmission equipment, Western's prices were lower than those of general trade suppliers of telecommunications manufacturing.[2] Most state commissions accepted those studies as indication of Western's efficient and economic performance.

But was AT&T's captive supplier turning out new, progressive state of the art equipment and plants? Was Western Electric innovative and progressive as a manufacturer? The answer to this question was that Western Electric research and development was derived from Bell Laboratory, the premier research laboratory in the world. As its mandate Bell Laboratory not only designed high quality and reliable equipment, it also conducted research that was on the cutting edge of the telecommunications state of the art. Western Electric was the beneficiary of BTL's world renown reputation. In turn, Bell Laboratory's research and development was passed to the general subscribing public. AT&T's plant, equipment, and products derived from Western Electric, were in turn monitored by the preeminent laboratory in the world.

Few regulatory agencies possessed the temerity to question Bell Laboratory's engineering judgement or performance. Insulated from market entry and market competition, the telephone company essentially determined the introduction of products. The retirement of plant and equipment are all subject, of course, to regulatory oversight and approval. Private monopoly, utility regulation stood as the U.S. answer to wasteful competition.

In a predivestiture world, both telephone service and telephone manufacturing enjoyed a monopoly status. As noted, telephone service was regulated directly in terms of operating expense, plant, depreciation, and earnings on capital investment. Some state commissions attempted to impose limits on Western Electric's profits on grounds that the firm enjoyed risks no higher than that of the regulated utility. But those decisions were occasional and rare.

More important, a 1956 Consent Decree reinforced not merely the regulation of telephone plant and service, but resurrected a boundary between telephone manufacturing and computer manufacturing.[3] This decree ruled that Western could engage in no manufacturing activities unless its customers, the Bell operating companies, could offer the service as a regulated tariff activity. Stated in the negative, if a Bell operating company could not diversify the unregulated common carrier activities, then that boundary line, that restriction, that prohibition applied to Western Electric's portfolio of products as well. In a predivestiture world, the dichotomy between regulation and competitive markets applied with equal force to Western Electric's product line.

In a predivestiture environment, global manufacturing equipment markets were separate and separated. Western confined its sales largely to the domestic Bell operating companies. Bell's Northern Electric confined its sales largely to Bell Canada, although that soon changed. European manufacturers sold products to their parochial PTTs (Postal, Telephone, and Telegraph Agencies) and few European manufacturers, with the possible exception of ITT, entered the U.S. equipment market as alternative suppliers to Western or other domestic manufacturers. Similarly, Western Electric viewed the European and other continental markets as far removed from its strategic horizon.

Finally, utility regulation was an accepted institution in a predivestiture world. No one questioned regulatory oversight over natural monopoly in local or toll services. And regulatory authorities could, if necessary, disallow the cost of products flowing between a captive supplier and a captive buyer in the name of protecting the telephone subscriber. But, as noted, such disallowance seldom occurred. The equipment market in the United States enjoyed a unique status; Western enjoyed a monopoly that was unregulated by either market forces or direct commission oversight.

POSTDIVESTITURE

Although Western Electric and AT&T remained part of an integrated structure, the spin-off of the twenty-three Bell operating companies into seven regional companies has, in effect, separated local exchange service from telecommunications manufacturing.

The Bell operating companies are now free to secure equipment on the open market. With a large imbedded base of Western Electric hardware, AT&T Network Systems (formerly Western Electric), still holds 50% of the Bell operating company equipment market. Nevertheless, divestiture has opened a market long perceived as off limits by outside manufacturers.

The Bell operating companies clearly inhabit a world of choice and option. Some industry observers suggest the Bell operating companies, restive in a predivestiture world, are today acting "like kids in a candy store."[4] From the perspective of the outside manufacturer, divestiture has served to create opportunities for equipment access and market entry.

A postdivestiture world has erected a new meausre of market efficiency. Manufacturing costs have fallen. That in turn has precipitated price declines in equipment and hardware. For example:

- central office exchanges have dropped in price from nine hundred dollars a line to three hundred dollars in the past five years.
- fiber optic repeater distances have increased from ten to thirty miles over the past five years.
- satellite terminal prices have declined from twenty thousand dollars to two thousand dollars in the past five years.
- PBXs, key telephone systems and telephone station equipment has also dropped in price dramatically over the past several years.[5]

The adjustment to entry and access has not been without trauma to AT&T Technologies, however. The company has reduced production costs, shut down six manufacturing plants, moved some production offshore, consolidated its distribution system, farmed out products to other suppliers, written off inventory as obsolete, realigned management, and accelerated its decision-making process.[6] Inevitably, as the company has reached for higher levels of efficiency, reorganization, and restructuring, the company has experienced layoffs and downsizing.[7]

Market competition also has affected manufacturing life cycles. Where once Western Electric, in conjunction with AT&T and Bell Laboratory, exercised sole discretion over the innovation process, a postdivestiture world reveals that market forces now propel the innovation process. Compressed development cycles have altered the cultural environment of Bell Laboratories—imposing such alien issues as profitability and market performance in a world of competitive alternatives.[8] Patent accumulation alone may no longer suffice as an index of commercial success. Indeed, Bell Laboratory transferred its academic journal on the economics of regulation to the Rand Corporation.

A postdivestiture world has also expedited the coalescence of computer and telecommunications markets. IBM, for example, now manufactures a variety of telephone subscriber equipment and switching hardware; AT&T Technologies now manufactures personal computers and mini-computer systems.[9] A postdivestiture world has freed AT&T to move into the world of computers and data processing, inviting IBM to position its manufacturing to the needs of telephone subscribers and operating companies.

Manufacturing coalescence has spilled into the international arena as well. Although in a predivestiture world telecommunications supply is often national and parochial, a postdivestiture world suggests an environment of open rivalry among offshore competitors. European suppliers have now penetrated the U.S. market and AT&T is diversifying into Europe and the Far East.[10] In the meantime, both product, industry, and spatial barriers continue to erode over time.

Finally, few state commissions today in the United States define manufacturing as a candidate for utility oversight. Regulation as a surrogate of equipment manufacturing clearly belongs to another era. Today equipment manufacturing is driven by market forces and market performance.

In sum, a postdivestiture world is one of entry, rivalry, borderless products, borderless markets, and international competition. Entry in manufacturing is now a global phenomenon, limited not merely to North America, Europe, or Japan. Today entry into telecommunications equipment is erupting in Brazil, India, and South Korea. And in the process, telecommunications equipment, computer hardware, IC circuits, and software packages are becoming indistinguishable.

NOTES

1. James R. Billingsley, *Values of Vertical Integration in the Bell Systems,* Wisconsin Telephone Company, Sixth Annual Seminar on Economics of Public Utilities, Oshkosh, Wisconsin, March 8, 1973, p. 23.

2. Ibid., p. 19.

3. Hearing Before the Antitrust Subcommittee (subcommittee No. 5) of the Judiciary, House of Representatives, *Consent Decree Program of the Department of Justice,* 85th Cong., 22d sess., April 15, 1958, 2, Vol. 2, p. 2,593.

4. "A Scramble to Supply the New Phone Companies," *Business Week* (December 5, 1983): 180.

5. *Assessing the Effects of Changing the AT&T Antitrust Consent Decree,* NTIA Trade Report, Department of Commerce, February 4, 1987, p. 21.

6. Anna Zornosa, "AT&T to Lay off 27,000 and Write Off 3.2 Billion to Reshape and Refocus," *Communications Week* (December 22, 1986): 2; "Why AT&T Isn't Clicking," *Business Week* (May 19, 1986): 89; Janet Guyon, "AT&T Ratings on Debt Issues Cut by Moody's," *Wall Street Journal,* February 27, 1987, p. 4.

7. *The Communications Industry,* Focus: The Northern Trust Company, July 31, 1986, p. 2.

> We believe AT&T faces three very difficult problems: 1) The company is engineering, not market or customer oriented; 2) The company lacks direction in its technology products area; and 3) Production costs are estimated to be too high by one third to compete successfully long term against major U.S. rivals (and higher yet versus Asian competition).

8. Michael Schrage, "Bell Labs is Long on Genius But Short in the Marketplace," *Washington Post,* March 1, 1987, p. H1.

9. Paul Duke and Dennis Kneale, "Compaq, AT&T Introduce Computers: Both Face Tough Competition," *Wall Street Journal,* February 18, 1987, p. 8.

10. John Gosch, " 'Siemens' Changing From a Tortoise to a Hare," *Electronics* (June 2, 1986): 38; Beth Kralin, "Battle Lines Drawn in World Phone Market," *Wall Street Journal,* April 6, 1984, p. 34. "AT&T Starts to Lose Its Innocence Abroad," *Business Week* (July 22, 1985): 30.

4

Networks as Corporate Strategy

Before the divestiture of AT&T, the telecommunications choices open to the firm, circuits, switching, terminals or software, were necessarily limited and constrained by monopoly and regulation. In an environment of competition, however, network options today are growing if not proliferating. For many firms, the network is emerging as a competitive response and an explicit competitive strategy. To examine the evolution of this strategy, we address the network as an internal response, an external response, and as a spatial or global corporate response. We suggest that an internal corporate strategy represents several dimensions of the entry process, namely telecommunications bypass, capacity reselling, third-party networks, and customers posing as rivals and competitors.

We conclude that in turn market entry alters the environment within which the firm operates and intensifies the degree of market competition. We also concude that the network invites the firm to redefine its customers, suppliers, and competitors.

THE NETWORK AS INTERNAL STRATEGY

In a world of deregulation, business firms confront at least three options for their network requirements. A first is the leased circuit or dedicated line choice. Here the firm rents local and toll switching transmission facilities, hardware, and equipment from the telecommunications carriers on an exclusive use basis. These networks can be employed for voice, data, or graphic transmission requirements. Dedicated networks did exist prior to the divestiture of the Bell System, but the equipment, features, and transmission alternatives open to the firm on a lease basis have expanded dramatically in an environment of deregulation.

The *T-1 lease line* has become a common choice for many corporations, becaue of its capacity and unit cost savings.[1] T-1 lease lines connect corporate headquarters with subsidiaries and affiliates and accommodate a mix of voice, data, and video transmission. Prior to the breakup of the Bell System, T-1 lines were confined essentially to the internal requirements of the carriers. Today carriers have introduced T-1 transmission service to corporate subscribers as a component of dedicated circuit use.

A second network choice permits the firm to own and purchase telecommunications equipment rather than lease circuits from the carrier industry. As a result, the firm operates its own internal corporate network. One advantage of the ownership option is that it permits the firm to circumvent the capital investment of the carriers as well as to avoid rising tariff costs and prices. Once a firm secures its own telecommunications equipment, the corporation abandons the investment of the carrier industry, and in the nomenclature of the industry engages in telephone bypass.

Firms may, for example, purchase satellite dishes called VSATs (very small aperture terminals) as one such telecommunications bypass alternative. The VSAT network permits the firm to connect disparate locations, and enables a corporate headquarters to coordinate information flows between and among divisions, subsidiaries, and affiliates. The VSAT choice is driven by the economics of owning a system versus leasing facilities from the carriers. And the VSAT choice may not be unattractive to some users. It is estimated that a VSAT network cost may average between three to four hundred dollars per month, versus a five hundred to eight hundred dollar per month carrier lease facility cost.[2]

Other firms link their operations through terrestrial microwave distribution as another form of telecommunications bypass. Still other corporations construct fiber optic networks as a choice, particularly if the firm is fortunate enough to own its own right of way. As expected, pipeline companies, railroad carriers, canal firms, and electric power utilities have developed fiber optic networks as an internal corporate strategy.

A third corporate strategy combines both carrier facilities and user-owned telecommunications, an option known as the *hybrid approach.*[3] Here the combination of lease facilities and equipment hardware are governed by the relative cost, usage, and needs of each corporate operation. A firm may elect to construct its own local distribution network but choose to rent or lease toll facilities from telecommunications companies; or the firm may invert the process if the economies of network ownership and leasing change. In any case, by definition, hybrid networks are configured as a function of the distribution requirements of each firm and the cost tradeoffs of owning versus leasing.

An internal corporate network enables a firm to coordinate a variety of activities—research, development, training, manufacturing, sales, or financial control. Several examples point to the potential for such application. K Mart, the retail chain, has erected a VSAT network for inventory control and point-of-sales device credit verification; Hewlett-Packard employs its network for corporate training and development; the convenience store chain 7-11 is employing VSATs to facilitate point-of-sales data and inventory order and control; Days Inn operates its own hotel reservations system through a VSAT network; Citicorp owns its own satellite to facilitate the transfer of credit card data from Sioux Falls, South Dakota to the bank's New York City headquarters; Merrill Lynch, in a joint venture, operates its fiber optic network within downtown Manhattan; Sears Roebuck combines both fiber optics and satellites to tie together some seven hundred odd stores, insurance, real estate, and brokerage operations.[4]

Corporate telecommunications networks have penetrated a cross-section of U.S. industries—banking, manufacturing, finance, brokerage, retail, insurance, air cargo, coal, rail. Such networks serve to reduce costs, coordinate intrafirm activities, expedite corporate responsiveness to product shifts, and augment a firm's marketing effort. As competition and technology interact, and as the number of equipment and hardware choices multiply, such options encourage the firm to consider the network as an explicit competitive response in an environment of increased competition.

THE NETWORK AS EXTERNAL STRATEGY

By contrast, an external strategy permits the firm to reach beyond its own manufacturing and customer applications. Here the network acts to supplement the revenues of the firm by inviting telecommunications use external to the corporate family. External strategy carries at least three components: capacity resell, customer bonding, and supplier linkage.

Capacity Resell

Selling excess network capacity is a natural extension of any corporate investment in telecommunications facilities. As frequently happens, any network may not operate at full capacity every hour of the day; or the network may experience excess capacity during all hours of the day. In any case, selling excess capacity to outside customers is an inviting as well as an incremental step. The network stands underutilized. Additional revenues from outside clients add to the cost-effectiveness of the firm's original make-buy decision.

In some instances, the firm may actually spin off its in-house network operation and form a separate affiliate with profit and loss responsibility. Once done, this new affiliate ironically finds itself competing with its former supplier, the telephone carrier.

Several examples point to this internal–external transition. Sears Communications Corporation advertises that it can provide user service requirements "across the entire spectrum of a client's telecommunication requirements."[5] That an external strategy is an extension of an in-house capital investment can be seen by the recent observation of a Sears employee: "Since we have invested in the expertise and a huge geographic distribution network, we felt we were in a good position to sell customers with ten to one thousand locations across the United States."[6]

The General Motors hybrid network illustrates the inviting prospect of selling excess capacity. The GM telecommunications network covers some 40 states, links some 250 thousand telephones, coordinated by some 500 telephone switches. General Motors not ony sells excess capacity on its network system, the company persuaded Holiday Inn to transfer its nationwide reservations system from Bell's leased lines to General Motors' private network.[7] Presumably, Holiday Inn switched its service to General Motors because of attractive price discounts.

Other firms sell excess capacity as well. Merrill Lynch is doing so via its fiber optic network in downtown New York. Recently Merrill Lynch formed a joint telecommunications venture through a fiber optic network and is diversifying into the Boston area.[8] In a sense, Merrill Lynch finds itself competing with both the New York Telephone Company and the New England Telephone Company. Federal Express and 7-11 have expressed interest in capacity resale. American Airlines operates AT&T's telemarketing program, a case where a buyer evolves into a competitor and then converts itself into a supplier.

Customer Bonding

A second external strategy permits the firm to link its corporate network to its users and customers as a means of differentiating its services from its rivals and competitors. In this way, a network coordinates computer to computer exchange of inventory, invoices, bills of lading, electronic mail, or electronic data interexchange. The latter, electronic data interexchange, permits the firm to reduce the inventory costs to its customers and to quicken the supply response to users' sales.

General Motors, for example, connects its corporate headquarters to some ten thousand auto dealers.[9] American Airlines has added software, financial, and accounting programs to its eight thousand travel agent users, leveraging its network to make available software programs and word processing services. Food wholesale and manufacturing firms employ networks to quicken their response to the inventory requirements of the retail and distribution outlets. Pharmaceutical firms place computer terminals on their customer premises to facilitate the order and attainment of pharmaceutical products.[10] Electronic Data Interexchange (EDI) is finding applications from railroad to trucking, plastic manufacturing to maritime industry, or automobile manufacturing to food retail.

Clearly, as a customer bonding vehicle, the corporate network accelerates the firm's response time to the delivery requirements of its clients. But that response carries a ripple effect. As one firm secures a competitive advantage in delivering electronic invoices, competitive firms' rivals are compelled to follow suit. The result is a generalized adaptation of new network facilities and use among more and more firms and industries.

Supply Linkage

Another specie of an external network permits the firm to link its operations to parts components, subsystems, and financial suppliers. Here the network enhances firm responsiveness to customer needs by extending that coordination deeper into its chain of suppliers. K Mart, for example, is pushing electronic data interexchange between some eight thousand suppliers and K Mart's retail stores.[11] General Motors has designated some eight banks to whom it will engage in electronic payments for some $4 billion monthly of its supply bills.[12] EDI thus migrates not merely from firm to customer, but from firm to customer's bank. Electronic transmission as a paper substitute promises to reduce costs, expand inventory turnover, and increase corporate revenues simultaneously.

Failure of an individual supplier to accommodate this information automation and financial document flow can carry a severe penalty. When the Mellon bank refused to adapt its computer payment system to Pittsburgh Plate and Glass, a supplier to General Motors, PPG shifted its account to the Pittsburgh bank and the Mellon bank lost a critical corporate account.[13]

A similar ripple effect is evident in the automobile industry. If one firm enjoys lower costs and fast responsiveness through supplier linkages, that benchmark impels competitors to replicate the same economies and the same user flexibility. A General Motors move toward EDI inspires Ford Motor Company and Chrysler to engage in the same process. Or as K Mart pushes electronic data interexchange, Penny's is not far behind.

Clearly the growth of computerized transactions between suppliers and firms spreads and migrates beyond inventory control. If an automobile manufacturer depends on some four thousand part suppliers then a supplier firm linkage migrates from the electronics industry to plastics, from chemical to textiles, from financial institutions to steel manufacturing. Thus firm–supplier linkages cut across diverse and seemingly unrelated industries. Indeed, EDI growth is expected to gain momentum as more and more industries recognize the cost economies of paperless transactions.[14]

SPATIAL STRATEGY

Corporate networks can circumvent spatial or geographic barriers to market entry. Citicorp, for example, employs credit card data, as we have noted, from South Dakota via its own satellite to New York.[15] *USA Today* employs its own satellite network to tap into thirty remote printing sites and thus establishes a national newspaper readership. Reservation systems for auto and hotel firms are network dependent and indispensable as an asset to gain spatial access.

If corporate networks embody a domestic transparency, in a global sense, they are equally distance insensitive. Thus banks, manufacturing, foreign exchanges, and equity markets underscore the critical role of the network as an informational infrastructure. As a mirror image of the domestic counterpart, global networks enable the firm to bond closer to its overseas suppliers and subcontractors. Texas Instruments, for example, imports software from India. The *Financial Times* uses satellites to tap into U.S. readership and *USA Today* penetrates both European and Asian markets via satellite relay. To repeat, the network as a spatial strategy enables the firm to establish connections between customers and suppliers on a global as well as a domestic basis.

IMPLICATIONS OF CORPORATE NETWORKING

What economic implications ride on the corporate network, whether internal, external, or spatial? Certainly, one spin-off of the network is that it constitutes a specie or form of market entry. When a firm invests in its own telecommunications switching, transmission, and software investment, the firm is vacating the capital investment of the telephone industry. Telecommunications bypass constitutes a form of entry and competition.

A buyer is now converted into an in-house supplier of telecommunications services. And the telecommunications carrier must view that transition with some apprehension. Indeed, entry impels the carrier to examine the validity of its own investment, hardware, cost, prices, and marketing endeavor.[16] One by-product of the corporate network both expands the telecommunications equipment market, and spurs plant innovation and efficiency decisions by the incumbent carriers. In short, as a form of market entry corporate bypass fosters and encourages carrier progressiveness.

Once a firm decides to resell excess capacity, the firm has altered and transformed its economic status. The firm has moved from a customer to a competitor of the carrier industry. Here market entry is direct and immediate. When for example, a General Motors, a Merrill Lynch, a Federal Express, or a Minnesota Electric and Power Company begins to sell excess telecommunications capacity, these strategies pose as a direct alternative to the carrier facilities and services.[17] Not only are more choices available to the public, but market entry has broadened telecommunications competition across the board. Thus capacity resell adds still another dimension to the degree and intensity of market competition.

As companies employ the network to accommodate their response to customer needs or to coordinate output with suppliers input, that strategy generates opportunities for third-party networks. Here firms create software interfaces that permit document exchange of incompatible computer systems. General Motors, General Electric, IBM, McDonald Douglass, and a host of software and hardware submarket manufacturers are introducing third-party networks through VANS—Value-Added Network Services.[18] That entry in turn generates new services, suppliers, software, a non-zero-sum game that broadens the options and revenues to all participants, carriers, firms, suppliers, and customers.

Finally, spatial networks erode distance or geography as a barrier to the entry process. U.S. firms are selling commercial data bases in Europe and Asian firms deliver newspaper to the United States by satellite. The London *Financial Times* is imported by satellite relay, and indeed the *Queen Elizabeth II* considered having satellite dishes for daily printing of the *Financial Times* on board as it travels from New York to London. Satellite and optic fiber transparency invites a globalization of newspapers, data, and information transfer.

Telephone bypass, capacity resell, value-added carriers, and global market penetration represent different aspects of the same entry process. The corporate network, in short, has internationalized the perception of cost, innovation and carrier responsiveness to new markets and customer usage.

It is a cliche to suggest that any corporate network infrastructure generates market interdependence. Financial flows, debt equity, and foreign exchange rates travel the speed of light. Information transparency does tend to subject government policies to a new and harsh benchmark, namely, foreign policy alternatives. U.S. tax policy on corporate borrowing, for example, in the 1960s expedited the movement of bank loans offshore to the European money market.[19] Today, the phenomenon of *stateless cash*, regulated and controlled by no individual nation, consists of buyers and sellers connected by computers, satellites, and customer-owned terminals. Such exchanges pump billions of dollars between banks and their corporate clients within microseconds. That networks interconnect markets is a tautology, but the reality of global transactions can be disconcerting. A rumor on the Tokyo money market precipitated a $15 billion withdrawal from Chicago's Continental Illinois within two weeks—an international bank run that ultimately resulted in the nationalization of the Chicago bank.[20]

October 19, 1987 has been described as the first global referendum as a commentary on the U.S. inability to deal with its twin deficits. Here networks—corporate, carriers, or hybrid—reinstate the transparency and interdependence of global markets and information flow.

As international markets coalesce, as market boundaries soften, as industry boundaries intersect, as the firm–supplier relationship is recast, the entry process continues as an institutional given. Corporations begin to reassess themselves, to redefine their markets, customers, and competitors. Today, manufacturing firms are moving into telecommunications; banks are diversifying into securities; consumer retail firms are moving into financial services; and local telephone companies are diversifying into corporate banking (see Table 4.1).[21] In a sense, the network serves as both a cause and an effect; a subtle transformation in the definitional content of the corporation. In another sense, the network is becoming a timeless, transparent global market. That development holds new opportunities as well as a new degree of international and domestic competition.

Table 4.1
Corporate Redefinition

	Old	New
General Motors	autos	home mortgages
		telecommunications
American Airlines	airline	education and training
		electronic freight tracking
Texas Air	airline	telecommunications
Sears	retailing	banking
		brokerage
		telecommunications
K Mart	retailing	financial services
7-11	convenience store	financial services
Federal Express	package delivery	telecommunication services
Citicorp	loans	investment banking
		stock quotation
Ford Motor Co.	auto	global shipping services
Merrill Lynch	brokerage	telecommunications
Pacific Telesis	telecommunications	investment brokerage
Sea Land	ocean shipping	telecommunications

NOTES

1. Josh Gonzo, "Purolator Changes Net Path," *Network World* (July 20, 1987): 1.

2. Jay C. Lowndes, "Corporate Use of Transponders Could Turn Glut to Shortage," *Aviation Week and Space Technology* (March 9, 1987): 122.

3. Mary Johnston, "How to Grow A Hybrid," *Network World* (August 3, 1987): 25.

4. Robert A. Bennett, "Citicorp's Satellite Challenge," *New York Times,* March 24, 1983, p. 1.

5. Sears Roebuck & Co., *Introducing Sears Company, The New Force in Telecommunications Service*, 1985.

6. Pam Powers, "Sears Resells Excess Space on its SNA Net," *Network World* (March 23, 1987): 8.

7. Kathleen Healy, "Thank You for Using Westinghouse," *Forbes* (November 30, 1987): 208.

8. Karyl Scott, "Merrill Lynch, Fidelity Team for Bypass Net," *Network World* (February 29, 1988): 1.

9. Leonard Hagmann, "EDS to Build General Motors a Dealer Satellite Net," *Communications Week* (October 19, 1987): 63.

10. Peter Keen, *Competing in Time* (Cambridge, Mass.: Ballinger, 1986), 46.

11. Tony Seideman, "K Mart Suppliers Get Word: Automate," *Journal of Commerce* (December 16, 1987): 1.

12. Tom Ferris, "How GM's Payment Network Will Communicate Data to Eight Banks," *American Banker* (October 12, 1986): 1.

13. B. B. Wallace, "EDI Gives Competitive Edge," *Network World* (June 8, 1987): 326; Jim Brown, "Banks Increase Use of EDI," *Network World* (January 25, 1980): 82.

14. David Meyer, "EDI Use to Double Yearly," *Communications Week* (September 28, 1987): 20.

15. Mary Galligan, "South Dakota's New Love Affair with Big Banks," *US News and World Report* (January 30, 1984): 4.

16. "The Rewiring of America," *Business Week* (September 15, 1986): 188.

17. Bill Richards, "Minnesota PTC Explores Joint Venture to Create Telecommunications Network," *Wall Street Journal*, December 14, 1984, p. 17; "Fiberoptics Network uses Former Oil Pipelines," *Journal of Commerce* (April 14, 1988): 3A.

18. Tony Seideman, "Data Technology Comes of Age as Action Supersedes Theory," *Journal of Commerce* (December 3, 1987): 1.

19. Adrian Hamilton, *Financial Revolution* (New York: The Free Press, 1986), 54.

20. "U.S. Throws Full Support Behind Continental Illinois in Unprecedented Bailout to Prevent Crises," *The Wall Street Journal*, May 18, 1984, p. 3.

21. Peter Wilson-Smith, "Master of Change Welcomes City's Inevitable Revolution," *London Times*, December 14, 1984, p. 27.

5

Firm Entry as a Process

Firm entry intensifies market competition and market competition accelerates price and nonprice rivalry. Both processes place a premium on the firm's ability to adopt new manufacturing techniques and to institutionalize product introduction. An environment of intensified rivalry carries several consequences; the coalescence of products, the technical infusion of products, a contraction of product development time, a shortening of product life cycle, and an acceleration of both innovation and product obsolescence. Consider the process of shifting comparative advantage.

SHIFTING COMPARATIVE ADVANTAGES

Firm entry on a global basis reflects shifts in comparative advantage over time. The process can be segregated into several stages (see Figure 5.1). A first stage begins with a domestic product supplier (F). The domestic firm buys input resources from domestic suppliers (S) and combines resources into final products—the typical relationship between buyer and seller. In the past, the S-F relationship has tended to be stable and long-standing.

However, domestic firm F must constantly monitor its options for low cost factor inputs. That scrutiny invites the firm to consider the alternative prices offered by the offshore supplier S'. If offshore suplier S' can deliver parts and components cheaper than S, its domestic counterpart, or if the quality of the offshore firm exceeds that of the domestic supplier, then the offshore firm wins the bid to supply subsystems.

A third stage is discernible when offshore supplier S' acquires technological know-how, capital, labor expertise, management talent, and

Figure 5.1
Entry Process Evolution

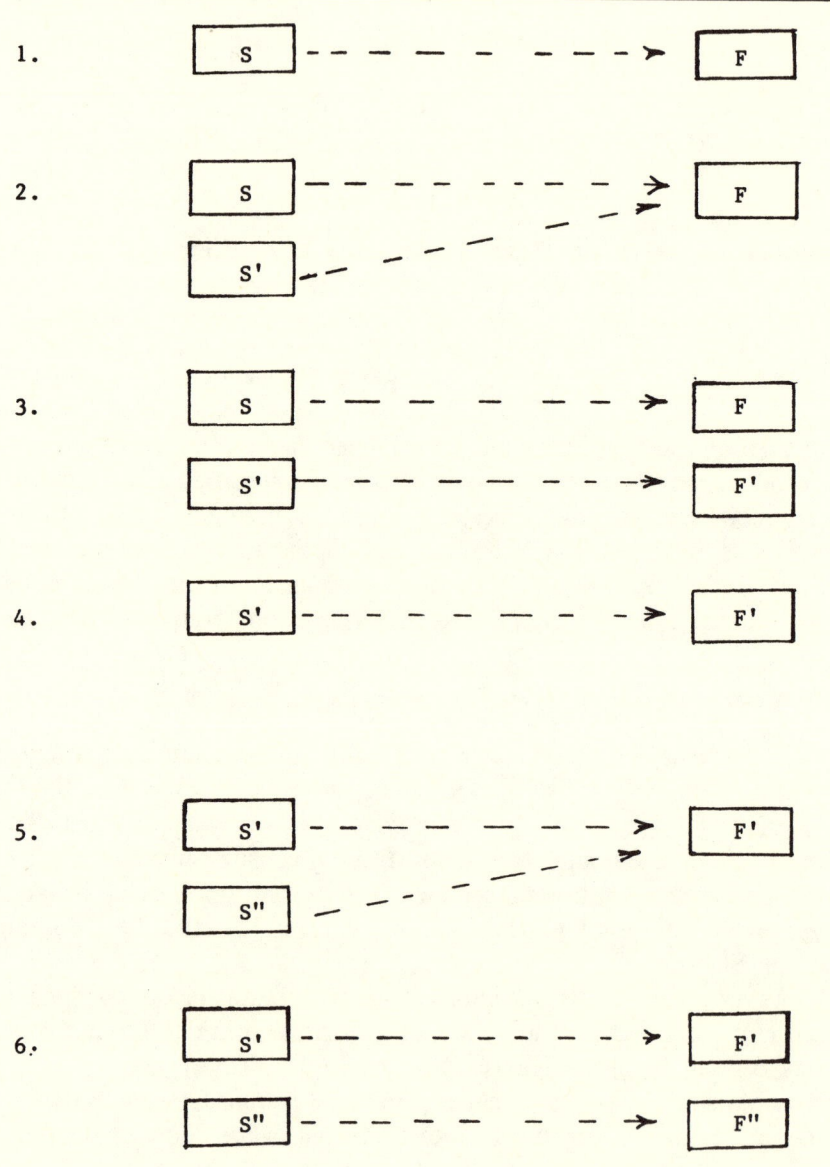

financial resources. Final product design and manufacturing beckons. The offshore supplier becomes restless in the role of subcontractor. Eventually the offshore supplier S' driven by the incentives of added value and higher profits integrates forward from component to total system or product manufacturer, F'. Firm F now confronts the old supplier, not as a subcontractor or a resource supplier, but as a direct and immediate competitor and rival (F'). $F's$ new status enhances, multiplies, and intensifies the competition to F.

A fourth stage is a replay of the first stage. Here offshore firm F' converts its domestic inputs into a product or service output. Again the firm constantly scans the resource environment for further cost reduction opportunities. Such a search reaches beyond domestic affiliates or suppliers. It can lead to an examination of offshore sourcing, S''. Once located, the firm either moves its parts plant to another country or perhaps shuts down its integrated affiliate and throws orders to an offshore supplier—stage five.

Finally, a sixth phase, analogous to the third entry phase, finds offshore supplier S'', acquires the skill to integrate forward into final product assembly, or F''. Once completed, the input supplier converts itself from a lower level of the production chain to a direct competitor of its former client (F'). Now both firm F and F' confront competition from F''.

This comparative advantage evolution carries with it both a geographic and a product dimension. Geographic out-sourcing of factor inputs is an experience common in the United States, whether U.S. components are secured from Brazil, Mexico, Japan, or South Korea. The search for input out-sourcing may be driven by wage rates, exchange rates, enhanced productivity, or superior work ethic. Whatever the driving force, shifts in relative input costs prompt the firm to embrace opportunities for reduced production costs.

The next phase occurs when the offshore supplier integrates forward from input subcontract to output rival. Here firms in Mexico, Brazil, Japan, Taiwan, or Hong Kong alter their relationship to their original customers. Now firms reside as direct rivals to their former clients. Now Japanese TV sets suppliers compete with U.S. manufacturers.

Phase three occurs when firms in Hong Kong, Singapore, Japan, and Taiwan find themselves searching for additional cost reduction opportunities. Such a search can take them from the domestic market to offshore suppliers such as those located in Thailand, Indonesia, Philippines, Malaysia, or the People's Republic of China. Firms in these geographic areas become resource suppliers to final product manufacturers in Hong Kong, Singapore, Japan, and Taiwan.[1] Such a regional migration toward resource input suppliers may be facilitated through an intermediary. Taiwan companies, for example, have established textile and shoe manufacturing plants in, of all places, the People's Republic of China. They do so, however, through third-party brokers in Hong Kong.[2] Through this process, subassemblies move from firm to firm, area to area, and country to country. The comparative advantage of one nation often dissolves in the face of competitive alternatives of another country. The result is a discernible shift in the tiers of suppliers. The supply firm incrementally changes its status to that of a direct competitor.

The United States has experienced this transition, not merely within domestic regions of the country, but between continents as well. Auto components suppliers have gravitated from the United States to Japan, to Korea and then Thailand. Similarly, Japan is experiencing competition from firms in Malaysia and Taiwan.

Technological transfer is energized by a combination of market entry, shifts in competitive advantage, and alterations in the firm–supplier relationship. Whether in design, development, manufacturing, marketing, or service, technology diffusion moves from north to south, from west to east. And interestingly enough, the technological transfer process can be inverted. Witness the growing U.S. interest in Japanese products and know-how in such areas as materials research, robotics, optics, telecommunications, and factory automation systems.

SPECIFIC PRODUCTS

The locus of industrial shifts in textiles, shipbuilding, steel, shoes, and automobiles illustrates the migration of technology, the placement of production, and the recasting of the buyer–seller relationship. Shifts in comparative advantage are common in office automation products, telecommunications handsets, consumer electronics, and genetic engineering.

Similarly, migrations have occurred on a geographic level. Telephone handsets, for example, have traditionally resided as a U.S. manufactured product. Offshore suppliers erupted at the low end of this product in such areas as basic telephone handsets, key telephone sytems, telephone answering devices, and in some cases, small private line branch exchanges or customer switching equipment. The locus of production from the United States to Japan has subsequently shifted from Japan to Taiwan, Singapore, and South Korea. A similar movement can be detected in segments of factory automation, office automation, word processing facsimile equipment, personal computers, to say nothing of the thousands of electronic subsystems and components that feed final product assembly operations.

Nor is technological migration confined or restricted to so-called commodity-type products. Rocket launchers and the hoisting of communication satellites illustrate the dynamics of the market entry process. For decades, the United States enjoyed essentially a launching monopoly in the West, albeit underwritten by the National Aeronautics and Space Administration (NASA).

In the past three years, however, launching capability and know-how has widened and diffused. In 1986, the French offered commercial launching services to all comers. The People's Republic of China then entered the launching market. Now the Soviet Union is offering launching services. Predictably, such entry has not been without its effects on price. The French offered discount prices on their launches prior to the Challenger accident in 1986. Thereafter they raised rates by 40 percent. The People's Republic of China offers booster prices some 50 percent less than that of U.S. launching fees.[3] And now the Soviet Union has announced commercial rocket propulsion systems on the order of $10 to $20 million dollars a launch, prompting some U.S. government officials to suggest the Soviets are engaged in predatory pricing.[14]

Launching capability is contemplated by other nations and other firms including Japan, India, Brazil, and even Australia. Indeed, the USSR has indicated it will place rockets on domestic launching sites of a host country as a means of entering the market and developing competitive alternatives.[5]

The development of smaller missile capability in South Korea, Taiwan, and Israel testifies that propulsion expertise has migrated. Recently the U.S. government attempted to quarantine the knowledge of missile technology from gravitating to lesser developed nations.

Remote sensing satellite technology—aerospace photos in the vernacular—is closely aligned to the launching experience and know-how of the West. Once again, communication satellite sensing first originated in the United States by a government monopoly. Subsequently, the United Staes privatized NASA's Landsat operation and has announced a policy of private entry, private ownership, and competition with the United States.

Even so, international rivalry in remote satellite sensing images has intensified since 1986. In that year the French announced a remote sensing service for sale to customers. The U.S. Department of Defense is one such client.[6] As discussed in Chapter 7, the French satellite resolution is three times the clarity of its U.S. rival, Landsat. Yet in 1987 the USSR announced its intention to sell remote sensing pictures even more sharply defined and clearer than that of its French or U.S. rival.[7]

Additional entry candidates are on the horizon. Remote sensing satellites have been announced by West Germany, Canada, Japan, India, Brazil, and the People's Republic of China.[8] All have indicated an interest in selling services for both domestic and international consumption.

The scramble for clients and customers has thus intensified over time. In satellite launching, for example, industry observers have stated that Brazil will "sell to anyone."[9] And in selling remote satellite sensing, a French official has observed: "We don't ask what they're doing with the pictures. We just sell the data."[10] As expected, price discounts have erupted in remote satellite sensing images.

Labor intensive input software illustrates the dynamic interaction of migrating technology and comparative advantage. As computer telecommunications becomes software intensive, as products—to use the trade jargon—become "more feature rich" apropos centralized data bases, such developments increasingly depend on software engineers and programming as a factor input. Traditionally, software engineering had resided as a domestic industry within the United States.

However, U.S. firms invariably search for reduced factor costs. Consequently, the Asian Rim and India have developed a presence in software development centers. Given its labor intensity, India possesses a growing competitive advantage in this segment of the information market. A $400 million software system in the United States, for example, can be purchased for some $36 million in India.[11] The Miami Police Department's software system is a product of the India software programmers; and Texas Instruments, operating a software subsidiary in Bangaladore, India, imports that software into the United States via satellite relay. In a somewhat related development, American Airlines imports key punch ticket processing from its Barbados data processing subsidiary via satellite transmission at night. And now American Airlines has extended its operation to other Caribbean islands including the Dominican Republic.[12]

Candidates selling products in nations with relatively low per capita income and low wage earnings reside at various stages of the production sequence. Each nation embodies a particular comparative advantage. Peru, for example, manufactures personal computers that it sells to the Soviet Union. Brazil exports fiber optical cable to Cuba.[13] Malaysia manufactures silicon rectifiers that it sells to the United States. The Philippines assembles loud speakers; Thailand, color televisions; India, digital telephone PBXs; The People's Republic of China, GM auto parts. Whether in office automation, factory automation, telecommunications, data base services, biotechnology, materials research, or consumer electronics, market entry is an ongoing process that is international in reach and dimension. Few firms, here or abroad, remain oblivious to the shifting reality of comparative advantage.

EFFECTS ON MARKET ENTRY

Several implications ride on this ongoing entry phenomenon. Clearly, market entry changes the environment inhabited by the firm. These changes include products embedded with more technology, a contraction of the development time, a shortening of product life cycles, a premium placed on corporate innovation, adaptation, and responsiveness.

Product Fusion

Consider first the phenomenon of *product fusion*. Product fusion occurs when several separate products are combined into a single unit. Stated alternately, one product is capable of performing more and more features traditionally associated by separate, individual units. Word processing equipment is a case in point. In the 1980s Wang Laboratories introduced the Wang Office Assistant, a stand alone word processing system. The product combined the software features of word processing, retained the keyboard and the feel of an electronic typewriter, and through a proprietary operating system incorporated data processing, personal file, data base manipulation and some graphic capability, all associated with the personal computer.[14] Wang's Office Assistant fused three separate and distinct products into one—a word processor, an electronic typewriter, and a personal computer.

IBM has subsequently introduced a three for one product three years later, followed by the Japanese firm, Cannon. Such firms combine chips, floppy discs, operating systems, software capability, display technology, diskette memory, and printers into a single product with multiple operating features. Product fusion as a phenomenon is common in office automation, telecommunications medical equipment, and consumer electronics.

Similarly, the evolution of so-called dumb products to intelligent products illustrates the imbedding or fusion of more and more features within a single product. In 1970, for example, the average U.S. automobile was virtually devoid of electronic components and parts. Ten years later the

U.S. automobile industry employed components of some four hundred dollars, ranging from electronic devices for display for exhaust monitoring equipment and the like. By the mid 1990s an auto is expected to include one thousand dollars worth of electronic components and microprocessors.[15] And such innovation is international in reach and scope. *Forbes* reports:

> Nissan is said to be close to introducing a heads-up display that will project dashboard instrument readings on the windshield using an electrical projection system. The Japanese are also believed to be working on mulitplexing technology whereby data from sensors and microprocessors pulse through wires in bursts.[16]

General Motors is similarly experimenting with opto-electronic systems, heads-up display units, satellite positioning locations, digital electronic maps and antennas that combine AM/FM, cellular radio, and satellite reception.[17] In short, the automobile industry, through enrichment of its products and infusion of technology, is adopting some of the traits and characteristics of the aerospace industry. Whether in toys, cameras, watches, or consumer electronics, products incorporate speech synthesis, opto-electronics, high speed electronic circuits, and memory capability. The same process finds application in telecommunications. McDonald's, for example, the fast food retailer, is exploring digital telecommunications network services, ISDN, linking its restaurant point of sales devices to its corporate headquarters.[18] Such a link will permit inventory control, sales, marketing and financial data transfer.

Development Cycles

As firms experience market entry, and as the number of competitors multiply, a premium is placed on the firm's ability to quicken decision making, that translates into both process and product innovation. The entry process compels firms to reduce costs, to engage in both price and nonprice marketing, and to explore new market opportunities. Competition inevitably spills into the innovation process. As a result, product development cycles, the period of time to conceive and bring a product into fruition, is cut and reduced over time (see Table 5.1).

As more and more firms enter an industry, product life cycles shrink and contract. Telecommunications illustrate the duality of product innovation and product obsolescence. Twenty years ago, telephone switching equipment enjoyed a life of some twenty, thirty, or even forty years.

Table 5.1
Product Development Cycles

Company	Product	Cycle Time
Xerox	Copiers	6 years to 2 years
Allen-Bradley	Electrical equipment	7 years to 2 years
Rolls Royce	Turbine blades	5 years to 2 1/2 years
Proctor & Gamble	Consumer products	1 year to 3 months
IBM	Personal computer	4 years to 2 years
Epson	Personal computer	2 years to 18 months

Source: Christopher Lorenz, "Holding Rivals at Bay with Quick Draw Tactics," *Financial Times,* July 10, 1987, p. 24; Peter Behr, "Fast Moving Technologies Giving Products Shorter Life," *Boston Globe,* March 24, 1985, p. A96; Christopher Lorenz, "Scrum and Scramble—the Japanese Style." *Financial Times,* June 19, 1987, p. 19; Christopher Lorenz, "Seizing the Initiative in a Struggle For Survival," *Financial Times,* June 17, 1987, p. 12; "Seven Wary Views From the Top," *Fortune* (February 12, 1987): 62; Barbara Bradley, "The Flexible Factory Reshapes American Industry," *Christian Science Monitor,* June 1, 1987, p. 19.

Today the economic life of even large exchange switching equipment is now less than ten years. Office automation life cycles approaches four to five years, although firms can enhance product life through additional hardware and software features.[19]

SECTOR SHIFT?

The United States has experienced a subtle movement in the derivation of technological change attendant on the entry process. Traditionally, the public sector, specifically military research, paced the development of new products. Commercial products trickled down from government sponsored R&D. Technology pushced the state of the technical art in computers, satellites, nuclear power, space technology, semiconductors, and opto-electronics. In many instances that process continues today.

On the other hand, competition is so intensive in the private sector that a subtle shift has occurred in the locus of the innovation process. Many commercial products—for example, toys, cameras, automobiles, personal computers, telecommunications networks, automatic teller machines, smart cards, genetic engineering—are more advanced than that employed in military products. In some cases, "the commercial marketplace occasionally leads the military market for applications of such technology as microelectronics, software, and instrumentation."[20] A British study recently observed a similar realignment between public and private technology: "The military no longer provides as important a demand pull as it did in the former years of microelectronics. The commercial and industrial market requiring very little cost, high performance products, is now the leading edge of technology."[21]

This transition may apply to more and more private products, and industries. If the trend continues, the fact that West Germany and Japan allocate a higher percentage of commercial research and development relative to their gross national product than the United States holds ominous competitive implications in the decade to come.[22]

To sum up, the entry process, whether domestic or offshore, is an ongoing phenomenon. The search for low cost input costs spreads technology geographically, softens distinctions between products, and destabilizes a once durable buyer–seller relationship.

Comparative advantage is hardly static. Cost economies move from Europe to the United States, from the United States to the Asian Rim, from the Asian Rim to the so-called little tigers, Malaysia, Thailand, Philippines, and now the People's Republic of China. How long it takes a firm to evolve from a component supplier to direct competitor depends on the nature, the circumstance, the type of capital and human investment, and relative exchange rates. But the search for factor inputs is unrelenting and ongoing. In the process, comparative advantage continually alters the relationship between products, firms, and nations.

Competition also erases former product distinction, reduces product development time, places premium on responsive innovation, contracts product life cycles, and alters the sourcing of technology between economic sectors. A National Academy of Engineering report on the semiconductor industry observed recently that the developmental cycle of Japanese firms in the semiconductor industry now exceeds that of U.S. firms.[23] At the same time, the U.S. share of international technology has begun its decline from 50 percent in the 1960s to an estimated 30 percent in the 1990s.[24] Technological shifts carry with it changes in comparative advantage. It may not be surprising that the U.S. technology balance of payments will drift from a surplus in the 1980s to a deficit in the future.

Any diminution in the entry process is unlikely to take place in the foreseeable future. The United States stands to experience more rather than less competitive pressure in the 1990s.

NOTES

1. Cristina Lee, "Asian Manufacturers Shift Production Abroad," *Journal of Commerce* (January 6, 1982): 1; Paula Doe, "The Far East: Beware of the Baby Dragons," *Electronic Business* (January 1, 1988): 100; Patricia Gray, "Asian Computer Firms Invade the U.S. Market for Personal Machines," *Wall Street Journal,* January 10, 1986, p. 1.

2. Bob King, "Chinese Triangle Lures Taiwan," *Financial Times,* December 17, 1987, p. 6.

3. Peter Marsh, "China's Long March Into Orbit," *Financial Times,* October 20, 1987, p. 21; Craig Couault, "Chinese Expand Launch Facilities to Attract Satellite Customers," *Aviation Week and Space Technology* (July 13, 1987): 120.

4. Les Dorr, "Russki Business," *Space World* (July 1987): 31-33.

5. William Dullforce, "Moscow Offers Satellite Launches," *Financial Times,* May 23, 1982, p. 2.

6. William J. Broad, "Private Cameras in Space Stir U.S. Security Fears," *New York Times,* August 25, 1987, p. C1.

7. William J. Broad, "Soviet Space Photographs Stir U.S. but Agency Plans to Buy Them Faces Barriers," *New York Times,* September 27, 1987, p. 40.

8. "Japanese Launch Initial Remote Sensing Program," *Aviation Week and Space Technology* (February 23, 1987): 29.

9. "The Scary Scramble to Build Nuclear Missiles in the Third World," *Business Week* (January 11, 1988): 59; David Buchan and Tony Walker, "Cairo Rocket Plan Fuels Proliferation Fears," *Financial Times,* December 26, 1987, p. 3, Sydney Shaw, "Private Eyes in the Sky," *The Village Voice,* May 17, 1987, p. 1; "Brazil's Space Program Remains Dynamic Despite Fiscal Woes," *Aviation Week and Space Technology* (August 24, 1987): 75.

10. Mark Hosenball, "U.S. Fears French 'Sky for Hire,' " *London Times,* October 27, 1986, p. 22.

11. Alan Cane, "India's Development of Telematics," *Financial Times,* November 25, 1987, p. XI; Mary Jo Foley, "Offshore Programming: Here We Go Again," *Electronic Business* (October 15, 1987): 104.

12. David Ludlum, "Offshore Data Entry Pays Off," *Computer World* (June 9, 1986): 103; Carole Shifrin, "American Diversifies Operations Based on Airline Related Skills," *Aviation Week and Space Technology* (April 20, 1987): 38.

13. Barbara Dorr, "Peru to Sell PCs to Moscow," *Financial Times,* January 9, 1987, p. 4. "Cuba and Brazil in Cooperation Deal," *Communications International* (May 1987): 10.

14. Linda O'Keefe, "New WP Products from Wang Labs," *The Seybold Report on Office Systems* (February 18, 1985): 1; "PTS—Praise the Secretary," *Gartner Group, Inc.,* August 14, 1987, p. 1.

15. Kenneth Goodina, "General Motors: When Captive Technology is a Competitive Edge," *Financial Times,* September 25, 1987, p. 14.

16. Marc Beauchamp, "Here They Come Again," *Forbes* (February 8, 1988): 82.

17. Robert W. Henkel, "FYI," *Electronics* (May 14, 1987): 8.

18. Mary Petrosky, "ISDN at Home Under The Golden Arches," *Network World* (September 29, 1987): 33; "Golden Arches Planned for USSR," *Journal of Commerce* (January 22, 1987): 5A

19. William M. Bukeley, "Computer Add-ons Give New Life to Models Lacking Latest Features," *Wall Street Journal,* August 30, 1987, p. 25.

20. James Dukowitz, "A Business Perspective on Export Controls," *Signal* (August, 1983): 99; "Military Spending Questioned," *New York Times,* September 11, 1986, p. D5.

21. Geoffrey Owen, "High-Tech Chance for Europe," *Financial Times,* September 1, 1986, p. 15.

22. "Non Defense R&D Expenditures As a Percentage of Gross National Product (GNP) by Country," National Science Foundation, 1987.

23. Jack Robertson, "Semiductor Spectre," *Electronic News* (September 22, 1987): 10; Charles H. Ferguson, "High Technology Product Life Cycles, Export Controls and International Markets," National Academy of Science, *Balancing the National Interest* (Washington, D.C.: National Academy Press, 1987), 60.

24. Testimony of Lionel H. Olner, Under Secretary for International Trade, Department of Commerce, Senate Hearings Before the Permanent Subcommittee on Governmental Affairs, 98th Cong., 2nd sess., April 12, 1984, p. 202.

6

Telecommunications Services and Manufacturing

In any struggle between a policy of competition and a policy of monopoly the national security argument has invariably sided with monopoly in local exchange, monopoly in toll exchange, monopoly in manufacturing, and with minor exceptions, sole source procurement. In taking such a position, the national security argument has backed the principle of facilities regulation, services regulation, and integrated supplier regulation. In a word, the national defense argument has served to buttress the regulatory status quo, the move against market entry, and the case against investment diversity and economic innovation. Consider first, an examination of the national security argument in telecommunications services.

TELEPHONE SERVICES

The common ownership of a firm supplying telecommunications services and of a firm manufacturing equipment, the traditional organization of the industry, has vexed public policy for some eighty years. Conventional wisdom had it that one firm alone supplies telecommunications services effectively and efficiently. But was the argument valid in equipment manufacturing? Was telecommunications fabrication and supply also a natural monopoly? If so, should not manufacturing be subject to regulation? And if not, should telecommunications manufacturing be subject to the forces of competition?

The structure and practices of AT&T in the United States argued for neither. Telecommunications constituted a regulated monopoly; but manufacturing was not a natural monopoly. This position presents a problem because, given AT&T's ownership of Western Electric, the Bell operating companies invariably bought most of their equipment from their own hardware supplier. And if the Bell operating companies did elect to buy non-Western equipment, Western Electric served as the purchasing agent in that transaction. Predictably outside suppliers felt disadvantaged by both AT&T's integration and procurement policies. Invariably, they concluded that the Bell market was closed to competitive access.[1]

Western enjoyed privileged access to the specifications, the budgets, and the planning forecasts of the Bell operating companies. Western also funded two-thirds of Bell Telephone Laboratory's budget. Given the buying practices of the Bell System, outside vendors viewed AT&T and the Bell operating companies as beyond competitive reach.

Congress struggled with the industry's vertical structure issue in the late 1920s and 1930s. An early draft of the communication act sought competitive bidding procedures, but that requirement was struck down after AT&T testified that bidding interfered with managerial prerogatives.[2] The final communication act did request that the FCC look into the matter of telephone company buying practices.

In the 1930s the FCC inaugurated an investigation of AT&T and Western Electric. Four years later in 1938, a staff recommended that commission jurisdiction be extended to Western Electric's manufacturing operations.[3] But that recommendation was found unacceptable or unworkable. And then the matter died. Germany marched into Poland, World War II commenced, and the nation turned its attention toward preparation and wartime production.

In 1949, however, the antitrust division of the Department of Justice filed a complaint charging that AT&T had leveraged its telephone monopoly into a manufacturing monopoly.[4] That monopoly was Western Electric. The department recommended harsh surgery in the tradition of American Tobacco and Standard Oil, namely a separation of Western from the Bell operating companies, divestiture of Western into three separate companies, and a requirement that the Bell operating companies, purchase future equipment on the open market.

On March 7, 1952, Dr. M. J. Kelley, president of Bell Telephone Laboratory, offered a memorandum for the Secretary of Defense requesting that the antitrust suit be postponed for some eighteen months during the Korean conflict on grounds of national security. The March 7 AT&T memo to the Department of Defense suggested that "an adequate telephone system is clearly essential to this nation's defense."[5]

Two weeks later, the Secretary of Defense, Robert Lovett, requested that the Department of Justice postpone the Bell suit until after the Korean Conflict.

About a year later on July 3, 1953, AT&T sent another memo to the Department of Defense, with the observation: "The pending antitrust case seriously threatens the continuation of the important work which the Bell System is now carrying forward in the interest of national defense."[6]

On July 10, 1953, the Department of Defense letter from Secretary Wilson to the Attorney General contained the following: "The pending antitrust case seriously threatens the continuation of the important work which the Bell System is now carrying forward in the interest of national defense."[7]

But by 1955 the Department of Justice and AT&T were moving to a settlement of the 1949 antitrust suit. In January of 1956, the department announced a consent decree that permitted AT&T to retain ownership of both telephone service and telephone manufacturing activities.[8] In sustaining its manufacturing integration, AT&T agreed to confine its future telephone services to common carrier communications—that is, to regulated activities. Although the Department of Justice noted that AT&T's patent portfolio was to be made available to the public, the settlement, in preserving the Bell integrated system, was regarded as a victory for AT&T management. Among other reasons, the integration of utility manufacturing was sustained on grounds of national security.

Although the Defense Department actively opposed the AT&T antitrust settled in the late 1940s, the department was discretely quiet as the FCC struggled with the policy of market access by terrestrial carriers, satellite carriers, and value-added carriers. Any policy that sanctioned entry, competition, and diversity in long haul facilities conflicted with the premise that a regulated monopoly of all facilities, all investment, all service, was grounded on scale efficiencies and scale economies. Despite opposition by AT&T and state regulatory agencies, in the 1960s the FCC began to solicit firm entry into specialized terrestrial markets, specialized satellite markets, and value-added or resale services.

One reason for this policy reversal was found in a relatively unknown inquiry known as Computer I.[9] Inaugurated in November 1966, Computer I questioned whether the policy, practices, and investment of the telephone industry could accommodate the needs of data processing and the computer industry. Stated differently, it was a network oriented toward voice or analogue service adequate or even compatible with the needs of computer applications. Could such a voice network accommodate computer time-sharing, remote data base, credit verification, computer reservation systems, brokerage services, electronic transfer funds, and computer-to-computer data exchange.

AT&T responded that its analog network and its policies and practices embodied as its tariffs were more than adequate to meet the needs of the data processing industry. The Bell System noted that digital machines, through data modems, permitted data access to primarily a voice network.

The FCC, however, was deluged by responses to its inquiry from banking, brokerage, data processing, aerospace and computer manufacturing, and data terminal industry. (In fact, the commissioner farmed out the reply briefs to the Stanford Research Institute for analysis and recommendation.) Invariable industry responses cited a growing disparity between telephone company practices and the data processing requirements.

It was Computer I and its submissions that conditioned the FCC as to the merit or demerit of a policy of soliciting telecommunications entry. The needs of a new clientele were apparently not being met satisfactorily by incumbent carriers—their facilities or services. That perception led the commission to be more receptive to the application of new facilities, new value-added carriers. Moreover, liberalized entry found support in the Presidential Task Force under President Johnson in the late 1960s.[10]

These policy movements did not challenge telecommunications and its fundamental structure on a frontal assault. But each policy change represented small, incremental, hesitant steps toward diversity and market competition. Cumulatively the FCC began to introduce toll competition in limited, selected markets. Such policies ignited heated debate. However, the Department of Defense, rarely engaged in the policy controversy of the 1960s, remained discretely silent as company briefs traversed through the FCC, went up for the full commission decisions, and then spilled into judicial review. The one exception occurred when the Defense Department defended Bell's 80 percent price cut as a counter move to private microwave.

AT&T opposed any policy sanctioning entry, no matter how limited. The telephone company insisted that competition would drive up costs, lift rates, deteriorate service, and compromise for end-to-end service responsibility. Market entry would, in AT&T's judgement, end a policy of rate cross-subsidization between toll and local users. The Bell System, in resisting a policy of entry, argued that the FCC was pursuing a contradictory policy of regulated competition.

Yet AT&T's opposition to market entry risked running afoul of the nations' antitrust statutes. And private suits did begin to erupt in the 1970s. Then in November 1974, the Department of Justice filed a suit alleging that AT&T, through the ownership of its toll and its local exchange facilities, had frozen out competition with AT&T's long lines or toll carrier.[11] By denying access to local exchange facilities, the Department of Justice asserted that AT&T had excluded specialized intercity carriers unfairly.

Once again, the Department of Justice sought divestiture as an antitrust remedy. But unlike the 1949 suit, the 1974 complaint went to trial. The Department of Justice presented its case and witnesses. When the government completed its case, AT&T asked the court for dismissal on grounds that the company was subject to pervasive state and federal regulation. Harold Greene, the presiding judge, refused to dismiss the suit and the Bell System began its affirmative case in 1981.

In April 1981, the Department of Defense wrote a letter to then Assistant Attorney General Baxter. The letter stated "It is the position of the Secretary of Defense that the pending suit against the American Telephone and Telegraph Company be dismissed."[12]

Later, the Department of Defense, in a memo to the White House noted the national security implications of corporate restructuring:

> The Department of Defense can unequivocally state that divestiture as currently proposed by Justice, that is separation of local exchange from intercity functions, would cause substantial harm to national defense and emergency preparedness telecommunications capability.[13]

The memo, in short, defended Bell's status of regulated monopoly.

The Department of Defense's memo, made available to AT&T counsel, was introduced into the antitrust case as a defendant exhibit. Judge Greene, informed that the Department of Defense released its study to AT&T almost exclusively, admitted the Department of Defense memo into evidence, but with the observation, "The evidence indicated that the Department of Defense relied almost entirely for the technical portions of its study upon AT&T."[14]

The Defense communication agency's counsel later testified that the Defense Department would have been foolish not to talk to AT&T in the memo's preparation.[15]

In telecommunications service, then, the national security argument has been invoked in support of and in defense of regulated monopoly. The Defense Department has actively defended the policies and practices of the integrated carriers, first in the 1949 suit and later in the 1974 suit. In the process, the national security argument has supported policies dividing markets between regulated and competitive services, defended rate of return regulation, advocated cost-plus pricing, sanctioned exclusivity in research and development, and approved monopoly in facilities and telecommunications services. In short, national security and telephone monopoly have been treated as inseparable and indivisible.

TELECOMMUNICATION MANUFACTURING

The national security rationale has also been extended to telecommunications manufacturing. Over the years, the Department of Defense supported AT&T's confinement to regulated markets only. And by opposing divestiture or open bidding, the Defense Department has tacitly rstricted equipment competition. Indeed Defense has pleaded for more rather than less public regulation of telecommunications manufacturing. In a word, the national security argument has opted for a utility-supplier status quo.

Telecommunications manufacturing was central to the Department of Justice's 1949 suit that alleged AT&T had leveraged a telephone franchise into a manufacturing monopoly. As a result of the 1956 settlement, the structure of equipment market was not disassociated from market definition. The Consent Decree ruled that AT&T's services were to be confined to regulated communications carriers' activities—a market condition that applied with equal force to Western Electric.

At the time, Bell operating companies' orders more than occupied Western Electric's plants and production. But over time, computer and telecommunications technology began to coalesce and overlap. Telecommunications began to embody digital characteristics and software dependency. But just as the operating companies were precluded by the Consent Decree to sell services in nonregulated markets, that same constraint applied to Western Electric's product line as well. Western was confined to regulated telecommunications hardware.

Over and above foreclosing the Bell equipment market, the 1956 Consent Decree also served as a structural model for the independent or non-Bell companies in the industry. Non-Bell holding companies began to acquire their own integrated suppliers as well. And captive suppliers enjoyed captive customers. The result saw the national defense argument both concentrate and cartelize telephone manufacturing in the United States. Moreover, the Consent Decree restricted Western Electric to regulated equipment insulating IBM from direct competition from the telephone industry. Little wonder then that when the market was opened up, post-divestiture offshore suppliers moved to exploit product and technological disparities in customer premise equipment and central office switching.

As noted, the FCC attempted to introduce competition in private microwave (above 890) and customer premise equipment in the early 1960s.[16] Through frequency allocations, that option permitted corporations to buy and own their own point-to-point microwave communication systems. The FCC attempted to diversify the supply side of telecommunications manufacturing. However, failure to enforce the interconnection private networks dial-up public network rendered the private microwave a weak and inconsequent force in the marketplace.

However, entry into the customer premise equipment market was another matter. Conditioned by the Computer I inquiry, the FCC sanctioned the attachment of customer-owned equipment to the dial-up network. That decision set the stage for an acrimonious debate: Could the user attach telephones by coupler versus through direct connection under a FCC equipment certification program? Ten years after Carterphone, the court opened the market through a certification plan and non-Bell PBXs, key telephone systems, automatic call directors, standard telephones, and so forth began to experience new vitality and growth. The decision held that customer premise suppliers could sell directly to the residential and business customer.

There is some debate as to whether the Commission's specialized carrier decision or its Carterphone decision was more instrumental in altering the environmental setting of the U.S. telecommunications market. From the Defense Department's perspective, however, this debate remained academic. Defense elected to distance itself from actively participating in a policy debate of investment pluralism, diversity, or choice.

By contrast, the national security argument did actively participate in the FCC's investigation of AT&T's buying practices. Known as Docket 19129, the FCC investigation originated as a rate case filed in the mid-1960s and focussed on the reasonableness of telephone rates. How could the FCC determine whether telephone rates were optimal if neither regulation nor market forces set Western Electric's prices? Phase II of Docket 19129 took as its mandate the examination of equipment costs, specifically Western Electric's costs and prices.

An FCC Trial Staff introduced case studies suggesting that competitive access to the equipment market benefitted both equipment buyer and equipment seller. The staff, among other recommendations, pushed for opening up this close market on utility manufacturing, whether by spin-off, competitive bidding, or a combination of each.[17]

The Department of Defense rejected both options. Rather, the Department of Defense insisted that the Commission disallow Western Electric's earnings to a level no higher than AT&T's or regulated profits. As the Defense Department's brief noted:

> The evidence presented in this proceeding overwhelmingly demonstrates that the business and economic risks of Western Electric are considerably below those of other manufacturers and that, in any event, Western Electric's risk cannot be separated from and is equal to that of Bell system as a whole. We do not require, therefore, a greater rate of return on investment related to its sales to Bell System Companies than the rate of return required with respect to the interstate operations of the Bell System Companies. Western Electric's charges, greater than those sufficient to maintain the same rate of return permitted AT&T for its overall interstate operations should, therefore, be disallowed for rate-making purposes.[18]

Although the Commission rejected the Department of Defenses' rate disallowance proposal, such a recommendation clearly pushed Western Electric toward the status of a public utility.[19]

The FCC struggled with the procurement issue from 1965 to 1982. Again, the Commission focussed on whether outside manufacturers could gain access to the integrated market of AT&T and Western Electric via a separate entity known as the Bell Systems Purchase Product Division (BSPPD). Created in 1974 the BSPPD was Bell's response to the charge that vertical integration foreclosed the independent supplies market. Presumably, BSPPD would facilitate that access.

When the Commission's staff recommended that BSPPD take bids from both Western Electric and general trade suppliers, Defense invoked the national security argument once again. Defense rejected competition bidding on grounds that the FCC's proposal was tantamount to a de facto divestiture of Western from AT&T.[20]

This position was not unlike the Defense Department's observation as to the essence of telephone equipment in the government suit. As the Defense Department observed:

> The products of telephone equipment therefore must be considered along with the production of the military departments in appraising the importance of the contribution of the Bell System to the national defense and in weighing the burdens and the responsibilities imposed upon management by the defense effort.[21]

The procurement issue surfaced a final time before the FCC when fiber optics became an attractive alternation to cable and microwave transmission. In the late 1970s, AT&T announced a fiber optical network from Atlanta to Cambridge, MA., divided into two phases. AT&T placed its first order, from Atlanta to New York, with Western Electric. Despite the legacy of the FCC's investigation of buying practices, an AT&T official observed: "We have never seen a need for bidding in the past."[22]

But Corning Glass and Harris complained to the FCC that Western Electric would wind up with the bulk of the nation's fiber optic capacity. The FCC asked for cost comparisons. AT&T responded that Western constituted the low cost producer.

In June 1981, however, AT&T reversed itself. The company agreed that it would open procurement on Phase II from New York to Cambridge and invited vendors to bid on the fiber optic network. Fujitsu, a Japanese supplier, submitted a bid one third lower than Western Electric and apparently won the award. But on December 11, 1981, the national security argument was invoked. A Department of Defense study to the FCC observed:

> National defense and security and emergency preparedness needs can best be served by developing a strong domestic fiber optic technology base and Western Electric's construction installation of these specific segments appear to be the most reasonable approach considering the economic construction of the interconnecting links."[23]

The Department of Defense study to the FCC stated that "AT&T has shown that Western Electric will benefit the emerging U.S. lightwave industry, will provide employment opportunities, will serve the national defense interests identified by DOD."[24] The Defense Department later modified that position by suggesting that the FCC should limit this to domestic suppliers only.

Events moved quickly thereafter. AT&T withdrew the Fujitsu bid, placed the award with Western, and the FCC justified the process by noting that Western would farm out fiber optic components to domestic suppliers.

IMPLICATIONS

How then, can one summarize the application of the national security argument to equipment manufacturing? Here the Defense Department's position has paralleled its stance taken in telecommunications service;

namely, that vertical integration was essential for national defense, that competitive bidding was unworkable, and that competition was subservient to national security needs. By supporting the 1956 Consent Decree, the Department of Defense concentrated and cartelized the telephone manufacturing market, and artificially separated telecommunications from computer technology. True, information technology was soon to erode, if not erase that line over time. Nevertheless, Defense policy continued to defend centralization in manufacturing, research, and equipment ownership. The national security argument held that monopoly control should transcend a policy of market competition.

Why did the Department of Defense assume this position? Perhaps the answer can be found in the department's interest in cost-plus. Rate base economics is attractive to the Defense Department to the extent that AT&T, hardened and rerouted transmission and switching plants around densely populated areas. However, that cost was born not merely by the Department of Defense. It was spread through all rate payers, businesses, and subscribers alike. In a sense, the Defense Department enjoyed a rate subsidy—that is, the department did not incur the full cost of hardening or diversifying telecommunications investment.

By contrast competitive entry disrupted that subsidy to the extent that competition places a premium not as cost-plus but on cost-efficiency. One might assert that market entry spells transmission and switching diversity and pluralism—not an inconsequential national interest consideration. But the Department of Defense apparently did not find that proposition persuasive. As one observer noted: "In a competitive environment, common carriers trying to build switching and transmission facilities have no incentive to harden them."[25] Whatever the reason, over the years the Defense Department preferred to equate regulated monopoly with the imperative of national security.

NOTES

1. Before the Federal Communications Commission. In the Matter of Bell Supplier Practices; in the Matter of Bell Operating Company Procurement of Telecommunications Equipment. Docket No. 80-53, *Report an Order and Notice of Inquiry,* July 28, 1981, p. 2; *Comments of International Telephone and Telegraph Corporation,* October 15, 1981.

2. Hearings Before the Senate Committee on Interstate Commerce, *Commission on Communications,* 71st Cong., 2d sess., pt. 10, January 1930, p. 2,055.

3. *Proposed Report.* Telephone Investigation, Federal Communications Commission, Washington, D.C., 1938, p. 701.

4. *United States vs. Western Electric Co.* (Civ. No. 17-49), District of New Jersey, February 14, 1949.

5. Hearings Before the Antitrust Subcommittee (subcommittee No. 5) House Committee on the Judiciary, *Consent Decree Program of the Department of Justice,* 1958, p. 1,871.

6. Ibid., p. 2,036.

7. Ibid., p. 2,027.

8. Ibid., p. 1,723.

9. Before the Federal Communications Commission. In the Matter of the Regulatory and Policy Problems Presented by the Interdependence of Computer and Communications Services and Facilities. Docket No. 16979, *Notice of Inquiry,* November 10, 1966, p. 1.

10. *Final Report.* President's Task Force on Communications Policy, December 7, 1968.

11. *United States vs. American Telephone and Telegraph Co.,* 552 F. Supp. 131 (DD6 1982).

12. George H. Bolling, *AT&T, Aftermatch of Antitrust* (Washington, D.C.: National Defense University, Fort Lesley J. McNair, 1983), p. 20.

13. *Executive Summary.* Department of Defense Analysis of the Effect of AT&T Divestiture upon National Defense and Security and Emergency Preparedness, June 30, 1981, Defendant's Exhibit D-1-141, pp. 2-3, 11, 23.

14. *United States vs. American Telephone and Telegraph, et al.* (Civ. A. No. 74-1698), *Memorandum,* Harold H. Greene, 524 F. Supp., 1981, p. 1,333.

15. Testimony of Randolph MacPherson, *Telecommunication Reports,* August 17, 1981, p. 11.

16. Before the Federal Communications Commission. In the Matter of the Allocation of Frequencies in the Band Above 890 Megacycles. Docket No. 11866. *Report and Order,* July 29, 1959.

17. Federal Communications Commission. In the Matter of AT&T, the Associated Bell System Companies, Charges for Interstate Telephone Service, AT&T Transmitted Nos. 10989, 11027, 11697. Docket No. 19129 (Phase II), *Initial Decision.* Administration Law Judge David I. Kraushaar, p. 166 (cited as initial decision).

18. Ibid., *Proposed Findings of Fact and Conclusions of Law of the Department of Defense and all Federal Executive Agencies of the United States,* Office of the Judge Advocate General, Department of the Army 1976, p. 90.

19. FCC, *Final Decision,* 1977, pp. 5-8 (cited as final decision).

20. Before the Federal Communications. In the Matter of Bell System Practices; in the Matter of Bell Operating Procurement of Telecommunications Equipment. Docket No. 80-53, *Comments of the Department of Defense,* October 15, 1981, p. 6.

21. *DOD Executive Summary*, p. 1.

22. Edward Meadows, ''Japan Runs into American Inc.,'' *Fortune* (March 22, 1982): 51.

23. Before the Federal Communications Commission. In the Application of American Telephone and Telegraph Company, et al., File No. W-D-C-3071, *Opposition,* American Telephone and Telegraph Co., December 30, 1981, p. 29.

24. Ibid., p. 29.

25. Johnson J. Lane, "Phone Fibers, Fujitsu and the FCC: A National Light at the End of the Northeast Corridor," *Law and Policy in International Business,* 13, No. 2 (1983): 684.

7

Jurisdictional Gridlock

Since the 1970s, the national security argument has dominated government decision making in the federal establishment. Moreover, the national security as a rationale for regulation is no longer confined to explicit defense matters alone. The argument is applied by the civilian or nondefense agencies of government as well. What, for example, separates classified from unclassified information; what is the definition of commercial dual use products that embody both civilian and military applications; what constitutes an effective export licensing policy; who should be the final arbiter in issuing licenses for dual use goods; what U.S. agency should coordinate export control with our European allies (COCOM); who should design encryptographic algorithms and electronic keys; who should control the resolution clarity of remote satellite images; who should monitor the buying practices of the Bell operating companies?

These issues have precipitated bureaucratic infighting on matters and questions of jurisdictional turf. Since the 1970s Defense has gained increasing jurisdictional ascendency over other federal agencies as final arbiter of national security matters. But the preeminence of the Department of Defense has not been without struggle or controversy. Depending on the issue, a battle over regulatory turf has involved intra and interagency disputes:

- Department of Defense versus Department of Defense
- Department of Defense versus Department of State
- Department of Defense versus Department of Commerce
- Department of Commerce versus Customs (Treasury)

- National Security Agency versus National Bureau of Standards (Department of Commerce)

DEPARTMENT OF DEFENSE VERSUS DEPARTMENT OF DEFENSE

By 1979 the Pentagon's review of export policy was assigned to the Office of Defense Research and Engineering (DRE). Dr. Richard DeLauer, Assistant Secretary under the Reagan administration, viewed firms' commercial exploitation of technology as critical, and hence favored a policy of licensing liberalization.

Explaining his position before a House subcommittee, Dr. DeLauer testified that "To lock it (technology) away for purposes of protecting it I think is counterproductive. It will disappear. When you open the safe years later, you will find it is not there. It is dust."[1] Relaxing U.S. export policy was not universally shared by others within the Department of Defense. Mr. Richard Perle, Assistant Secretary for International Security Policy (ISP), pushed for a more stringent control policy, and testified:

> We have sought to bring a greater recognition of the danger posed to the security of the United States and its allies by Soviet acquisition of advanced Western technology that finds its way very quickly in some cases, rather faster than we are able to incorporate the same technology, into the weapons systems of the Warsaw Pact.[2]

In the summer of 1983 Mr. Perle created an export review function parallel to that within the ISP section of Defense. Mr. DeLauer objected that such an office constituted a "serious misallocation of resources."[3] The struggle over jurisdictional control of export licenses within the two Departments of Defense was thus joined. The question of jurisdictional supremacy between ISD and DRE came to the desk of Caspar Weinberger, Secretary of Defense. The secretary ruled in favor of ISP with Defense Directive 2040.

> It shall be Department of Defense policy to treat defense-related technology as a valuable, limited national security resource. Consistent with this policy and in recognition of the importance of international trade to a strategic US defense industrial base.[4]

Director 2040 established a new organization, the International Technology Transfer Subpanel. The panel functioned to approve export control policies. Although Under Secretary DeLauer was placed on the panel, his position was both not-voting and advisory.

DEPARTMENT OF DEFENSE VERSUS DEPARTMENT OF STATE

A jurisdictional turf struggle also erupted between Defense and the Department of State in the early 1980s. For decades, the State Department had represented the United States in promulgating export control policy with our European allies and Japan, the so-called Coordinating Committee for Multilateral Export Control known as COCOM. The committee reviewed licenses destined to Soviet bloc nations. COCOM originated with the creation of the Marshall Plan. Recipient nations agreed that each COCOM country would monitor and limit certain strategic goods flowing to the Soviet bloc countries.

Assisted by the Department of Defense, the Department of State has articulated and defended U.S. positions at COCOM meetings in Paris. A key assignment of COCOM was to classify and deny product shipment to the Soviet bloc. The organization operated by consensus rule. No firm could sell a product unless all thirteen COCOM Members approved. A single veto cancelled any nation's attempt to export COCOM products to the Soviet bloc.

In the late 1970s, COCOM began to revise its computer list largely because the 1976 definition was considered obsolete. Subsequent generations of PCs, minicomputers, and mainframes had altered the processing speed and memory dramatically.[5] The question before COCOM, then, was one of redefinition and product upgrade.

William Root, Under Secretary of State, had participated with COCOM members in hammering out what was thought to be a consensus on computer reclassification. But the Department of Defense interceded and rescinded the U.S. reclassification plan. Overruled by Defense, Mr. Root subsequently tendered his resignation.

The former member of the State Department testified that the Department of Defense was pivotal in determining U.S. export policy.

Mr. Root contended that Section 10G of the 1979 Export Control Act (later incorporated in the 1985 act) assigned Defense essential veto power over another federal agency's determination of export control. Should a president decide to overturn a Department of Defense position on export control, the President must, under section 10g, issue a report to Congress as to the reason for overriding the Defense Department's objections. Secretary Root was to observe:

Section 10G in the existing export administration act (1979), which gives the Defense Department a form of veto over security cases, should be repealed. This section provides the President must report to Congress if he overrides a Defense Department objection to export. Presidents have not done so in the past nor are they likely to do so in the future because it would reveal that the Commander in Chief is not master in his own house.[6]

DEPARTMENT OF DEFENSE VERSUS DEPARTMENT OF COMMERCE

The Department of Defense has also been critical of the Department of Commerce's export licensing policy of private, commercial products—so-called dual use products. Defense has alleged that the licensing policies of the Department of Commerce of both products and technology has served to benefit the economy of Soviet bloc nations.

When the 1979 Export Act expired in 1984, the dispute over export licensing became public when Congress considered new legislation. The quarrel between Commerce and Defense found its mirror image on Capital Hill. A Senate bill assigned export control to the Department of Defense; a House bill assigned control to the Department of Commerce. However, the emerging conference committee recommendation contained a ban on U.S. loans to South Africa. When the President exercised his veto over the South African embargo, the Export Act died accordingly.

The administration's subsequent legislative effort did give Defense authority to review applications for export licensing. The act also incorporated Defense's position that the indexing (loosening) of technical standards remain fixed.

During this period, the Department of Defense insisted that it be assigned jurisdictional review over Commerce's export policy—specifically, distribution licenses.

Distribution license regulation applies to U.S. firms only, and is thus unilateral. And it is also obvious such licenses apply to private products destined for offshore buyers. But it was Defense's position that Commerce's license policy was overly relaxed and liberal. Defense sought license control and review of Commerce's activities on grounds that "Distribution licenses have been a major siphon directing our technology to the Soviets."[7]

In 1984, the Department of Commerce proposed a review of license policy. The department suggested that distribution licenses be abolished, that firms send a list of their customers to the Department of Commerce and drop shipments to end users be banned or restricted as an ongoing policy.

Industry participants generally opposed Commerce's new proposals. Most firms guard their customer lists jealously. Some respondents asserted that they would not reveal their customers list because of inadvertent government leaks. Corporations also insisted that regulations would delay delivery of products to overseas clients. And most industry representatives opposed the proposed ban on drop shipments to direct customers rather than consignees. In calling for a ban on drop shipment, Mr. Archey of the Commerce Department recalled: " 'I don't understand drop shipment. I don't think anybody out there understands them anymore. Let's see what the hell we can stir up,' and we did."[8]

By September 1984 the Department of Commerce modified its original distribution license proposal. Commerce proposed that distribution licenses be continued as a matter of policy. Furthermore, the department would not demand customer lists from export firms. Nevertheless, the department requested that each corporation monitor product reexport or transshipment. In line with that policy, the department announced it would set up an internal audit program to track corporate adherence to the Commerce Department's export rules.

With export legislation stalled in 1984, the Department of Defense managed to enlarge its jurisdiction over Commerce in one area: the licensing of sales to non-COCOM but free-world nations. A presidential order assigned Defense review of exports to so-called "leaky grapes," Hong Kong, Austria, Finland, Lichtenstein, Singapore, South Africa, Switzerland, Syria, Taiwan, India, Iraq, and Libya.[9] By presidential order the Department of Defense can monitor such exports as:

- electronic and semiconductor equipment
- test and measuring equipment
- microcircuits and integrated circuits
- computers
- silicon and other components
- sapphire substrate

A presidential order assigned export license control over private, commercial products destined to non-COCOM nations represented a jurisdictional win for Defense, and a loss to Commerce.

Then the Department of Commerce struck back. Just as the Department of Defense extended its jurisdictional reach into commercial VLSI circuits, Commerce extended its jurisdictional reach into military systems. Commerce imposed export control regulation on nuclear missile systems, their electronic components (e.g., analog to digital converters) and specific technical data.[10] Interagency quarrelling is not without offensive as well as defensive strategy.

DEPARTMENT OF COMMERCE VERSUS CUSTOMS (TREASURY)

A jurisdictional war also surfaced between the Department of Commerce and the Bureau of Customs, Department of Treasury. The Department of Defense alleged that Commerce's enforcement of export controls was overstretched and essentially ineffective. In an unusual interagency transfer, Defense allocated $25 million to augment Custom's export enforcement program.[11] And Customs enforcement activity came alive. Commerce had cleared a computer license to Digital Equipment Corporation (DEC) to export a computer to West Germany. Apparently the machine was routed to South Africa and then to the Soviet Union. But Customs impounded the computer shipment with much public fanfare. Both Secretary Weinberger and Secretary Regan (Treasury) held a press conference on the DEC equipment. (Data General, a DEC rival was to observe later that the equipment contained obsolete, 12-year-old component technology).[12] In any case, Customs' action reinforced the perceived ineffectiveness of Commerce's enforcement program.

But Commerce soon responded with export enforcement. The department created a department assistant secretary for export control, increased its enforcement regulation and resources by 400 percent. It then reexamined its effort and concluded: "We have had results that are extraordinary."[13] For good measure Commerce accused the Customs Bureau of allowing eighty-seven Hughes helicopters to be shipped to North Korea. Thereupon Customs responded that Commerce was becoming like "newspaper writers."[14] Commerce's rejoinder was that Customs be awarded the "Chutzpah of the Year Award."[15]

Interagency rivalry intensified over the pending export control legislation. The issue of jurisdictional turf was joined when the House bill assigned enforcement to the Commerce Department, the Senate bill to Customs. In fact, the Customs Department described the House bill as "a KGB relief act."[16] But Secretary Baldridge alleged that Defense, in releasing reports to the National Technology and Information Service, was "tolerating a massive give-away project of sensitive information to the USSR."[17] In a classic congressional compromise, the final legislation assigned licensing enforcement to both Treasury (Customs) and Commerce.

NATIONAL SECURITY AGENCY VERSUS NATIONAL BUREAU OF STANDARDS

Point-of-sales devices, personal computers, minicomputers, and computer work stations increasingly serve as communication terminals. Corporations and government agencies are becoming network dependent as information is transmitted over copper cable, satellite relay, microwave relay, and optical fiber.

Encryptographic key and algorithms are classified under Defense Department policy and for obvious reasons. Here the National Security Agency, (NSA) created in 1952, has assumed a central role in protecting U.S. secrets and in monitoring the attempt by adversaries to penetrate and compromise that information. Within the federal government, NSA's role is pivotal and central. The agency designs encryptographic algorithms and electronic keys for Defense application.

Unauthorized access is equally critical to corporate computer networks, whether employed in manufacturing, transportation, retail credit cards, or banking. Hence privacy is of paramount importance. An encryptographic standard for private sector use evolved as a cooperative endeavor between IBM and the National Bureau of Science, Department of Commerce. Known as DES (Data Encryption Standard), the standard was made public in 1977.[18] Firms employed the algorithms for their data communications networks. Manufacturers supplied products with appropriate electronic keys and circuits. The private sector thus owned, operated, produced equipment, and utilized encryptographic products for network security.

However, the National Security Agency became concerned in the 1980s that government networks might be susceptible to Soviet penetration, that the public DES standard might be compromised by Eastern bloc snooping. Indeed there was fear that commercial corporate networks of the United States might be even more vulnerable to unauthorized penetration.

In 1984 NSA announced it would design a new algorithm and electronic key known as CCEP.[19] Such a product would be government owned and classified. The NSA would franchise firms to market products and the agency would retain control over electronic keys. By implication, corporations concluded that NSA would no longer support the public DEC standard for encryptographic application.

There was also the implication that the CCEP standard, because it embodied a defense classified algorithm, would not be exported to offshore corporate subsidiaries. Given its overseas diversification, banks became concerned about the consistency, if not viability, of their data networks. Would such networks require more than one security standard? Would networks be subject to government control? The NSA's position was obviously pivotal. Its three hundred employees outnumbered the resources of some thirteen professionals at the National Bureau of Standards. Thus, a struggle over jurisdictional turf ensued between Commerce and NSA. Congress soon stepped into the act; several bills were introduced that assigned primacy of the National Bureau of Standards over NSA's security standards.

A jurisdictional struggle also focussed on the definitional content of information. For decades, classified information has been the prerogative of the Department of Defense. But what of nonclassified matters deemed "sensitive,"—such items as medical records, social security records, or federal reserve money transfers. Such information is confidential; should it be classified or at least subject to national security regulation?

In 1977 a President Carter directive assigned jurisdiction of sensitive, unclassified information to the Departments of Defense, and the National Telecommunications and Information Agency (NTIA), Department of Commerce. Because of budget restrictions NTIA proved ineffective in defining information content. By 1984, a presidential directive assigned the Defense Department jurisdiction over government, unclassified, sensitive material that monitored such government data bases as the National Technical Information Service (NTIS), the Defense Technical Information Service (DTIS), and NASA.[20]

Regulation of government data banks tightened under the 1984 directive. The National Security Decision Directive (NSDD) did not deal with classified government information. Rather, its focus was on unclassified public documents. Such regulation became part of a generalized endeavor by Defense to exercise oversight in NASA, NTIA, and the National Defense Information Center. Indeed, NASA announced a list of so-called 'no-no' list firms in the private sector—largely because of suspected overseas customers.

In sum, federal regulation has been extended to information content and telecommunications products. The regulation of exports, foreign customers, licensing within COCOM, approval of encryptographic equipment, the content of nonclassified information, have in turn precipitated internecine warfare among and between Defense, Commerce, and State;

between the National Bureau of Standards and the National Security Agency; and between Commerce and Treasury.[21] If one trend in this inter-agency struggle can be discerned, it is that the Department of Defense's regulatory jurisdiction has broadened and predominated over time.

That preeminence has resulted from directives from the Secretary of Defense, executive orders from the President, directives from the National Security Council, and congealed by budget fund transfers from the Defense Department to the Treasury, and from the Defense Department to COCOM.

How did the Department of Defense acquire such jurisdictional authority? First, the preeminence of Defense's ISP over DRE has been a tribute to the bureaucratic infighting of ISP personnel. In the struggle over Defense Department regulatory policy, ISP has emerged as a locus of control and authority.

Second, the quarrel between State and Defense over COCOM policy was, according to some in the State Department, preordained by section 10G of the 1979 Export Administration Act. That section places the burden on the President to justify overruling a Department of Defense position. Few if any presidents have been willing to wash bureaucratic laundry before a congressional committee.[22] By default, the argument goes, the Defense Department exercises essential veto power of national security issues within the federal government.

A third element, the federal budget, must be assigned to resources. When a government agency takes the King's shilling, it does the King's bidding. Defense, for example, transferred $25 million to the Department of Customs for Project Exodus. Defense budget allocations outran the resources of other agencies. When the Defense Department assigned personnel and $2 million to COCOM, group decisions were often responsive; and in the budget struggle between NSA and the Bureau of Standards, the Department of Commerce was hardly competitive.

Finally, the jurisdictional decision to decide classified, sensitive information regulation was consolidated by the Department of Defense by a National Defense Security Directive of 1984, though later rescinded.

In sum, the Defense Department's preeminence has been driven by agency directives, executive orders, budget resources, and congressional mandates. More often than not, Defense has emerged as the arbiter in deciding the content and reach of national security regulation. Ironically, the spectacle of interagency turf fighting has generated a policy by-product. Other government agencies—civilian agencies—attempting to protect their jurisdictional integrity, have endeavored to out-Pentagon the

Pentagon. As a result, even a benign agency such as the Federal Communications Commission proposed to curtail the buying freedom of the regional Bell operating companies by invoking the principle of national security. Thus, within the federal establishment, one can detect a growing adaptation of national security as a regulatory doctrine.

NOTES

1. Testimony of Dr. Richard D. DeLauer, Undersecretary of Defense for Research and Engineering: Senate Hearings Before the Permanent Subcommittee on Investigations, Committee on Governmental Affairs, *Transfer of Technology,* 98th Cong., 2d sess., April 27, 1984, p. 27.

2. Ibid., p. 56, Richard Perle.

3. Ibid., p. 29, Richard DeLauer.

4. Ibid., p. 38.

5. William A. Root, "State's Unwelcomed Role," *Foreign Service Journal* (May 1984): 28.

> During the past six years, State had been particularly ineffective in leading negotiations on the most important item on COCOM's agenda: the updating of computer controls. The U.S. position has simply been the Defense Department's position.

6. William A. Root, "Trade Controls That Work," *Foreign Policy* (Fall 1984): 80; John P. Hardt and Jean F. Boune, "U.S. Export Control Policy and Competitiveness," Proceedings of the CRS Symposium, Congressional Research Service, April 30, 1987; "Shortly after a Defense handpicked a new U.S. delegate to COCOM arrived in Paris, the most competent veterans on the COCOM international staff were fired by the United States." Remarks of William A. Root, p. 99.

7. James Gordon, "Commerce Department Plans to Enforce New Distribution License Rules," *Aviation Week and Space Technology* (July 15, 1985): 93; Fred McGrail, "Export Controls: New Rules for an Old Problem," *Electronic Business* (April 15, 1986): 38.

8. Before the Department of Commerce, Transcript of Proceedings. In the Matter of: Hearings on Proposed Changes to the Distribution License Procedures, October 9, 1984, Boston, Massachusetts, p. 59.

9. Michael Schrage, "Pentagon Wins Trade Fight," *Washington Post,* March 24, 1984, p. 1.

10. Jack Robertson, "Government Close-up," *Electronic News* (January 11, 1980): 8.

11. Martyn Chase, "Defense Takes Charge as Export Battle Heats Up," *Electronic Business* (June 1, 1984): 28.

12. Letter, Edson D. de Castro, President, Data General, to the Honorable

Malcolm Baldrige, U.S. Department of Commerce, Washington, D.C., January 29, 1984.

13. Ted Agres, "U.S. Stands to Lose Big in Interagency Turf Wars," *Research and Development* (May 1985): 53.

14. Ibid., p. 53.

15. Ibid.

16. Edwardo Lachica and Gerald F. Seib, "Agencies vie over Exports in Technology," *Wall Street Journal,* February 2, 1984, p. 3.

17. Ibid., p. 55.

18. Office of Technology Assessment, Congressional Board of the 100th Cong., *Defending Secrets, Sharing Data: New Locks and Keys for Electronic Information,* OTA–CIT–310 (Washington, D.C.: U.S. Government Printing Office, October, 1987), 14.

19. Tom Athanasiou, "Encryption, Technology, Privacy and the National Security," *Technology Review* (August/September, 1986): 59.

20. Hearings Before the Subcommittee on Transportation, Aviation and Materials, House Committee on Science and Technology, 99th Cong., Computer Security Policies, June 27, 1985; Judith A. Turner, "Pentagon Planning to Restrict Access to Public Data Bases," *The Chronicle of Higher Education* (January 21, 1987): 10.

21. Ross Gelbspan, "Military Looks to Rerail Bill Limiting NSA's Role on Data," *Boston Globe,* October 5, 1986, p. 12.

22. James K. Gordon, "Three Agencies Will Cooperate to Cut Export License Delays," *Aviation Week and Space Technology* (May 6, 1985): 111; *East-West Technology Transfer: A Congressional Dialog with the Reagan Administration,* Joint Economic Committee, Congress of the United States, December 19, 1984, p. 16.

8

Regulation versus the Private Sector

While federal agencies quarrel incessantly over jurisdictional control of national security regulation, from the perspective of the private firm, federal regulation gives all the appearances of a united front. Certainly, over the past two decades, the tension between national security regulation and the private sector has intensified and grown. The question remains, what theory or rationale underlies government intervention into the buying and selling decisions of the firm? Moreover, what is the application of theories in the aggregate?

THEORY OF REGULATION

Consider the rationale of government control of product exports. By definition, some products are obviously military and classified. No one questions the national security imperative of battlefield tanks, tactical fighter planes, or Stinger missiles. Other products are deemed to reside at the opposite end of the polar spectrum; that is, products that are commercial or nonmilitary by definition. Presumably, a middle classification of products embodies both commercial and military features and capability. Such products are termed *dual use.*

Dual use products, producer as well as consumer goods, may range from robots to speed boats, from heart monitoring equipment to hang gliders, from telephone PBXs to personal computers, from "love boats" to genetic engineering. Some go so far as to assert that a pure commerical product is nonexistent, that every product embodies the potential of a dual function. The rationale for dual use regulation is that such products enhance the military capability of our adversaries and thus merit vigilant oversight, scrutiny, and control.

But what about manufacturing know-how, knowledge, and information? What is the principle that extends regulation to commercial data banks, technical research papers, or college graduate courses? If information lends itself to regulation, what demarcation separates classified from unclassified information?

The National Security Council has insisted that private services, like commercial products, also reside within a broad continuum of classifications. At one end, government information is classified and secret. At the other end, government information may be public or nonproprietary. It is once again the middle ground that resists easy classification and invites regulatory oversight. The middle ground consists of information, though unclassified, that may be intimate to the nation's national security interest. Hence the government has invoked "unclassified but sensitive" as a new category. Government data banks and commercial data banks fall into this middle nomenclature.

Commercial bibliographic services, stored in computers, accessed by remote terminals, are essentialy an automated extension of library bibliographic services. Such information is, of course, available to the public. Nevertheless, the mosaic theory of national security is invoked in the name of regulatory oversight. The mosaic theory holds that though components of information may be benign, data patterns can be cancerous. In the words of the Department of Defense, "The . . . individual abstracts or references in government or commercial data bases are unclassified, but some of the information taken in the aggregate may reveal sensitive information concerning U.S. strategy, capabilities, and vulnerabilities."[1] The national security argument holds that sensitivity invites, indeed mandates, some form of government supervision and oversight.

Similarly, research papers, graduate courses, and technical information that reside in the private sector can, as a composite, reveal sensitive national security issues. For example, private academic papers that explore encryptographic codes may border on a military content, and graduate courses on composite material technology can impinge on national security issues.

If a firm's selling action can trigger a question of national security, can a firm's purchase of parts, components, and subsystems also broach security issues—particularly if products come from offshore suppliers? Here the argument holds that foreign dependency weakens the nation's industrial base—particularly under conditions of national emergency, a position that applies with equal force to know-how services as well as products and goods.

In sum, commercial dual use, the mosaic thesis, and foreign dependency invite federal regulation of the buying and selling decisions of private goods and services. The application of these principles has precipitated an adversary relationship between government agencies on one side and the private sector on the other. On the export side, corporations have resisted policies promulgated by the Department of Defense, the Department of Commerce, the National Security Agency, the National Security Council, the Federal Communications Commission, the National Aeronautics and Atmospheric Administration, and both houses of Congress. On the buying or import side, federal agencies have set quotas, run cartels, and engaged in international price fixing schemes that invariably create product shortages or surpluses.

REGULATORY POLICY—EXPORTS

Private Sector versus Department of Defense

Private corporations have, at various times, stood in opposition to the regulation of commercial products by the Department of Defense. In the mid-1980s Defense asserted that export licenses issued by the Department of Commerce (dual use products) should be rescinded; that licensing should be granted on an individual, case by case basis. Each export ought to be assigned on its individual merit. Corporations responded that abrogating distribution licensing policy was akin to asking a person to seek a driver's license every time an individual decided to step in a car. Predictably, business firms regarded microlicensing of export products as overly restrictive and stood in opposition to such blanket regulation, particularly with respect to sales to Western or non-Communist nations.

Nevertheless, the Department of Defense, concerned over export leakage to the Warsaw Pact, sought to extend the regulation of dual use products beyond NATO to non-NATO countries including Finland, Sweden, Hong Kong, Singapore, and Austria.[2] Over the objection of the firms in the private sector, defense has broadened the content of commercial dual use products such as commercial robots, telecommunications switchboards, commercial software, composite materials, medical x-ray equipment, integrated circuits, and personal computers.[3] A recent Defense proposal to expand control over IC chips prompted industry trade groups to insist that this "is a sweeping attempt to expand (DOD) reach to dual use (commercial) devices, production, equipment and materials . . . all developed for the commercial market."[4]

Any conflict between Defense and the private sector turns on the definitional content of a particular product. Does not a telephone switchboard also serve as a command and control device? Does not an Apple II also serve to guide a cruise missile? Does not tennis racquet carbon composite technology also find application in stealth technology? Cannot an X-ray microprocessor be used in airborne radar? The debate over content does not cease with existing commercial products. As new product generations come on stream, as products become embedded with microprocessors and memory, as product life cycles contract and shorten, any controversy over definitional content is likely to persist.

Private Sector versus Department of Commerce

Corporations oppose the regulatory policies and practices of the Department of Commerce as well. The Siberian Pipeline Case is a case in point. Dresser-France, a subsidiary of U.S. Dresser, had contracted to send compressors to the Soviet Union. As the compressors were being loaded on French ships, the U.S. Department of Commerce issued a retroactive ban on the exports to the Soviet Union. The French government, however, ordered Dresser-France to honor the company's contract.[5] Caught in the middle, Dresser sought court action to vacate the Commerce Department's order. The court refused, stating that Dresser had to accede to the department's due process, an evidentiary docket, intervening parties and the appointment of an administrative law judge. The government of France insisted that Dresser-France deliver the compressors. When the company complied, the French subsidiary found its computer linked to the parent headquarters cut off.[6] The code of the parent firm's computer having been altered, Dresser-France was unable to gain access to a technical data base in Pittsburgh. The company subsequently lost sales on bidding for other products in non-Eastern bloc countries. In the meantime, the Department of Commerce counseled other American firms to police their rivals to reinsure the integrity of the unilateral pipeline embargo. A Commerce official advised, "I encourage you to contact the department if you know of any development in your area which we should be aware."[7] In 1984 the Department of Commerce, in response to pressure from the Defense Department, proposed to tighten its licensing of exports on dual use products. In January of that year, the department sought to abandon general distribution export licenses, to abolish drop shipments to end users, and to request U.S. firms to submit lists of their confidential customers and clients.[8]

Respondents opposed the abolition of distribution licenses. Firms insisted that shipment that bypassed the consignee direct to the end customer was mandated by competitive necessity, and they refused to turn over proprietary customer lists to the Department of Commerce. An IBM submission commented that their customer list of two hundred thousand overseas users changed constantly. Indeed, the company added five thousand new customers each quarter.[9] Commerce eventually retracted corporate user lists on the grounds that its computers lacked sufficient storage capability.

Private Sector versus National Security Agency

If any industry is network dependent, it is the banking industry. Telecommunications and computers are today inseparable. Predictably, the banking industry has opposed regulation in the name of data security. The National Security Agency's (NSA) decision to ban the public DES security standard and to substitute its own classified code has thus united the commercial banking industry. The Office of Technology Assessment (OTA), an arm of Congress, recently observed "there is some early evidence that NSA has already begun to encounter difficulty in satisfying the needs of the private sector beginning with the banking industry."[10]

NSA proposed to develop a new classified algorithm and that control of the the encryptographic code would reside in the possession of the government. NSA would not merely retain the electronic key, but the key would be designated as a classified product. A Congressional OTA report noted that "the bankers found the prospect of NSA retaining control of the cryptographic keys to be an unacceptable transfer of bank responsibility to a government agency."[11]

The banking industry is also apprehensive that NSA will block the export of encryptographic products. Such a rule suggests that banks employ one encryptographic standard for domestic networks, another for international networks. Two standards conjure the specter of what bankers term a "network nightmare." As one Bank of America official stated, "Tell your government agencies to use your CCEP gear—but don't mess with my DES."[12] NSA has reluctantly agreed to support the public available DEC standards for at least the near future.

Private Sector versus National Security Council

Private sector firms also stand opposed to data regulations issued by the National Security Council (NSC). In the fall of 1984, Directive NSDD 145 stated that government information, "unclassified but sensitive," stood as a candidate for National Security oversight.[13] Under the directive, the National Security Council was accorded jurisdictional control over the monitoring, dissemination, and regulation of government civil data and information.

However, NSDD 145 also implied that a standard of unclassified, sensitive might very well find application to private sector telecommunications networks and services as well. That definition, announced in the fall of 1984, was expanded in November 1986 to include government-derived information such as human, financial, agricultural and technical.

The Information Industry Association—whose members included periodicals, newspapers, telephone companies, book publishers, stock quotation systems, scientific institutions, data retrieval companies—objected to this new regulatory reach. The association was especially concerned that the National Security Council regulation would find application and jurisdiction within the private sector. This apprehension was not diminished when a member of the Department of Defense observed that ''the federal government is going to pursue very heavy protection of unclassified, sensitive, national security related information.''[14] In addition, an assistant deputy secretary of Defense commented that commercial data base services were, though unclassified, sensitive to national security considerations. Few commercial firms could avoid the threat of direct regulation. A Defense Department official observed, ''The question is not whether there will be restrictions or controls on the use of commercial market on-line data base—the question is how such restrictions or controls will be applied.''[15]

Then in the fall of 1986, the FBI and the Air Force visited Mead Data, operating an on-line commercial bibliographic service. As a company employee recalled, ''They asked whether we would be willing to disclose lists of our customers. We said no.''[16]

The Department of Defense explored several options with respect to commercial private sector data bases. A first would require that commercial data bases be defined as classified but sensitive informaton and hence regulated. A second option held that commercial data bases install software to permit the identity of both customer and the subject material queried. A third option qualified commercial data bases as candidates for export licenses.

NEXUS, operated by Mead Data, for example, is a computerized index of public magazines and newspapers. That such information could be gleaned from the public library apparently was not at issue. Rather, the question was ease of access. Yet a Defense official commented: ''If that means putting a monitor on NEXUS-type service, then I'm for it.''[17]

In the spring of 1987, the NSC announced it would rescind the extension of regulation in the private sector, and the Information Industry Association relaxed. Nevertheless, academic papers, proceedings, conferences, graduate programs, though unclassified, have invited national security oversight. Several nonclassified research papers were withdrawn from the International Society of Photo-optic Instrumentation Engineers Conference in 1982 on grounds of national security.[18] In other instances, attendees had to prove they held citizenship in the United States.

Private Sector versus the National Oceanic and Atmospheric Administration

Corporations have also resisted national security regulation of private remote satellite imaging systems. As noted in Chapter 5, remote images convert digital signals into images, pictures, or photographs. Since the 1960s the Landsat scanning has been a government monopoly under the direction of the National Aeronautics and Space Administration. Under the Carter Administration, Landsat was transferred to the National Oceanic and Atmospheric Administration (NOAA) in preparation for privatization of remote sensing operations. In 1984 Congress passed the Land Remote Sensing Commercialization Act. A consortium of Hughes and RCA (EOSAT) bid and won the contract to operate a private system on the assumption they would receive an operating subsidy from the Department of Commerce.

Remote satellite sensing is a classic dilemma of product duality. Are the satellite pictures commercial products or are they military secrets? (Road maps in the USSR are classified documents.) Should the clarity, the resolution, the availability of remote images invite Defense oversight and regulation? Under President Carter, presidential directive imposed limits on the clarity or meter resolution available to the general public. The 1977 Executive Order ruled that images of less than ten meter resolution would be off limits for private distribution or consumption.[19] The fact that Landsat's technology was confined to thirty meter resolution appeared to make the Carter directive somewhat academic.

The Chernobyl nuclear explosion changed all that. The world demanded information. The Soviets were discretely silent. Landsat's thirty meter resolution, through available, was eclipsed by a ten meter resolution of the French Spot satellites.[20] Spot's images of Chernobyl, enhanced by Swedish value-added companies, were displayed on U.S. television news programs. Some newscasters (CBS) speculated that the Soviets had experienced a nuclear meltdown.

In the meantime, the U.S. began implementing rules for the commercialization of remote sensing images. The NOAA inaugurated an inquiry as to the national security dimension of private photos. Should such images reside in the competitive marketplace; should such images be subject to Department of Defense oversight and review?

The Department of Defense sought power to exercise a broad review and oversight. As the Defense Department brief stated:

> The Department of Defense considers it essential that the Secretary of Defense should be permitted the maximum discretion to determine the system with applicable first amendment standard, those conditions necessary to address national security concerns of the United States.[21]

But a consortium of news media, the Radio/Television News Directors Association (RTDNA) asserted that under the first amendment, any Department of Defense scrutiny constituted prior restraint.[22]

In the summer of 1987, NOAA issued its findings. All private U.S. remote images would be subject to Defense review.[23] Despite a brief from the State Department insisting that NOAA's regulation include foreign government operations, NOAA's regulation applied to U.S. entities only.[24] The French satellite consortium SPOT, selling images three times the clarity of EOSAT, was ruled to reside outside the regulatory reach of NOAA's jurisdiction. Once again, a federal regulation had blanketed U.S. firms with unilateral oversight—permitting offshore rivals to engage in price or nonprice competition.

Offshore competition in remote sensing quickened and erupted from an unexpected quarter. The USSR offered to sell five meter resolution remote sensing to U.S. customers including agencies of the U.S. government. Soviet photos were also price competitive. U.S. firms charged $170 per thirty meter image; the USSR charged $46 for a five meter resolution image.[25] In early 1988, the Reagan Administration relaxed its national security meter stipulation of a ten meter limit. A White House memorandum noted that such relaxation was meant to encourage the development of U.S. commercial systems competitive with or superior to foreign-operated civil or commercial systems.[26] EOSAT has applied for a five meter imaging system oriented to the television news industry.[27] And remote sensing satellites have been announced by Japan and the People's Republic of China. Clearly, international entry had eruped in yet another market where the United States had enjoyed preeminence.

REGULATORY POLICIES—IMPORTS

Private Sector versus Department of Commerce

National security oversight finds application to the buying practices of U.S. firms, particularly if subcontractors are offshore suppliers. A regulatory imperative is invoked in the name of avoiding U.S. dependence on foreign suppliers. The Semiconductor Industry Association, for example, charged that Japanese IC suppliers of D-Rams were dumping chips in the United States, that is, selling at prices below costs. Such dumping threatened the economic viability of major semiconductor suppliers in the United States and thus eroded the defense industrial base of the country. The Department of Commerce concluded after an inquiry, that the Japanese firms had indeed engaged in chip dumping.

Commerce recommended and implemented an IC chip marketing agreement. Japan would submit its costs to Commerce, and Commerce would add on an 8 percent markup—thus setting prices of Japanese and U.S. chips at fair market value.[28] Under its agreement, Japanese firms may charge above but not below the Commerce set price. Within a short period of time D-Ram prices rose from two dollars to eight dollars by August of that year, a 400 percent price jump.[29]

But a year later, Commerce charged that the Japanese had violated the pricing agreement. In retaliation, Commerce embargoed the import of Japanese microprocessors, TV sets, and electric power tools. A Government Accounting Office (GAO) report was later to observe that:

> Although the arrangement was developed to provide remedies under U.S. trade laws responding to unfair foreign trade practices, the strength of will behind this development and enforcement is buttressed by national security concerns. Despite the national security concern, there has been no consensus as to what the semiconductor industry should look like to meet these national security goals. There might be greater assurance of success if such a consensus were reached and the trade initiatives were coordinated at the outset with other actions deemed necessary to insure the viability of the U.S. semiconductor manufacturing industry at the level that satisfies the national security objectives.[30]

Buyers of IC chips insisted that input chip costs were hurting their export sales. The American Electronics Association, a group of computer suppliers and manufacturers, insisted that its members might place their assembly operations offshore in order to remain competitive with overseas rivals.

Other industry associations opposing commerce's IC sanctions, included in the North American Telephone Association (firms that manufacture telephone equipment), the Scientific Apparatus Makers Association, and the Computer Business Equipment Manufacturers Association, buyers of components and subsystems from offshore suppliers.[31] Nevertheless, the Department of Defense has reaffirmed its position that the U.S. IC industry not be dependent on offshore suppliers.[32]

That was in 1986. Two years later, sales of personal computers and computer work stations have exploded, spilling over into a demand for DRAM chips. The "dearth" of such critical components is curtailing the sale and export of U.S. products and DRAM prices are soaring. The *Financial Times* report that "Japanese producers are being begged to increase their exports and U.S. chip makers are forming partnerships with producers in the Far East to increase supplies."[33]

The Department of Commerce, supported by the Department of Defense, sponsored a global IC cartel in 1986. A chip surplus in that year has been converted into a global chip shortage in 1988, which was administered and imposed by federal regulation.

The Department of Defense, also proposes to underwrite ($1 billion) the establishment of a consortium of U.S. chip suppliers research and development. A Defense science board recommended the subsidy on grounds that failure to place U.S. firms on an R&D government subsidy would "have profound consequences for American future national security and economic growth."[34]

Nevertheless, telecommunications, computer, and peripheral suppliers within the United States observe that federal funding may impose a long-term burden on U.S. firms' ability to compete in international markets. The Secretary of Commerce has expressed reservation as to whether an eight hundred employee consortium, pushing military chip development, is the appropriate response to global chip competition.[35] The government sponsored joint venture is now located in Austin, Texas.

The Private Sector versus Congress

Private firms have also resisted product embargoes imposed by Congress. The Toshiba violation of COCOM rules is a case in point. COCOM rules forbid exporting of milling equipment that has direct military applications. Milling tools and software that reduce the noise level of submarine propellers is banned under such regulatin. The Toshiba Mahcine Co., a subsidiary of Toshiba, in concert with Kongsberg of Norway, supplied milling hardware and software to a Leningrad shipyard. The illicit transaction was exposed by a Toshiba employee.

Angered by the sale, the United States Senate voted ninety-two to five to embargo Toshiba Products from the United States for a minimum of two years.[36] Toshiba sales approach about $2 billion in the United States. Indeed, on prime time television members of the U.S. Congress took sledgehammers to Toshiba radios.[37]

But as buyers of Toshiba parts, components, and subsystems American firms lobbied against the two-year embargo. The Computer Communications Industry Association, the Computer Business Equipment Manufacturers Association, the National Association of Manufacturers, essentially argued that without inputs from Toshiba, U.S. exports would be handicapped. Apple Computer stated that Toshiba was the only source of peripheral devices for its computer system, and GE, AT&T, Hewlett Packard, IBM, Honeywell, Motorola, United Technologies, and Xerox in addition to forty other firms opposed the embargo.[38]

In the meantime, a Norwegian investigation disclosed that other NATO nations, U.K., France, Italy, and West Germany, had sold similar milling equipment to the USSR, emphasizing once again that U.S. allies are also commercial competitors.[39]

Private Sector versus the Department of State

Corporations have also stood in opposition to the policies of the State Department. State, through the Office of Munitions, monitors the exports of U.S. products under ITAR (International Trade and Arms Regulation). The Office of Munitions with the advice and assistance of the Department of Defense regulated U.S. exports.[40]

The Challenger accident interrupted satellite launching in the United States. The shuttle was to replace expendable launch vehicles (ELV), the traditional vehicle that hoisted satellites into orbit. When the Challenger went down, the United States soon found that U.S. expendable launching vehicles, through disuse, could not pick up the launching slack immediately. Then NASA subsequently announced that the military would receive first priority on subsequent shuttle flights.

A backlog of satellites began to accumulate within the United States. Some firms in desperation turned to the French. Despite the fact that the French jacked up prices by 40 percent, the France Ariane Rocket enjoyed a $2 billion, two year backlog.[41] Other U.S. firms turned to the People's Republic of China for boosters. In 1986 the USSR offered its Proton

Booster as an alternative launching vehicle. Proton charges of $17 million per launch were pegged at more than half the cost of a $50 million U.S. launching.[42] In fact, the Soviet Union licensed an American agent to solicit orders for its launching facilities and services.

U.S. government officials expressed concern that the U.S. satellites transported to the Soviet Union would be vulnerable to the loss of technical secrets. Soviet officials countered that U.S. or corporate officials could accompany and guard the U.S. satellite mated with the Proton launcher.

Nevertheless, several U.S. companies have expressed interest in the Proton launcher including General Electric, and Hughes, a division of General Motors. In testing before a House Space Subcommittee, a Hughes aircraft official stated:

> To be competitive, we must consider procuring launch vehicles overseas if their product is satisfactory and their costs low. If our government sets up rules to prevent that—in order to protect our nascent commercial launch industry—then we risk losing both our commercial satellite and launch vehicle business to Europe, Japan and others.[43]

However, a State Department official stated unequivocally that ''all satellites, manned to unmanned, commercial or military—are by definition munition list articles.''[44] The State Department, however, did rescind the ITAR provision applied to the People's Republic of China and Western Union's commerical satellite will be hoisted by the Chinese Long March. U.S. firms have reportedly attempted to reverse the State Department's prohibition of securing offshore launching boosters from the Soviet Union. In the meantime, West Germany is negotiating a booster lease from the Soviet Union.

Private Sector versus the FCC

Bell operating companies that buy telephone equipment from offshore suppliers have encountered the national security argument from none other than the Federal Communications Commission. As discussed in Chapter 3, the once freed Bell operating companies have elected to purchase central office switches from a variety of domestic and offshore manufacturers. Siemens Corporation, a German supplier, has been particularly successful in penetrating the Bell operating market.

In 1986, ITT, a supplier of digital switching systems, decided to vacate the equipment market and sell its European manufacturing subsidiaries to the French government. France, in turn, announced that it was going to privatize—sell—CGCT, a former ITT subsidiary, previously nationalized by the French. AT&T, attempting to diversify into European manufacturing, placed a bid for Compagnie Générale d'Electricité (CGCT) ownership. Siemens, the German supplier, also sought to purchase CGCT shares.

Equipment restructuring found France's organization in Germany and German and U.S. corporations attempting to make acquisitions in France. There was every indication that AT&T might be placed at a competitive disadvantage in its acquisition policy. In January 1987, the FCC injected itself into the proposed French sale of CGCT.[45] The Commission announced an investigation of the offshore buying practices of the regional Bell operating companies (RBOCs), an inquiry supported by the Department of Defense.[46]

The FCC docket requested that Bell purchases of offshore equipment be cleared by the agency in the name of "efficiency, equity and national security goals."[47] The docket presented an opportunity for U.S. labor unions such as CWA (Communications Workers of America) to repeat its call for U.S. protectionism. The CWA brief replied that the FCC should disallow from any Bell operating investment rate base any foreign or offshore switching equipment.[48] Presumably, a RBOC could buy a Siemens central office switch but could not be permitted to earn a return on that capital investment.

The regional Bell operating companies, opposing competitive bidding before divestiture, now became the strongest and most vocal advocates of open access to equipment manufacturing. Bell South's reponse was typical:

> The policy of Bell South with respect to procurement is to seek out and buy technically suitable goods and services at the lowest overall cost without regard to source of manufacture. Bell South believes this procurement policy is fully consistent with the goals of the Communications Act. Discrimination against suppliers on the basis of geographic location or foreign ownership would be inconsistent with Bell South's obligations to its rate payers and investors.[49]

Nevertheless, the FCC has declared that any RBOC purchase of offshore telecommunications equipment be registered at the agency's Washington office.[50] And recently the Department of Commerce has warned that RBOC joint ventures with European telecommunications suppliers carries with it a national security concern.[51]

Private Sector versus Department of Defense

On occasion the national security argument has also transcended the nation's antitrust statutes. The Department of Defense has blocked or approved mergers on grounds of national security. When Minebea, the Japanese firm, acquired New Hampshire Ball Bearing, the Department of Defense intervened on grounds that national security issues of research and trade had to be resolved.[52] Defense later approved the merger. Defense opposed the sale of Fairchild Camera and Instruments by a French company, Schlumberger, to a Japanese company, Fujitsu, on grounds of foreign dependency.[53] And the Department of Defense banned the sale of a Harris Corporation subsidiary to a British firm, Plessey, on national security grounds. Even NTIA, the Department of Commerce, has expressed concern that foreign acquisitions of U.S. telecommunications affiliates should be regulated because, "a majority of U.S. telecommunications manufacturers might be foreign and also have significant U.S. national defense implications."[54]

In sum, the private U.S. sector has found itself again and again resisting a form of jurisdictional creep driven by national security concerns. U.S. firms have fought the export rules of the Department of Defense, the Department of Commerce, the National Security Agency, the National Security Council, and the National Oceanic and Atmospheric Administration. Many firms have resisted import restrictions, government price fixing schemes, and import quotas whether sponsored by the Department of Commerce, the U.S. Congress, the Federal Communications Commission, or the Department of State.

In sum, federal agencies curtail and limit the freedom of firms to buy, sell, and compete for customers and markets. Such regulatory intervention is driven by three supporting propositions: dual use, sensitive information, and foreign dependency. But what are the broad implications of this national security rationale?

THE IMPLICATIONS OF NATIONAL SECURITY THEORY

Defense, Commerce, and State assert that commercial products embody national security elements. But what if any commercial product is immune from national security regulation? Thane Gustafson, a former Rand economist, suggested that the distinction between civilian and military products is elusive. He noted:

> As soon as one shifts one's focus from weapons systems to the technologies embodied in them, virtually any high technology product, process or skill becomes militarily relevant. From there it is but a short step to declare all advanced technologies to be subject to export controls.[55]

In a sense, the dual use theory asserts that virtually all products in the commercial sector are candidates for regulation: robots, automobiles, hang gliders, crystal computers, medical scanning equipment, speedboats, word processors, imaging satellites, fiber optics, switching equipment carbon composites, genetic engineering.

A similar observation can be made with respect to trade in international areas. A Defense official observed that the Department of State enforcement of the international traffic and arms regulation statute is such that "the ITAR, if enforced to the letter would cover virtually everything done in the United States."[56]

Product blurring and diffusion may explain the growing list of private sector products that invite and attract export oversight. All of this suggests that the military critical technologies list (MCTL) of seven hundred pages, the size of a telephone directory, may not be large enough.[57]

Moreover, what services qualify for regulation under the mosaic theory that information is benign in the particular but subversive in the aggregate? If the National Security Council insists that collections of public newspapers and magazine articles merit federal regulation, then does not such a standard imply that virtually all information falls under the mosaic principle. And does not the mosaic thesis remove any constraint to regulatory oversight? Perhaps the mosaic theory explains why the FBI has requested New York public librarians to monitor patronage use of certain books and specific subjects.

Finally, what is the reach and breadth of the foreign dependency principle? If virtually all goods and services are endowed with elements of national security, does not that suggest that most all imports of goods and services qualify for some aspect of security regulation? And if so, does not this imply that regulation of autombles, steel, and textiles marks a first step—that national security mandates that machine tools, robots, integrated circuit chips, satellite imaging, and boosters also merit some form of government intervention? Carried to its extreme, such a policy argues against economic specialization, comparative advantage, and foreign trade competition. Foreign dependency, in short, is a rationale for economic autarchy.

Irrespective of the principle invoked, how does the national security argument effect and condition the operations of U.S. firms in the private sector? This issue is discussed in Chapter 9.

NOTES

1. Testimony of Donald L. Latham, Assistant Secretary of Defense, U.S. Department of Defense. Hearing Before the Subcommittee on Transportation, Aviation and Materials. House Committee on Science and Technology, *Computer Security Policies,* 99th Cong., 1st sess., June 27, 1985, p. 3; Walter Seeley, p. 77; Ross Gelbspan, "Information Policy: Reagan Seeks Controls on Database Access," *Boston Globe,* April 20, 1987, p. 35.

2. Eduardo Lachica, "New U.S. Technology Export Guidelines Broaden Pentagon's License Review Role," *Wall Street Journal,* March 22, 1984, p. 10; Michael Schrage, "Pentagon Wins Trade Fight," *Washington Post,* March 24, 1984, p. A1.

3. "OECD Warns of Curbs on Software Trade," *Financial Times,* October 3, 1985, p. 4.

4. Jack Robertson, "DOD Eyes Comm'l MPU Exports," *Electronic News* (July 27, 1987): 1.

5. "The Siberian Dispute and the Export Administration Act: What's Left of Extra Territorial Limits and the Act of State Doctrine?" *Houston Journal of International Law,* 63 (1983): 65.

6. "Dresser-France's Data Flow Cut During Pipeline Sanctions Row," *Transnational Data Report* (April/May, 1983): 12; " A Delivery That May Be Dresser-France's Last," *Business Week* (October 18, 1982): 50.

7. "U.S. Seeks Export Data for Pipeline Suppliers," *New York Times,* October 1, 1982, p. D1.

8. Department of Commerce, International Trade Administration, Docket No. 40110-4107, *Amendments to the Distribution License Procedure,* Proposed Rule with Request for Comments, September 12, 1984, Federal Register, p. 35,790.

9. Correspondence from Edward G. Law, IBM World Trade Corporation to Vincent Greenwald, Office of Export Administration, U.S. Department of Commerce, Washington, D.C., April. 6, 1984, p. 5. "We estimate that for IBM alone the list will initially amount to two hundred thousand names with more than five thousand new names each quarter."

10. "Database Access Controls Considered," *Computer Law and Tax Report* (February 1987): 3.

11. Office of Technology Assessment, Congressional Board of the 100th Cong., *Defending Secrets, Sharing Data: New Locks and Keys for Electronic Information,* OTA-CIT-310 (Washington, D.C.: U.S. Government Printing Office, October 1987), 107.

12. Charles C. Howe, "Into the Night," *Datamation* (June 1, 1986): 24.

13. Testimony of Donald C. Latham, *Computer Security Policies,* p. 2.

14. "IIA Uncovers Major Department of Defense Database Restrictions," *Information Times,* December 1986, p. 1.

15. Ibid.

16. David E. Sanger, "Rise and Fall of U.S. Data Directive," *New York Times,* March 19, 1987, p. A18.

17. "Pentagon Considers Data Access Controls," *Transnational Data and Communications Report,* August 1986, p. 5; Kenneth Allen, "S.I.: Sensitive Information," *Information Times,* October 1980, p. 3.

18. "An Ominous Shift to Secrecy," *Business Week* (October 18, 1982): 142. "Only two days before a San Diego meeting of the Society of Photooptical Instrumentation Engineers, The Defense Department prevailed on authors to withdraw some 170 of 626 unclassified technical papers from presentation."

19. Frederic B. Henderson, III, "Private Sector Satellite Remote Sensing: Barriers to Commercialization," in Robert Aamoth, et al., *American Enterprise, The Law and the Commercial Use of Space,* vol. 2, National Legal Center for the Public Interest (1986), 93; "Space Surveys Group for Sales," The Economist, July 6, 1985, p. 76.

20. Elaine Williams, "France Demonstrates Satellite System," *Financial Times,* Oct. 26, 1982, p. 5; "Ariane Space Puts Mass Order for 50 Big Rockets," *International Herald Tribune,* October 8, 1987, p. 9; Philip Reuzin, "Ariane Rocket's Success May Give Europe Lead Over U.S. Firms in Satellite Market," *The Wall Street Journal,* September 19, 1987, p. 5.

21. Department of Defense, Office of General Counsel, Washington, D.C., *Memorandum for Deputy Under Secretary of Defense for Policy Attention,* George Schossberg, December 31, 1986.

22. Before the Department of Commerce. In the Matter of the Licensing of Private Remote Sensing Space Systems. Docket No. 51191-5191, National Oceanic and Atmospheric Administration, *Comments of Radio-Television News Directors Association et al.,* May 23, 1983 (cited as NOAA Docket).

23. National Oceanic and Atmospheric Administration, Department of Commerce, *Final Rule, Licensing of Private Remote-Sensing Space Systems,* Docket No. 51191-7064, 1987.

24. NOAA, *State Department Comments,* Docket No. 51191-7064, December 29, 1986.

25. "Soviet Sale of Space Photos," *New York Times,* January 3, 1982, p. 35.

26. "U.S. Ends Restrictions on Satellite Photos," *Journal of Commerce* (January 27, 1988): 2A.

27. "EOSAT to Mount Challenge to Landsat Restrictions," *Aviation Week and Space Technology* (November 2, 1987): 26.

28. Bruce P. Malashevich, "Chip Trade War—U.S. Waterloo? *Journal of Commerce* (August 27, 1986): 11A.

29. Calvin Sims, "Chip Prices Skyrocket; Tokyo Accord Blamed," *New York Times,* September 9, 1986, p. P1.

30. United States General Accounting Office, *International Trade, Observations on the U.S.-Japan Semiconductor Arrangement,* April 1987, p. 9.

31. Louise Kehoe, "Famine Bites Computer Makers," *Financial Times,* February 18, 1988, p. 16.

32. Beth Karlin, "Is the U.S. Too Dependent on Foreign Semiconductors?" *Electronic Business* (April 15, 1987): 24; "Weinberger Cites Need to Boost Chip Industry," *Aviation Week and Space Technology* (May 18, 1987): 24.

33. Jack Robertson, "Sanctioning Dependence," *Electronic News* (April 27, 1987): 9.

34. Bruce D. Nordwell, "Defense Science Board Urges Semiconductor Consortium," *Aviation Week and Space Technology* (March 2, 1987): 94; Charles H. Ferguson, "Sink or Swim with Semiconductors," *New York Times,* August 18, 1987, p. A25.

35. Richard Bambrick, "DOD Funds for Servatech Draw Commerce Objections," *Electronic News* (June 29, 1987): 1.

36. Stuart Auerbach, "Senate Approves 2-year Ban on Toshiba's Sales in U.S.," *Washington Post,* July 1, 1987, p. 1.

37. Editorial, "Bashing Toshiba, Hurting America," *New York Times,* September 15, 1987, p. A34.

38. Susan F. Rasky, "Top U.S. Corporations Lobbying Against Curb on Toshiba Imports," *New York Times,* September 14, 1987, p. 1; Stephen Dryden, "How Toshiba is Beating American Sanctions," *Business Week* (September 14, 1987): 58.

39. Clyde H. Farnsworth, "Five More Companies Named in Toshiba Case," *New York Times,* October 22, 1987, p. D2; Eduardo Lachica, "Norway Finds Allies Violated COCOM Controls," *Wall Street Journal,* October 22, 1987, p. 34.

40. U.S. General Accounting Office, *Arms Exports, Licensing Reviews for Exporting Military Items Can Be Improved,* September 1987.

41. Les Dorr, "Are the Profits Really There?" *Spaceworld* (July 1987): 34; Edwin McDowell, "European Failures Leave Space Effort Mired in Frustration," *New York Times,* April 5, 1986, p. C1.

42. Theo Pirard, "Marketing The Proton," *Satellite Communications* (June 1987): 36.

43. Statement from Steven D. Dorfman, Hughes Aircraft, Committee on Science, Space and Technology, Subcommittee on Space, Science and Applications, U.S. House of Representatives, September 17, 1987, p. 4; William Broad, "Industries Fight Ban on Using Soviet Rockets," *New York Times,* October 1, 1987, p. 1.

44. "State Dept. Denies License to Export U.S. Satellites to the Soviet Union," *Aviation Week and Space Technology* (July 27, 1987): 59.

45. Bob Davis, "U.S. Communications Chief Warns Germany of AT&T," *Wall Street Journal,* November 12, 1986, p. 2.

46. Before the Federal Communications Commission. In the Matter of Regulatory Policies and International Telecommunications. Docket 86-494, *Notice of Inquiry and Proposed Rule Making,* January 30, 1987, p. 3. Also *Comments of the Department of Defense,* April 17, 1987, p. 1: "DOD also agrees with the Commission's recognition that telecommunications is critical to our nations economic development and national security."

47. Ibid., p. 3.

48. Ibid., *Comments of Communications Workers of America,* April 6, 1987, p. 3.

49. Ibid., *Comments, Bell South,* April 17, 1987, p. 8.

50. Bob Davis, "FCC Orders Phone Companies to Report Yearly Purchases of Foreign Equipment," *Wall Street Journal,* February 26, 1987, p. 7.

51. "Assessing the Effects of Changing the AT&T Antitrust Consent Decree," *NTIA Report,* U.S. Department of Commerce, February 4, 1987, pp. 125, D 54.

52. Robert S. Greenberger and David Wessel, "Pentagon Asks Review of Japan Firm's Bid to Acquire New Hampshire Ball Bearing," *Wall Street Journal,* October 5, 1984, p. 22.

53. Jack Robertson, "DoD Aide Seeks Policy as Foreign Buyouts of U.S. Firms," *Electronic News* (February 23, 1987): 1.

54. *NTIA Report,* p. 54.

55. Thane Gustafson, "Effects and Dangers of Technological Transfer," in Gary K. Bertesh, John R. McIntyre, Ed., *National Security and Technological Transfer* (Boulder, CO: Westview Press, 1984) p. 116.

56. Stephen H. Unger, "The Growing Threat of Government Secrecy," *Technology Review* (February 1982): 38 (Statement attributed to Defense Department official, Larry Sumney).

57. National Academy of Science, Committee on Science, Engineering and Public Policy, *Scientific Communications and National Security* (Washington, D.C.: National Academy Press, 1982), 7.

9

The Double Squeeze

What is the effect of a growing tension between federal regulation on one side and the private sector on the other? Two consequences are apparent. First, private firms experience an economic squeeze as regulations reduce a firm's total revenues and lift total expenditures. In addition, U.S. firms experience an opportunity cost resulting from the delay and the compliance burden imposed by tiers of competing regulatory agencies. Both economic and government actions impose a cost-price squeeze on the U.S. firm. Resources for future product development atrophy. Markets disappear as offshore rivals find that their revenues rise, costs fall, and research and development resources expand.

As the U.S. government witnesses the competitive erosion of firms in the private sector, federal assistance is extended and tariffs, quotas, embargoes, subsidies, offered to aid and abet a domestic industrial base in the name of national security. U.S. firms become increasingly dependent on government largess. Corporations tend to become wards of a benign state. The irony is that the state promulgates a cure for a disease caused by federal regulation.

THE ECONOMIC SQUEEZE

U.S. national security regulation rests upon two premises. First, commercial products merit export regulation and control; and second, that unilateral regulation can be imposed without any competitive consequences.

At the outset, it is important to reemphasize that the regulation of military products is not at issue. Rather, it is the regulatory status of commercial products that is at stake—regulation extended to robots, genetic engineering, word processors, butcher glovers, medical X-ray machines, telephone switching gear, and children's toys. Because of product duality, Congress has mandated that export licenses be sanctioned by the Department of Commerce and reviewed by the Department of Defense.

Furthermore, the federal regulation of an expanding list of commercial products is unilaterally applied to U.S. firms. Western allies—competitors—are not burdened by comparable rules, oversight, control, or enforcement. To that extent, U.S. corporations bear a burden disproportionate to their overseas competitors.

Given the regulatory disparity for commercial products, U.S. firms invariably find themselves placed at a competitive disadvantage. If Commerce, Defense, or State bans a commercial product export, an offshore rival firm enjoys, by default, the gain of sales and revenues. And if a U.S. firm is cleared to ship a part, component, or subsystem to a European customer, the fact that customer reexports may be subject to U.S. restriction imparts the element of risk and uncertainty, especialy when delivery promptness constitutes a vital ingredient to user loyalty. Whether regulations are issued by State, Commerce, or Defense, there is evidence that overseas customers are designing out U.S. components in their products and systems. A recent Naitonal Academy of Science study comments on this "de-Americanization" of overseas products:

- Fifty-two percent reported lost sales primary as a consequence of export controls.
- Twenty-six percent had business deals turned down (more than two hundred and twelve separate instances) by free world customers because of controls.
- Thirty-eight percent had existing customers actually express a preference to shift to non-U.S. sources of supply to avoid entanglement in U.S. controls and
- More than half expected the number of such occurrences to increase over the next two years.[1]

Episodic cases also suggest regulatory bypass:

- *The London Economist* noted "The design of Britain's telephone exchange, System X, were told to minimize the number of American components in the creation so as to minimize potential trade hassles."[2]
- A French firm, employing a Data General computer for a medical cat scanner observed that with the next generation it would, "design us out," according to Data General personnel.[3]
- The late Secretary Baldridge observed, "I have seen letter written by CEOs

(Chief Executive Officers) of major foreign companies instructing their managers to design out U.S. parts from their products."[4]

- British Aerospace advised Hewlett-Packard that it would avoid U.S. parts and components.[5]

- Siemens, a German electronics firm, built its own array processor in order to avoid U.S. regulations.[6]

- A Hong Kong telecommunications agency shifts to non-U.S. components.[7]

- French telephone manufacturers seek independence from U.S. IC chips and microprocessor suppliers.[8]

And in remote commercial data base, an OTA study suggests that competitive options exist: "Commercial data base firms have expressed concern that if the U.S. decides to limit foreign access allies will seize upon this diminution of U.S. presence to strengthen their own data base industries."[9]

Unilateral embargoes do not constitute a free good. The 1981 embargo imposed on the export of U.S. oil and gas equipment to the USSR (since lifted) exacted the following losses:

- Five hundred million dollars Fiat-Ellis technology and kits for crawler tractors.

- One hundred and seventy-five million GE rotors.

- One hundred million dollars Cameron Iron Works blow-out preventors.

- Eighty-eight million loss to Caterpillar pipe layers.[10]

If regulation reduces the ability of U.S. firms to compete for sales and customers, then import regulations—whether tariffs, quotas, or embargoes—elevate costs incurred by firms in purchasing parts and components. Fair market chip prices, unilateral embargoes on export products, bans on satellite launching, restrictions on fiber optic purchases raise the cost incidence to U.S. firms as resource buyers. National security regulation exacerbates a price-cost squeeze. Corporate earnings diminish and the ability to engage in research, development, and subsequent product innovation is attenuated. To the extent offshore rivals avoid or circumvent product controls, they enjoy robust revenues, lower costs, higher earnings, and research resources.

The economic cost of unilateral embargoes to the U.S. firms may not be trivial. Before the embargo on oil and gas equipment to the Soviet Union, Caterpillar Tractor enjoyed an 85 percent market share of pipe laying equipment in the USSR.[11] Today, Kumatsu, the Japanese firm, enjoys an 85 percent share of the Soviet market. Today Kumatsu has a presence in the U.S. domestic market and is contemplating plants in—of all places—Peoria, Illinois. One could make the case that Kumatsu's U.S. penetration was underwritten in part by profits form its Soviet sales. In any case, U.S. firms bear an economic burden disproportionate to their overseas rivals—namely, unilateral regulation of private sector products destined for private sector consumption.

THE REGULATORY SQUEEZE

U.S. policy exacts a regulatory squeeze on U.S. firms that, if indirect, is nevertheless real. Here the firm—comporting with rules, regulations, filings, due process, license applications, the burden of proving non-munition qualification, and the obligation to monitor customer shipments—incurs the cost of regulatory privatization. This cost goes beyond Commerce's budget increase from $7.3 million to $39 million in seven years or its personnel rise from 203 to 510 in the same period.[12] It goes beyond the Defense Department's budgetary growth devoted to regulating private commerce. Such budget costs are borne by the general taxpayer and are explicit. Compliance costs, by contrast, are borne by individual firms and can in some estimates approach twenty times the size of public sector budgets; that is, a one dollar budget cost exacts a twenty dollar compliance cost on the private sector.[13]

When, for example, the Department of Commerce relaxed its requirement that U.S. firms reveal customer lists, Commerce held that U.S. firms monitor customer reexport policies. Commerce, in turn, audits U.S. companies or determines whether the department's policy meets compliance. Presumably, Defense reviews Commerce. In a sense, U.S. export companies have been deputized by Comerce to enforce government strictures and policies.

But who bears the incidence of this legal compliance? Obviously, the U.S. firm ultimately must post prices that cover government regulatory costs. And although it is true that the larger firm may bear that cost with comfort, the small or medium size corporation may regard compliance cost as a significant barrier to export markets. The small entrepreneur may not even make the attempt. It is conceivable that unilateral federal regulation is a concentrating force within the private sector of the economy.

Regulation also poses a cost of delay. In an environment of global competition, shortening product life cycles, decreasing market boundaries, an emphasis on customer response and regulations can inhibit corporate reaction to customers enjoying a universe of options. If a U.S. firm cannot address the needs of its client expeditiously, offshore suppliers will meet that requirement with dispatch. Time is thus a precious commodity. From the perspective of Commerce, with Defense and State locked in jurisdictional struggle, however, time is often viewed as inconsequential. But what may be free good to a GS-15 translates into lost foreign sales and foregone earnings to the U.S. firm. Perhaps this explains why many U.S. corporations employ Washington "fixers" who "walk" licensing documents through the U.S. regulatory maze (see Figure 9.1).[14]

Licensing delays may be regarded as a nonissue if all firms are equally disadvantaged by due process. But if the French or Japanese bureaucracy proves more agile than Commerce or Defense, such delay does have a bearing on the U.S. firm's ability to compete, to generate sales and subsequent earnings. (Forty percent of all U.S. manufacturing is subject to export licensing.)[15]

In sum, unilateral regulation of commercial products constitutes a force that lifts corporate costs and depresses corporate revenues. It is as if the U.S. government engaged in a conspiracy with offshore rivals to handicap the freedom of the U.S. firm to compete in a global setting. To the extent such regulation is unilateral, to the extent embargoes are retroactive, to the extent tiers of agencies multiply control and oversight, U.S. firms are clearly disadvantaged in competing against their overseas rivals.

Alternatively, U.S. policies confer a cost-price bonus to offshore rivals. Little wonder that as European firms witness more and more U.S. products subject to unilateral regulation; as the Japanese note the time meter as U.S. licenses trundle through federal "in trays," as members of the COCOM tabulate the cumulative burden of privatized cost, overseas rivals perceive U.S. regulation as the coming of a second Marshall Plan.[16]

Figure 9.1
The Regulatory Maze

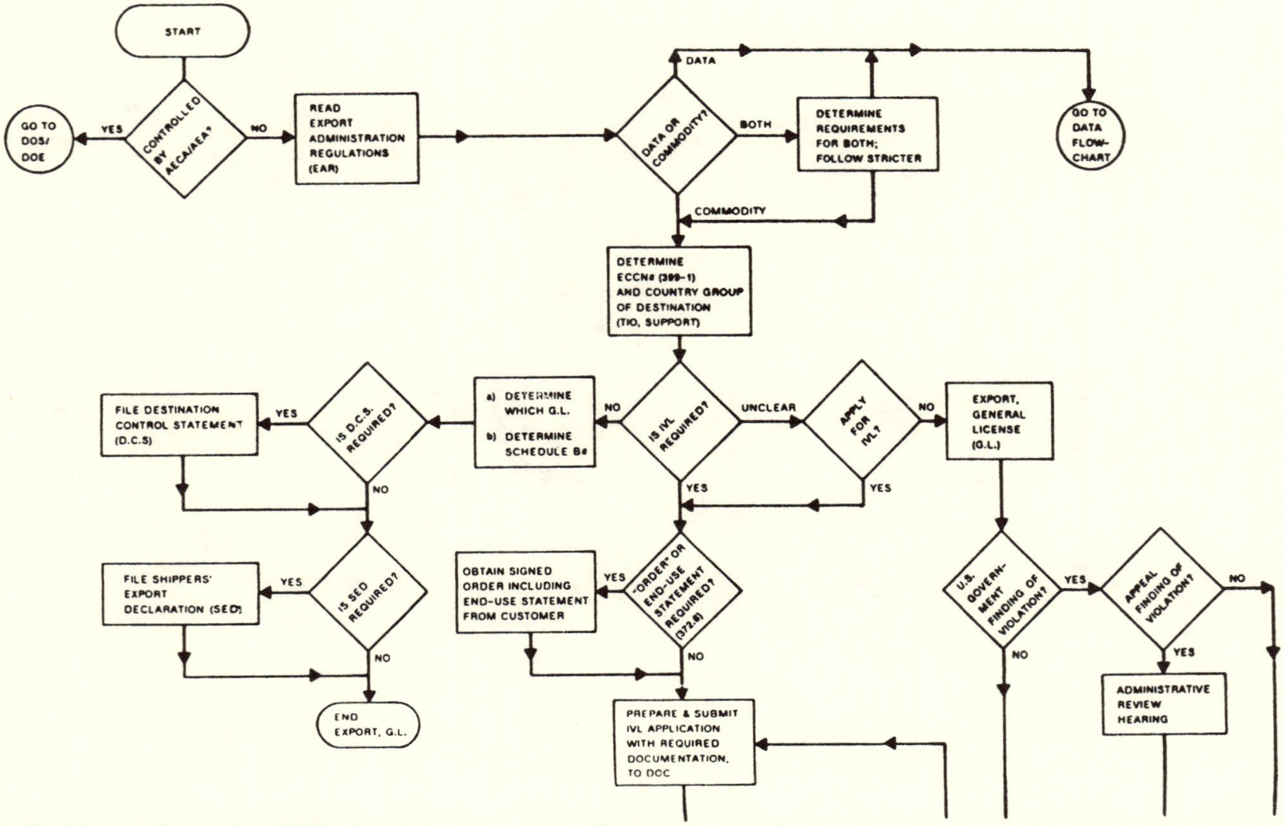

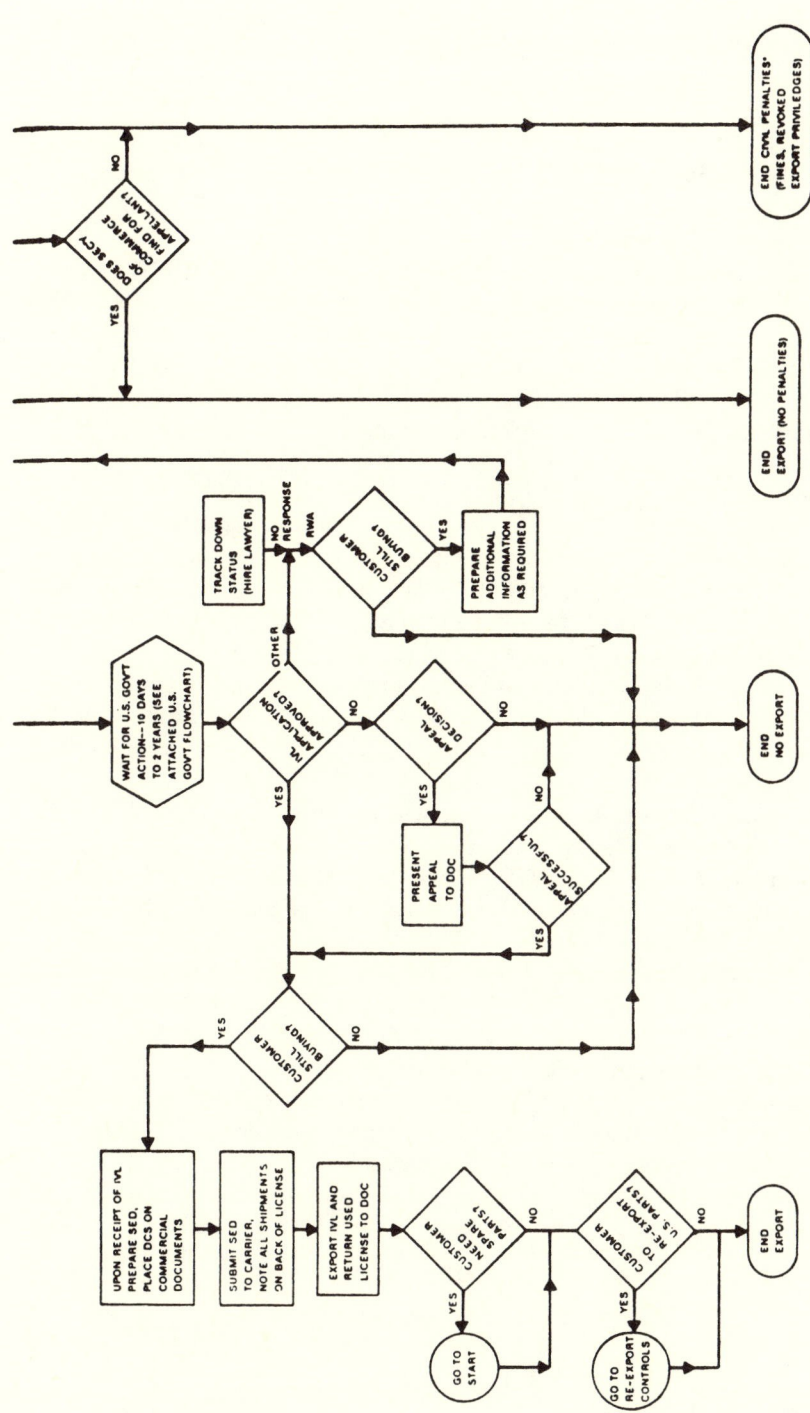

Source: National Academy of Engineering, *Balancing the National Interest* (Washington, D.C.: The Academy Press, 1987), 76–77. Reprinted with permission of National Academy Press.

NOTES

1. National Academy of Sciences, Committee on Science, Engineering and Public Policy, *Balancing the National Interest* (Washington, D.C.: National Academy Press, 1987), 11.

2. "High Tech for the Russians," *The Economist* (February 15, 1986): 63.

3. Robert J. Samuelson, "Backward Policies Restrict Our Exports," *The Los Angeles Times,* March 7, 1985, p. 1.

4. Donald Lambro, "Baldrige Battling Export Restrictions," *The Washington Times,* March 10, 1987, p. 3D.

5. James M. Dorsey, "Export Rules Biting into U.S. Businesses," *The Washington Times,* March 19, 1987, p. 2A.

6. Ibid.

7. Willie Schatz, "A Modern Moving Story," *Datamation* (July 15, 1984): 69; Raymond Snoddy, "Cable and Wireless to Limit Electronic Components from U.S.," *Financial Times,* April 10, 1984, p. 6.

8. David Marsh, "France May Cut Reliance on U.S. for Chips," *Financial Times,* April 30, 1984, p. 8.

9. Office of Technology Assessment, Congressional Board of the 100th Cong., *Defending Secrets, Sharing Data: New Locks and Keys for Electronic Information,* OTA—CIT-310 (Washington, D.C.: U.S. Government Printing Office, October, 1987), 1.

10. President's Export Council, *Coping with the Dynamics of World Trade in the 1980's,* December 1984, p. 323.

11. Homar O. Blair, "Export Controls on Non Military Goods and Technology: Are We Penalizing the Soviets or Ourselves," *Texas International Law Journal* 21 (1986): 320.

12. "America's Domestic and International Role in Protecting the Free World's High Technology," *Business America* (January 18, 1988): 7-8.

13. Murray L. Weidenbaum, *The Future of Business Regulation* (New York: American Management Association, 1979), 22-23.

14. See Letter to the Editor by Stan Yalof, President of Tetrahedron, Associates, Inc., San Diego, California, *Electronic Business* (December 10, 1984): 24.

15. National Academy of Sciences, "Balancing," p. 10.

16. F. Karl Willenbrook, "Information Controls and Technological Progress," *Issues in Science and Technology* (Fall 1986): 93.

10

Issues and Options

The national security argument stands in contrast to an environment of global competition and market entry. What is the nature of this opposition? What alternatives are open to public policy? What is the current policy direction of the United States? Can regulation be effective over the long term? First consider the trend toward global markets.

The postdivestitute world of U.S. telecommunications is one of telecommunications entry, softened boundaries between computers and telecommunications, realigned telephone prices and costs, an environment of shorter product life cycles, a revitalization of corporate efficiency and innovation.

In addition, a postdivestiture environment invites and solicits entry into telecommunications manufacturing. Market access has accelerated hardware–software innovation, expanded the buying options of the Bell operating companies, and expedited a globalization of product availability and diversity.

Furthermore, corporate telecommunications networks have emerged as a competitive strategic tool. Telecommunications networks as in-house systems employ the network to bond the firm closer with customers and suppliers. The network also leverages the firm to spatial markets and remotely located customers. To the extent that networks are geographically blind, the corporate network has evolved into an international strategy as well. At the same time the network permits the firm to bypass or separate itself from captive suppliers and subcontractors. Network bypass represents another form of market entry.

Moreover, information technology, expertise, know-how, and capability are migrating not merely across domestic boundaries within the United

States, but are also diffusing internationally—to the West, the East, and the newly industrialized nations. Information barriers to market entry are softening, declining, and eroding. With technological diffusion aided and abetted by networking, few U.S. corporations today exercise total exclusivity or enjoy total technological know-how. It's a cliche to assert that information technology is now of global proportion.

But in this global environment, what is the status of the conventional national security argument? The record demonstrates that the national security argument opposed the deregulation of U.S. telecommunications industry stood silent as to the incentives of market entry, supported cost-plus rate of return regulation, passively sanctioned long depreciation lives, pretended that industry boundary lines were immune to technological change, and ignored an environment of entry, access, and technological innovation.

In addition, the national security argument opposed deregulation of telephone manufacturing, diversity in telecommunications research and development, choice in telephone equipment purchases, and entry by off-shore suppliers. In defending monopoly in both telephone service and telephone manufacturing, the national security argument insisted that utility oversight be extended to telephone manufacturing—however indirect that regulation be applied.

The United States has also witnessed the spectacle of federal agencies struggling for regulatory turf, control, and jurisdiction. To be sure, the Department of Defense has emerged as central in promulgating its definition of national security. But as a rationale the national security argument has been emulated by the Department of State, Department of Commerce, the Customs Bureau, Federal Communications Commission, NOAA, National Security Council, and National Security Agency—all soliciting resources to enlarge their authority to intervene into the nation's private sector.

Furthermore, federal agencies compete to erode the prerogatives of U.S. firms' ability to both sell products in competitive markets and buy from multiple overseas suppliers. In the name of national security, each federal agency has felt essential to out-compete sister agencies for regulatory jurisdiction and control. As competition erupted within the government sector, the cost of internecine federal warfare spilled into the U.S. private sector—redounding ultimately to the advantage of offshore rivals.

The national security argument also intruded into the buying practices of U.S. firms. Federal agencies competed with each other to curtail, restrain, and inhibit the freedom of private firms to secure resources at their most optimal price and quality. As regulatory rules became increasingly complex, increasingly burdensome, increasingly costly, increasingly time-consuming, federal policies blanketed more and more commercial exports, services, and imports. Today, the national security rationale holds that dual use applied to butcher gloves and kidney dialysis equipment, that private information found in public libraries merit vigilant oversight, that centralized self-sufficiency stands as the recipe to economic prosperity and economic well-being.[1]

It need not be emphasized that the trend of national security regulation stands in contrast to an environment of market and global competition. What is of concern is the effect incremental doses of regulation imposes on the vitality of the U.S. firm. On the sale side, few U.S. firms enjoy market exclusivity or monopoly status. Most encounter varying degrees of product substitutes, competition, and market entry, both real and potential. Regulations that deter, curtail, block, or otherwise inhibit the response of the U.S. firm to competition, diminish customer sales, corporate earnings, research and development, and capital investment. The Department of Commerce has acknowledged the United States is experiencing a "de-Americanization" of overseas products, that the U.S. firms are being relegated to the position of "supplier of last resort." A first consequence, then, of regulation is that U.S. firms' total revenues are penalized while offshore rival firms are rewarded.

A second consequence resides on the buying side of the equation. Whatever the form—limits on imports, quotas, embargoes, fair market values, legalized price fixing—such policies translate into higher costs to the buying firm and not incidentally lead to supply shortages of personal computers. By contrast, overseas rivals—to the extent they elect to secure parts, components, and subsystems at lower costs—can pass those economies forward as lower prices. Foreign competitors secure cost savings denied their U.S. counterparts.

Through audits, compliance requirements, due process, and judiciary appeals, firms must bear the burden of proving benign the national security consequence of private output. This cost burden increases as global competition intensifies, as product life cycles shrink, as product innovation accelerates internationally. In effect, the United States "privatizes" the cost of national security regulation. In effect, regulation constitutes a tax up in the U.S. firm. In effect, depressed total receipts and inflated costs squeeze the firm's earnings.

The long-term consequence of a double squeeze is disquieting. Depressed earnings lead to depressed revenues, resources, product innovation, and curtailed research and development. Alternatively, the earnings of overseas rivals are thereby expanded as resources are plowed into research, development, product innovation, and service enrichment. Firms residing outside the sphere or burden of regulation enjoy a competitive advantage vis-a-vis their American counterpart. In the name of national security, regulation ultimately penalizes the U.S. firm and rewards its overseas rival.

Consequently, the private sector of the economy is visited by a government mandated cost-price squeeze, what options are open to the government in the future? The following four come to mind:

- Maintain the status quo
- Abolish export regulations
- Abolish import regulations
- Extend U.S. regulation to foreign competitors

MAINTAINING THE STATUS QUO

A first alternative is ''steady as she goes.'' The U.S. economy appears buoyant, our standard of living enviable, economic growth satisfactory, job creation healthy. The status quo is not without its ominous trend, however. A status quo policy promises no relief to the firm from a policy of regulatory squeeze. Indeed, a status quo policy invites more state intervention in the name of economic self-sufficiency and industrial policy. U.S. firms subtly become addicted to federal dependency and largess. Dependency, in turn, saps the long-term ability of the firm to acquit itself in a competitive marketplace. Indeed, the trade deficit in high technology products suggests that U.S. firms can be expected to encounter more rather than less international rivalry in the future. Thus a status quo policy appears unsatisfactory if only because it mortgages the future for a protected, artificial present.

DEREGULATE EXPORTS

A second policy option is to deregulate the export regulations of private goods and services. The problem is that the content of dual use—commercial products—is becoming increasingly elusive. Federal policy has attempted to deregulate some products: medical equipment, personal computers, and key telephone systems. But each subsequent generation of products embodies more technology, more chips, more software, and product life cycles are contracting. If it is true that the average U.S. automobile will embody one thousand dollars worth of electronic equipment by the 1990s, the definitional content of a Chrysler New Yorker is bound to invite a spirited, if not acrimonious, congressional debate.

In any case, export deregulation is unlikely to occur because current regulatory policy rests upon a policy of linkage—connecting our policies to the behavior of the Soviet Union—a form of ethical outsourcing. The Department of Defense, for example, denied the export of environmental computers to a Soviet housing project because HUD (Housing and Urban Development) personnel neglected to contact Russian Refusniks.[2] And many historians remind us that the Soviet Union did not attain its present geographic size absent a policy of force, coercion, and subversion. Regulating U.S. exports to the USSR or to the Western World rests on the premise that Russians will cease to be Russians. Yet West Germany's Franz Joseph Strauss has observed that attempting to reform Russians is akin to "roasting snowballs."[3] If the United States enjoyed a technological monopoly, then unilateral export regulation might possess some bite and effectiveness. But the lesson of the 1980s is that the U.S. policy increasingly handicaps the ability of U.S. firms to compete internationally.

Military assistance, on the other hand, can and does elicit a response. Better that U.S. Stingers had been sent to the Afghan rebels in December 1979 than an economic embargo policy that rewarded Komatsu tractors at the expense of Caterpillar. In any case, any reduction of unilateral security regulation over private goods will be greeted by contempt from the U.S. political right. Current reevaluation of export controls by the House of Representatives has earned the title as "the Soviet Technology Relief Act" of 1987."[4] In sum, unilateral regulation of commercial products can be expected to be a part of American policy for the foreseeable future.

DEREGULATE IMPORTS

A third policy option is to deregulate the rules, practices, and policies that curtail the freedom of the firm to buy resources at the most optimal price. Often the performance of overseas part and component suppliers exceeds the performance of U.S. firms. Decontrolling imports, however, finds opposition from the political left. The arguments possess a familiar ring—foreign dependency, pricing below cost, domestic content, plant shutdowns, unemployment—which is all a mask for protectionism, the inability or unwillingness to permit U.S. firms to compete against overseas rivals. Rather than ask why government policies handicap U.S. firms, the U.S. political left (supported by the Defense Department) prefers to invoke the power of the state to run a semiconductor cartel in the name of economic self-sufficiency. In the case of Toshiba and Kongs-berg, the U.S. Senate voted ninety-two to five to ban Toshiba products from the United States as punishment for COCOM violations. Yet such a ban would deny Motorola access to 32 percent of its memory chip sup-plies. The fact that import regulation constitutes a tax on the earnings of U.S. corporations almost appears irrelevant. Abolishing unilateral import regulation, very much opposed by the political left, appears unlikely in the near future.

In a very real sense, U.S. national security regulation is driven by political consensus; the right supports export control, whereas the left supports import control. Both invoke state intervention in the name of national security. Nor is there countervailing political power willing to identify the short-term and the long-run costs of political intervention that throttle the competitive freedom of the U.S. firm. No political consti-tuency has examined whether short run regulation leads to long-term economic atrophy and hence the ultimate compromise of U.S. national security. Indeed, there is a consensus in the United States, embraced by both ends of the political spectrum, that mandates more rather than less government regulation, oversight, and control. Rather than securing competitive freedom for the U.S. firm, U.S. policy chooses to pursue policies that limit the action and discretion of its overseas rivals. A fourth alternative thus blankets foreign competitors with national security over-sight comparable to that imposed on U.S. firms. This option represents the current direction of U.S. policy.

REGULATE COMPETITORS

A first policy step extends U.S. regulation to our allies in COCOM. Rather than regulate U.S. firms unilaterally, U.S. policy levels the playing field by pushing for similar constraints on the buying and selling decisions of overseas competitors. If the United States unilaterally bans the export of computers, telecommunications, robots, and software, COCOM countries must be blanketed with such control and constraint. Presumably, if COCOM increases regulation, the United States will soften unilateral, third-party restrictions within COCOM nations. In the extreme, the U.S. government elects to purchase a product rather than witness a NATO country deliver a product to the Soviet Union—as was the case with Belgium milling machines in 1984.[5] Here the U.S. Depart-ment of Defense, at the taxpayers expense, becomes NATO's buyer of last resort.

Extending U.S. regulation to our NATO allies often poses delicate matters of extraterritoriality. U.S. rules that cover the reexport of, say, a British telephone switchboard to Hungary, remain controversial. But U.S. rules that regulate the movement of a product *within* the national boundary of an allied nation are likely to encounter some resistance. Such was the case with IBM in1983 when the company sent a letter to its U.K. customers advising that

> Transactions within the United Kingdom involving "Advanced System" are also subject to the obtaining of U.S. export approval. Such transactions include not only the initial installation of a new machine with a user, but also any subsequent dealing or transferring in such machines.[6]

Needless to say, the IBM letter ignited a lively question and answer period in a House of Commons debate.

And when the U.K. Department of Energy attempted to donate its obsolete U.S. computer to the University of London, the invocation of U.S. licensing approval elicited a spirited inquiry as to the content and meaning of British sovereignty.[7] Even U.S. friends and allies can be expected to resist federal regulatory intrusion. (Would the United States, for example, welcome the U.K.'s clearance to transfer a U.K. machine from Cleveland to Cincinnati?)

A second administrative level exports U.S. regulation to such non-NATO nations as Sweden, Finland, Austria. At the outset such negotiations are not without some economic leverage. The United States can shut off access to our domestic market unless nations conform to our internal national security rules and policy.

That such pressure is not without effect can be seen by U.S. negotiations with Sweden's Ericsson. Ericsson is currently selling telephone switching gear and mobile radio equipment to newly split off Bell operating companies. The United States stressed to the Swedes that entrance into the United States was conditioned on Sweden's ability to prevent reexport of sensitive products, even indigenous products, to the Soviet Union.[8] Swedish legislation acceded to the Defense Department's request.

A third administrative level of regulatory export extends the licensing burden to the newly developed nations: the Singapore, Hong Kongs, Taiwans, South Koreas, and Malaysias. A regulatory quid pro quo is suggested to each nation; abide by export regulation and domestic access will be granted. Such endeavors may carry with it an element of success in the short run. Clearly the United States is engaged in a policy managing, policing, and controlling an international technology cartel. The question is, how effective will that cartel be in the longer term? Here cartel theory can be instructive.

A cartel is cohesive as long as the self-interest of individual players remains subordinate to the firm's loyalty to the group. Alternatively, cartels disassemble when the interest of the individual firm exceeds that of its loyalty to the group. In the recent Toshiba case, for example, the shipping of milling equipment that quiet Soviet submarines, constituted an explicit COCOM violation. Nevertheless, a Norwegian investigation revealed subsequently, that Toshiba and a Norwegian firm called Kongsberg were not alone in violating COCOM rules. Firms that participated with Toshiba consisted of companies in the U.K., Italy, France, and West Germany. If corporations find that breaking from the cartel generates higher profits, then the pressure to cheat can overpower any commitment to group loyalty. Commercial self-interest may strike one as parochial and narrow, but is is a most enduring incentive. Recall that European firms broke the U.S. imposed embargo on the Siberian pipeline equipment. Even Mr. Richard Perle, a proponent of tight export control, identified the power of commerce in bargaining sessions with COCOM:

> It is not uncommon at COCOM meetings to find officials of European countries whose product line is being discussed and negotiated, seated behind their national delegations. The last thing in their mind is the security of the Western alliance."[9]

An official of a European manufacturer offered a more cynical view of COCOM regulatory compliance:

> We make the necessary statement that a machine we are shipping doesn't exceed the required degree of technology. But we know it does. So we lie. We make up a false form. The government knows it. Besides, I'm helping my country's economy.[10]

And Mary Fagan, a reporter for the U.K.'s *New Scientist,* documented the series of options that Japanese firm's employ to circumvent COCOM regulations.[11]

A dummy strategy simply falsifies the product destined to the Soviet inspectors pass the invoice because it does not list products on COCOM's banned list. Another method, called the *Mask,* occurs when a Japanese buries the banned part in a benign commercial product. The Soviet customer then digs the product out upon receipt.

A third strategy, termed the *Hand Luggage,* takes place when a Japanese employee takes small components through customs without official discovery. Ms. Fagan reported: "In multiple journeys to the USSR from Japan, employees carry small parts of a larger system in hand luggage that is easy to take through customs. This is becoming easier, says Kumagai, as components become smaller."[12]

A fourth strategy circumvention is known as the *Soviet Route.* A Japanese official gives the sensitive component to a Soviet official and he or she takes it back to the USSR.

A fifth strategy is termed the *Breakdown.* Here a particular machine may be listed on COCOM's banned list, but its individual parts are not so banned. The Japanese ships separate components to the Soviet Union and then help them assemble the machine on site.

Sixth strategy, labelled the *Provincial Route,* involves shipping a banned product via smaller, more provincial airports in Japan. Export officials in the provinces are less sophisticated than their counterparts at Yokohama or Kobi. Still another strategy, the *Third Party,* routes the banned product to Switzerland and then on to the Soviet bloc—a leakage that occurs through non-COCOM nations.

A final strategy is called the *Exhibition.* Here products for display are shipped to an Eastern bloc nation. The Japanese loan the display piece to the Soviets and technicians examine the relevant technology.

A second factor that disrupts cartel cohesion is the ongoing process of market entry. New players penetrate the market, price competition erupts as individual firms elect to pursue their commercial self-interest. Nonprice competition invokes the same response. As technology, know-how, experience, spread among more players, as more firms enter the game, they push product innovation, contract product life cycles, and intensify price and nonprice competitive response. Policing commercial products becomes more elusive as the number of players multiplies and the complexity of products proliferates. It is one thing to monitor NATO; quite another to monitor non-NATO Western countries, much less Taiwan, Brazil, Indonesia, South Africa, South Korea, India, and the People's Republic of China.

Having said this, regulating one's competitors remains an inviting and attractive policy prescription. A recent National Academy of Science report, suggested that export controls cost $9 billion and nearly two hundred thousand lost jobs, but nevertheless argued for the extension of COCOM regulation to non-COCOM nations. The report stated that non-COCOM Nations:

- assume responsibility for preventing exports to the Soviet Union and the Warsaw Pact countries of imported COCOM controlled items that do not have re-export authorization from the originating COCOM countries.
- monitor use of COCOM items in the Soviet Union and the Western Pack countries after obtaining re-export approval.
- control the export to proscribed destinations of indigenously produced products that are functionally equivalent to COCOM controlled items and
- cooperate in enforcement measures.[13]

It is questionable whether the United States will diminish its regulatory extension to private, commercial products in the near future—despite some relaxation of U.S. component content of overseas systems. Rather, the United States prefers a policy that blankets its allies and international rivals with trade controls.

Over and above the growing number of foreign rivals that qualify as candidates for regulation there is still a question concerning which commercial products invite federal scrutiny. The list is by no means limited or finite. Each subsequent generation of commercial products, developed in the private sector, embodies more chips, electronics, hardware, and software. Increasingly, the content of duality is dynamic and hence eludes easy definition.

And assuming for a moment that any consensus on product definition can be reached among rivals in a particular year, how long will that definition hold or remain valid in the future? If it is a reality that in an environment of global competition product innovation is accelerating, that the pace of obsolescence is quickening, how can the federal government monitor technological convergence, product fusion, and process innovation? The answer is inviting: Assign more and more resources to the regulatory effort of commercial products and control will be accomplished effectively and with dispatch. But such a policy also assumes that more and more of the nations resources be allocated to public control rather than private innovation. In a world of increased competition, such a prescripton borders on economic suicide.

All of this suggests that definitional content remains the heart of any national security regulation. A conventional definition holds that national security is control—government power to circumscribe the freedom of the firm to buy and sell. Such as policy contemplates more regulation, more rules, more sanctions, and additional policing, fines, and imprisonment. Such a definition is premised on a static, short-term view of national security—a veiled form of industrial policy that chooses national "winners" and "losers."

A second definition, by contrast, equates competitive freedom with national security: freedom to buy, sell, innovate, respond to consumer needs, and address the imperatives of rivalry in a global setting. Under this definition public policy must address the incentives that drive corporate efficiency and innovation. That definition assumes that the United States, despite seven hundred government laboratories, no longer exercises exclusive control over a broad range of technologies. That definition assumes that U.S. firms no longer enjoy monopoly status in markets or services. That definition asserts that over the long term the economic incentive to innovate, assume risk, and engage in entrepreneurship marks the *essence* of national security. If federal regulation diminishes, dilutes, throttles, or nullifies these incentives, then U.S. regulatory policy places the nation's economy at risk.

If uninhibited freedom to compete and innovate remains the vital key to economic survival and national security—and that is the thesis of this book—then sooner than later public policy must address a legacy of policies that unilaterally punish and debilitate U.S. firms in the private sector. These include the double taxation of U.S. savings, taxes on capital gains, federal disincentives to save, the Jackson-Vanik Act, the Foreign Corrupt Practices Act, taxes in corporate earnings, and federal expenditures that each year consume more and more of the nation's productive resources.

In an environment of global competition, it is not surprising that corporations experience bankruptcy every day, every week, and every month. That is to be expected. But nowhere is there the equivalent of a Chapter 11 in the public sector—the federal establishment. In 1984, for example, the nation dissolved the largest private telephone company in the world. The United States elected to pursue a policy of telecommuncations competition. Today, as an institution, the FCC embraces national security as a regulatory substitute for the public interest. We are witnessing the ironic spectacle of invoking the national security issue to recycle obsolete, insolvent regulatory institutions. Until a fundamental reassessment of the cost of these institutions is undertaken, the United States will enjoy a political consensus that throttles, stifles, and penalizes the ability of U.S. firms to compete in a global economy.

Thus far the United States has been in the dubious position of establishing a political consensus bent on atrophying the long-term national security interest of this nation. No countervailing opposition to this consensus appears on the horizon. As we move into the 1990s, the political left and right prefer to define regulation as a free good in the short run. Could it be that the long-run cost of that consensus forfeits economic freedom?

NOTES

1. Robert D. McFadden, "Libraries Are Asked by F.B.I. to Report on Foreign Agents," *New York Times,* September 18, 1987, p. 1; Judith Axler Turner, "Effort to Limit Access to Unclassified Data Bases Draw Criticism," *The Chronicle of Higher Education* (March 4, 1987): 12.

2. James M. Dorsey, "Export Rules Biting Into U.S. Business," *Washington Times,* March 19, 1987, p. 2A.

3. Theo Sommer, "Reform Grips Russia and China," *World Press Review* (January 1988): 14.

4. Richard Perle, "Making Sure Our Technology Stays Ours," *Wall Street Journal,* July 22, 1987, p. 20.

5. Steven J. Dryden, "Belgium Workers Ask Bigger Bailout for Loss of Machine Sales to Soviets," *The Washington Post,* October 6, 1984, p. A 13; "U.S. Freeze Delays Belgium Tool Purchase," *The Journal of Commerce* (September 28, 1984): 5A.

6. Kevin Cahill, *Trade Wars* (London: W. H. Allen, 1986), 4.

7. "High-Tech Trade Caught in Red Tape," *New Scientist* (July 24, 1986): 21.

8. Eduardo Lachica, "Secret Police, Neutral Nations Guard American Technology to Gain Import Rights," *Wall Street Journal,* January 15, 1987, p. 1; Eduardo Lachica, "U.S. Plans to Urge Non-Aligned Nations to Keep Advanced Gear from Soviet Bloc," *Wall Street Journal,* January 15, 1987, p. 20.

9. *Wall Street Journal,* p. 20.

10. Willie Schatz, "Yankee Bashing Time," *Datamation* (July 15, 1985): 46.

11. Mary Fagan, "Eight Ways to Break the Technological Embargo with the East," *The New Scientist* (September 17, 1987): 28.

12. Ibid., p. 29.

13. National Academy of Science, Committee on Science, Engineering and Public Policy, *Balancing the National Interest* (Washington, D.C.: National Academy Press, 1987), 149.

Appendices

Appendix A

Federal Register, Vol. 49, No. 13, Thursday, January 19, 1984
Proposed Rules

DEPARTMENT OF COMMERCE
International Trade Administration
15 CFR Parts 373 and 376
(Docket No. 40110-04)

Amendments to Distribution License Procedure

AGENCY: Office of Export Administration, International Trade
Administration, Commerce.

ACTION: Proposed rule with request for comments.

SUMMARY: The Office of Export Administration (OEA) proposes to amend the
"Distribution License" procedure, an authorization to export certain
commodities under an international marketing program to consignees that
have been approved in advance as foreign distributors or users. OEA
has determined that these regulatory changes, as well as the
institution of an extensive program of audits of Distribution License
holders and consignees, will better assure this licensing procedure
does not result in illegal diversion contrary to U.S. national security.
This rule would require submission of a more complete description of
the commodities to be exported under a Distribution License. This rule
also would ensure that exporters applying for a Distribution License
has sufficient experience with basic licensing procedures and
sufficient overseas business to comply fully with the Distribution
License procedure. Before these proposed changed are published in
final form, OEA will determine which will apply to existing
Distribution Licenses and which will apply only to new applications or
license renewals.

The proposed rule modifies the provisions dealing with direct shipments
to customers to approved consignees by limiting such shipments to the
country in which the consignee is located. This rule also proposes to
eliminate the provision that allows approved distributors to make
shipments under the permissive reexport provisions of # 374.2 of the
Regulations.

The public is invited to make specific comments on each proposed
change, and to specify and substantiate anticipated workload impact and
economic impact for each proposed change. Comments should specify no
only the impact if the proposed changes are applied retroactively to
all existing Distribution Licenses, but also the impact if the proposed
changes are applied only to new license applications and to license
extensions and renewals.

DATE: Comments must be received by February 21, 1984.

ADDRESS: Written comments (six copies when possible) should be sent to: Procedures Branch. Office of Export Administration, U.S. Department of Commerce, P.O. Box 273, Washington, D.C. 20044. Mark "COMMENTS" on the face of the envelope.

FOR FURTHER INFORMATION CONTACT: Vincent Greenwald, Office of Export Administration (Telephone: (202)377-3856).

SUPPLEMENTARY INFORMATION:

The period for submission of comments will close February 21, 1984. All comment received before the close of the comment period will be considered by the Department in the Development of final regulations. While comments received after the end of the comment period will be considered if possible, their consideration cannot be assured. Public comments will become a matter of public record. Comments that are accompanied by a request that the information be treated confidentially because of its business propriety nature or for any other reason will be accepted on the conditions described below.

Public comments on these regulations will be a matter of public record and will be available for public inspection and copying. In the interest of accuracy and completeness, comments in written form are preferred. If oral comments are received, they must be followed by written memoranda, which will also be a matter of public record and will be available for public review and copying. Communications from agencies for the United States Government or foreign governments will not be made available for public inspection.

The public record concerning these regulations will be maintained in the International Trade Administration Freedom of Information Records Inspection Facility, Room 401C-B, U.S. Department of Commerce, 14th Street and Pennsylvania Avenue, N.W., Washington, D.C. 20230. Records in this facility, including written public comments and memoranda summarizing the substance of oral communications, may be inspected and copied in accordance with regulations published in Part 4 of Title 15 of the Code of Federal Regulations. Information about the inspection and copying of records at the facility may be obtained from Patricia L. Mann, the International Trade Administration Freedom of Information Officer, at the above address or by calling (201)377-3031.

The Office of Export Administration (OEA) is especially interested in receiving comments on the business and economic effects of the proposed regulations. Because providing such comments may involve the disclosure of proprietary business information, OEA will accept comments on a confidential basis.

Persons may request confidential treatment of their comments involving proprietary information on paperwork burden, lost sales, or any other aspects of the business or economic impact of the proposed regulations. The request must include a full statement of the reasons why confidential treatment should be granted. The business or financial information for which confidential treatment is requested should be submitted to OEA on sheets of paper separate from any nonconfidential information submitted. The top of each page should be marked with the term "Confidential Business

Information." OEA will either accept the submission in confidence or, if the submission fails to meet the standards for confidential treatment, will return it.

A nonconfidential summary must accompany each submission of confidential summary must accompany each submission of confidential information. The summary will be made available for public inspection.

Information accepted by OEA as privileged under section 12(c) of the Export Administration Act and subsections (b) (3) or (4) of the Freedom of Information Act (5 U.S.C. 552(b) (3) and (4)) will be kept confidential and will not be available for public inspection, except according to law.

This rule proposes to establish a requirement that a foreign consignee submit a listing of countries in which U.S. - origin commodities received under the Distribution License will be sold (including names and addresses of customers); the listing will be update quarterly. The Office of Export Administration has submitted this proposal to the Office of Management and Budget (OMB) for review under Section 3504 (h) of the Paperwork Reduction Act of 1980. The public is invited to submit comment on this proposed reporting requirement to the Office of Information and Regulatory Affairs of OMB, New Executive Officer building, Washington, D.C. 20503, Attention: Desk Officer of International Trade Administration.

List of subjects in 15 CFR Parts 373 and 376

Exports.

Accordingly, the Office of Export Administration proposes to amend the Export Administration Regulations (15 CFR Parts 368-399) as follows:

PART 373 - (AMENDED)

373.1 (Amended)

1.   Section 373.1 is amended by adding the following sentence to the end of the first (undesignated) paragraph -

"* * * Improper use or failure to comply with the conditions of any special licensing procedure described in this Pat 373 may, in addition to any enforcement action, result in the loss of export privileges under that licensing procedures."

2.   in # 373.3, that part of paragraph (c)(1)(ii) that appears before (a), paragraphs (c) (1)(iii), (c) (2), and (d) (3)(ii) (D) and (G) are revised; and paragraphs (c) (4) and (5), and (d) (3)(iii) (A) and (B) are added, reading as follows:

373.3 Distribution license.

   (c) Eligible exporters and consignees.

   (1) * * *

(ii) An agent, representative, or any other person or firm distributing the commodities to be exported under this license pursuant to a written agreement, either with the U.S. exporter or its wholly-owned subsidiary, that has been in effect for at least one year and that -

*   *   *   *   *

(iii) An end-user importing the commodities for his own use or for use in the production or manufacture of commodities, who has been importing from the U.S. exporter for at least one year.

*   *   *   *   *

(2) Prerequisite experience and volume of business. In order to be considered for a Distribution License, a new applicant must have receive approval from OEA for at least fifty individual validated export licenses during the 12 months before applying for a Distribution License. These fifty individual validated licenses must have covered exports to countries that will be receiving U.S. exports under the Distribution License (see # 373.3(a)(1)).

*   *   *   *   *

(4) Unless a distributor meets the qualifications for reexports contained in § 373.3 (i), no commodities received by an approved consignee under a Distribution License may be reexported without specific prior written approval from OEA. The written approval may be included on the validated Distribution License, a validated form ITA - 6052, or a validated form ITA - 699P. In addition, no commodity received by an approved consignee under this License may be resold or reexported to any person located in any country not listed in Supplement No. 2 to part 373, until the consignee has obtained the following certification from the purchaser:

> We (purchasers) understand that the commodities obtained
> from (name of distributor) were authorized for export by the
> U.S. Government under a special Distribution Licensing
> procedure on the condition that such commodities would not
> be reexported without specific prior written approval of the
> U.S. Government. Accordingly, we acknowledge that the
> commodities obtained under (order No., Contract No., etc.)
> will not be reexported from (name of country) without such
> approval.

Such certifications must be retained by the approved consignee for a period of two years after the sales transaction. Consignee may be required to submit such certifications for inspection or audit by OEA. When a continual business relationship is anticipated, the certification may be modified to apply to all transactions, may be valid through the normal validity and extension period of the license, and shall be retained for two years beyond that period.

(5) Notification of special restrictions. It is the responsibility of the exporter to notify all consignees of any special conditions or restrictions applicable to goods received under a Distribution License.

*   *   *   *   *

   (d)   * * *
   (3)   * * *
 (ii)   * * *

*   *   *   *   *

(D) List separately on the application, or on an attachment, a general description of each type of commodity to be exported, the appropriate Export Control Commodity Number from the Commodity Control List (CCL) (Supplement No. 1 to # 399.1) for each, and the appropriate paragraph designation - (a), (a)(1), (a)(1)(ii), etc. - under the Export Control Commodity Number. Only commodities included in a CCL entry specifically listed on the application and approved by OEA may be exported under a Distribution License. (The listing of the CCL entries by Export Control Commodity Number and paragraph designation will generally constitute a sufficient description of the commodities being shipped. However, the exporter is encouraged to include as specific a description as possible in order to speed up the processing of the application.) OEA may impose more specific limits on the commodities covered by the license.

*   *   *   *   *

(G) Leave blank item 9(a), "Quantity," the processing code under item 9(c), and item 9(d), "Unit Price" and "Total Price."

*   *   *   *   *

(iii)

(A) Listing of customers. With each form ITA - 6052, attach a listing of the countries in which the foreign consignee wishes to sell U.S.-Origin commodities received under the Distribution License. This listing shall include the country in which the foreign consignee is located and the countries in the consignee's authorized sales territory, giving for each such country the names and addressed of every customer to which the distributor expects to sell. (Changes to this listing shall be submitted quarterly.) This listing is not required for customers located in countries listed in Supplement No. 2 to Part 373, nor is it required to end-users as described in # 373.3 (c)(1)(iii).

(B) Certification of sales territory. The ultimate consignee(s) listed in item 7 of the license application (or on the attached sheet) must submit written certification on the Form ITA - 6052, or on a separate attachment, of (1) at least 6 sales during the previous year within each country in the assigned sales territory, or (2) an average of 6 sales per year over the preceding 3 years within each country in that territory. Each time that a particular Distribution License is extended, the consignee must submit a written statement certifying the continued authenticity of the assigned sales territory and evidence that sufficient sales are anticipated in that territory to justify the extension of a Distribution License authorization.

*   *   *   *   *

3.   Paragraph (e) of # 373.3 is amended by redesignating paragraphs
(1), (2) and (3) as (2), (3) and (4) respectively, and by adding a new
(e)(1); paragraph (f) is amended by adding a sentence to the end of (f)(1),
changing the final period in (f)(2)(ii) to a semicolon and adding the world
"and", and adding paragraphs (f)(2)(iii) and (iv.), reading as follows:

373.3 Distribution license.

*   *   *   *   *

(e) Action on license applications, (1) Pre-approval review. The
Distribution License procedure authorizes multiple export transactions
without a review and approval of each individual transaction by OEA. Thus,
before approving such a License, OEA must be fully satisfied that the
persons benefiting from this special licensing procedure can be relied upon
to adhere to the conditions of the license and the Regulations, and that the
approval of the application will not be detrimental to U.S. interests. To
permit OEA to make such judgments, each application will be reviewed by OEA
and OEE to establish the reliability of the parties to the license. Such
review may entail an audit of past export transactions, inspection of
documents, and interviews in the United States and abroad. If OEA cannot
verify the appropriateness of this special licensing procedure or establish
the reliability of the proposed parties to the license, it may deny the
application or modify it by eliminating persons from the application or by
removing certain commodities or countries included in the application.
However, failure to obtain approval to participate in this special licensing
procedure does not preclude the filing of an application for an individual
validated license or reexport authorization.

*   *   *   *   *

(f) Action on Form ITA - 6052. (1) Validation. * * * OEA will advise
the exporter if any customers on the attached list (see # 373.3 (d)(3)(iii)
(A)) are not acceptable recipients of U.S. - origin commodities.

(2) * * *

(iii) Advise the consignee that he may not resell or reexport any
commodities received under the Distribution License in countries not listed
in Supplement No. 2 to Part 373 until the purchaser has furnished the
certification required by # 373.3 (c)(4); and

(iv) Advise the consignee of any customers listed on the attachment to
Form ITA - 6052. This notification should advise the consignee to submit to
OEA quarterly lists of any changes in customers, and also make clear that
the consignee does not need to report and await OEA approval before making
sales to new customers. Customers may be added at any time, as long as they
are listed in the next quarterly submission, and sales to listed customers
may continue unless the distributor is specifically notified that a customer
is unacceptable.

*   *   *   *   *

4. Paragraph (i)(4) of # 373.3 is removed, and paragraph (j) is amended by removing the phrase "or to a customer is another country who has been authorized to receive reexports under the provisions of # 373.3(1)" in the first sentence, and by adding a last sentence reading as follows: "in addition, if the shipment is to a country of destination not listed in Supplement No. 2 to Part 373, the certification described in # 373.3(c)(4) must be obtained by the consignee before the shipment of the commodities."

5. Paragraph (k)(1) of # 373.3 is amended by inserting the following sentence at the beginning of the undesignated flush paragraph following the indented certification:

"In addition the exporter shall submit a certification of sales territory (see paragraph (d)(3)(iii) (B) of this section).

6. Paragraph (k)(1) of # 373.3 is amended by inserting a new next-to-last sentence to paragraph (iii), reading as follows:

"* * * in addition, before an extension can be granted, the ultimate consignee must submit the certification required by paragraph (d)(3)(iii) (B) of this section. * * *"

7. Paragraph (1) of # 373.3 is amended by adding a paragraph (4)(i), reading as follows:

373.3 Distribution license.

* * * * * * *

(1) Records

* * * * * * *

(4) Inspection of records.

* * * * * * *

(i) The records of both U.S. exporters and approved consignees will be audited by OEA at regular intervals. As part of the audit procedure, a consignee may be required on occasion to submit to OEA a listing of all sales under this License during the previous month.

* * * * * *

8. The following entries are added/ revised in Supplement No. 1 to Part 373, "commodities Excluded from Certain Special License Procedures," each with a footnote reading "Distribution License is available for shipment to countries listed in Supplement No. 2 to Part 373.": Entry 1355 is added between 3336 and 1357; entry 1522 is revised, and an entry 1529 is added immediately following it; entry 1564 is added (following 1555), and an additional entry 1565; and entries 1572 and 1584 are added between 1570 and 1585, reading as follows:

373.3 Distribution license.

*   *   *   *   *   *

Supplement No. 1 - Commodities Excluded from Certain Special License Procedures.

*   *   *   *   *   *

1355 Sub-entries (b)(1)(ii), (iii), (v) and (x), (b)(2), and (b)(6)(ii) only.

Semiconductor material processing equipment; crystal pullers that are rechargeable without opening, or that are magnetic, or that are computer controlled; molecular beam epitaxial growth equipment; electron beam systems; all masks and mask-making equipment, except:

Hard surface coated substrates defined in paragraph (b)(2)(ii);

Photo-optical mask fabrication equipment defined in paragraph (b)(2)(v) that does not exceed the performance capabilities of U.S.-designed photolithographic step and repeat cameras and pattern generator systems introduced in volume into the market before December 31, 1976;

Manual types of mask inspection equipment defined in paragraph (b)(2)(vi);

Photo-optical Contact and Proximity mask align and expose equipment defined in paragraph (b)(2)(vii), and projection aligners that can produce useful pattern sizes no finer than 3 micrometers; and

Contact image transfer equipment defined in paragraph (b)(2)(x). Microcircuit and microcircuit assemblies test equipment denied in paragraph

(b)(6)(ii), except:

Analog test equipment for TV, OP amps and voltage regulators; A/D and D/A circuit test equipment; and

Digital test equipment with test data rates of 10 MHz or less defined in paragraph (b)(6)(ii).

*   *   *   *   *

1522 Lasers and laser systems and specially designed components and parts therefore, as follow: machine tools containing or which are designed to contain lasers described on the Commodity Control List under entry 1522A, single aperture lasers with an output greater than one thousand joules per nanosecond, and tunable diode lasers.

1529 Cesium frequency standards.

Instruments designed for use at frequencies greater than 26 GHz, and capable of being controlled by an external signal.

FFT signal analyzers with "zoom" capabilities having a resolution better than .02 Hz.

*   *   *   *   *

1564 Semiconductor devices that have a high-speed processing capability with a functional throughout rate of greater than $5x10^{11}$ gate-Hz/cm^2.

1985 * * *
1565 * * *

1565 Home personal and small business computers having an XPDR greater than 30 Mbps; specialized processing units that have an "equivalent multiply rate" in excess of 2 million (product) operations per second. (See # 376.10 (a)(4)(xxiv) for the definition of "equivalent multiply rate.")

1572 All electron beam recorders.

Analog recorders with the following characteristics:

Bandwidth greater than 2 MHz for longitudinal machines and video machines modified for transient free recording.

Specifically designed for underwater use.

Tape speed greater than 120 ips, consistent with limits imposed on bandwidth.

Having 28 recording channels.

A time basis error better than $\pm$ .2 microseconds, consistent with limits imposed on bandwidth.

High density digital recorders having a density of 16K flux reversals per inch or greater (one flux reversal – 1 bit).

1584 Cathode ray oscilloscopes having amplifier bandwidths greater than 350 MHz.

Oscilloscopes having cathode-ray tubes incorporating microchannel plate electron multipliers capable of operating at frequencies greater than 1000 MHz.

Digital oscilloscopes with sequential sampling of the input signal at an interval of less than 2 nanoseconds.

PART 376 - [AMENDED]

9.   Section 376.10 is amended by adding paragraphs (a)(4)(xxv) and (xxvi), reading as follows:

#376.10 Electronic computers and related equipment.

(a) Digital computers.

*   *   *   *   *

   (4) Definitions of terms.

*   *   *   *   *

   (xxv) "Equivalent multiply rate" is defined as the greater number of multiplication operations that can be performed per second, neglecting setup or pipeline filling operations. This rate is based on the maximum rate achievable fully utilizing all hardware architectural features (including multiple or staged (pipelined) arithmetic units); assuming optimal operand lengths of 16 bits or greater and optimal operand locations in the "most immediate memory"; and ignoring initialization, interrupts, and data reordering times:

   (a) If the basic multiplication operation includes multiple simultaneous multiplications either because of complicated computational arithmetic operations (complex multiplication, convolution, recursive filtering) or parallel pipelining, the "equipment multiply rate" is the basic multiply rate times the number of multiplies that can be performed simultaneously;

   (b) If multiple arithmetic units are used within a single processing unit, the "equivalent multiply rate" is the "equivalent multiply rate" of one unit multiplied by the number of units;

   (c) If multiple processing units of the same or different types (e.g., array processor, image enhancement processor) are contained in a system, the "equivalent multiply rates" of each of the processing units.

   (xxvi) "Most immediate memory" is defined as the portion of "main memory" most directly accessible by the central processing unit: (a) For single level "main memories," the "most immediate memory" is

                (1) The cache memory.
                (2) The instruction stack, or
                (3) The data stack.

*   *   *   *   *

(Secs. 4, t, 13 and 15, Publ. L. 96-72, 93 Stat. 503 as amended, 50 U.S.C. app. 2401 et seq.; Executive Order No. 12214 (45 FR 29783, May 6, 19800; Executive Order No. 12451 of December 20, 1983 (48 FR 56563, December 22, 1983)

Dated: January 16, 1984.

John K. Boidock,
Director, Office of Export Administration, International Trade Administration.

(FR Doc. 84-1537 Filed 1-18-84; 8:45 am)

BILLING CODE 3510-DT-M

Appendix B

35790 Federal Register/Vol. 49. No. 178/Wednesday, September 12, 1984/Proposed Rules

DEPARTMENT OF COMMERCE

International Trade Administration
15 CFR Parts 373 and 376

[Docket No. 40110-4107]

Amendments to the Distribution License Procedure

AGENCY: Office of Export Administration, ITA, Commerce.

ACTION: Proposed rule with request for comments.

SUMMARY: On January 19, 1984 (49 FR 2264-2267), the Office of Export
Administration (OEA) solicited public comments on a proposal to amend
the "Distribution License" procedure, which authorizes exports from
the United States of Certain commodities under an international
marketing program to consignees that have been approved in advance as
foreign distributors or users.

Subsequently, OEA received comments, consulted informally with industry
groups, performed audits of several Distribution License holders and
foreign consignees, and conducted an extensive review of the entire
Distribution License (DL) procedure. As a result of the foregoing, OEA
has determined that the changes incorporated in this new proposal will
not only materially strengthen controls on exports under the Distribution License, but will also alleviate burdens on the business community
that would not have contributed to an enhanced expert control program.

The public is invited to make comments on each proposed change, and to
specify and substantiate anticipated workload impact and economic
impact for each change. When possible, commenters should indicate any
anticipated increase in individual validated licenses and reexport
authorizations that would result from applicable regulatory proposals.

The Department anticipates that applicants with pending DL applications
and pending extensions will have 60 days from the effective date of any
new requirements to bring their applications into compliance with the
new requirements. A key element of the new proposal, which makes
possible further flexibility in the proposed regulatory provisions, is
the requirement for pre-license approval of an internal control program
containing the minimal elements specified by the Department. Within
six months of the effective date of any new regulations, the Department
would expect from all current DL holders a narrative statement
describing their internal control system. Comments on the
implementation of these regulations are encouraged.

In a separate Notice, the Department of Commerce will be announcing a
schedule for public hearings during the comment period. These public
hearings will be completed in time for interested parties to prepare
formal, written comments.

DATE: Comments must be received by November 13, 1984.

ADDRESS: Written comments (six copies) should be sent to: Betty Ferrell, Exporter Services Division, Office of Export Administration, U.S. Department of Commerce, P.O. Box 273, Washington, D.C. 20044. Mark "DL COMMENTS" on the face of the envelope.

FOR FURTHER INFORMATION CONTACT: Vincent Greenwald, Exporter Services division, Telephone: (202) 377-3856.

SUPPLEMENTARY INFORMATION:

Rulemaking Requirements and Invitation To Comment

In connection with various rulemaking requirements, the Office of Export Administration has determined that:

1. Since this regulation involves a foreign affairs function, the provisions of the Administrative Procedure Act, 5 U.S.C. 553, requiring a notice of proposed rulemaking, an opportunity for public participation, and a delay in effective date are inapplicable. Nevertheless, to help ascertain the economic impact of the regulation upon the general public, the regulation is being issued in proposed form and public comment is being solicited.

2. Revisions to the existing collection of information requirement (OMB control no. 0625-0052) contained in this proposed rule have been submitted to the Office of Management and Budget (OMB) for review under Section 3504(h) of the Paperwork Reduction Act of 1980. the public is invited to submit comments on this proposed reporting requirement to the Office of Information and Regulatory Affairs of OMB, New Executive Office Building, Washington, D.C. 20503, Attention: Desk Officer of International Trade Administration.

3. Because no notice of proposed rulemaking is required by law, this rule is not subject to the requirements of the Regulatory Flexibility Act, 5 U.S.C. 601 et. seq.

4. Because this proposed rule is being issued with respect to a foreign affairs function, it is not subject to Executive Order No. 12291 (46 FR 13193, February 19, 1981), "Federal Regulation."

The period for submission of comments will close November 13, 1984. All comments received before the close of the comment period will be considered by the Department in the development of final regulations. While comments received after the end of the comment period will be considered if possible, their consideration cannot be assured. Public comments will become a matter of public record.

Comments that are accompanied by a request that the information be treated confidentially because of its business proprietary nature or for any other reason will be accepted on the conditions described below.

Public comments on these proposed regulations will be a matter of public record and will be available for public record and will be available

for public inspection and copying. In the interest of accuracy and
completeness, comments in written form are preferred. If oral comments are
received, they must be followed by written memoranda, which will also be a
matter of public record and will be available for public review and copying.
communications from agencies of the United States Government or foreign
governments will not be made available for public inspection.

The public record concerning these regulations will be maintained in
the International Trade Administration Freedom of Information Records
Inspection Facility, Room 4001 U.S. Department of Commerce, 14th Street and
Pennsylvania Avenue, NW., Washington, D.C. 20230.

Records in this facility, including written public comments and
memoranda summarizing the substance of oral communications, may be inspected
and copied in accordance with regulations published in Part 4 of Title 15 of
the Code of Federal Regulations. Information about the inspection and
copying of records at the facility may be obtained from Patricia L. Mann,
International Trade Administration Freedom of Information Officer, at the
above address or by calling (202) 377-3031.

The Office of Export Administration (OEA) is especially interested in
receiving comments on the business and economic effects of the proposed
regulations. Because providing such comments may involve the disclosure of
proprietary business information, OEA will accept comments on a confidential
basis.

Persons may request confidential treatment for their comments involving
proprietary information on paperwork burden, sales, or any other aspects of
the business or economic impact of the proposed regulations. The request
must include a full statement of the reasons why confidential treatment
should be granted. The business or financial information for which
confidential treatment is requested should be submitted to OEA on sheets of
paper separate from any non-confidential information submitted. The top of
each page should be marked with the term "CONFIDENTIAL BUSINESS INFORMATION."

OEA will either accept the submission in confidence or, if the submission
fails to meet the standards for confidential treatment, will return it. A
nonconfidential summary must accompany each submission of confidential
information. The summary will be made available for public inspection.

Information accepted by OEA as privileged under subsections (b) (3) or
(4) of the Freedom of Information Act (5 U.S.C., section 552(b) (3) and (4))
will be kept confidential and will not be available for public inspection,
except according to law.

Proposed Revision of distribution License Procedure

On January 19, 1984 (49 FR 2264-2267), the Department solicited
comments on proposed revisions to the Distribution License procedure, a
comprehensive export licensing system for firms with international marketing
programs generally involving a number of foreign consignees/distributors.

Major changes to the Export Administration Regulations during the
1970's, such as elimination of monthly reporting requirements, reduction of
record keeping requirements, and relaxation of eligibility standards, have

reduced a number of the safeguards in the original program.

A thorough analysis of the DL procedure has confirmed that stronger safeguards are needed. The January 1984 proposal was issued with this purpose in mind. In addition, the Department concluded in 1983 that additional staff positions should be allocated to the special licensing unit in OEA and that an audit program should be re-established.

The aim of the proposal was to achieve the national security objectives of the United States by preventing the DL procedure from being used as a method to divert controlled commodities. It was also intended to impose effective controls without impeding legal U.S. trade. The DL regulations were issued in proposed form in January 1984 because the Department wished to obtain additional information on their impact.

The Department received about 250 responses to the request for comments. In addition, OEA gained much information on the process and the DL holders' control programs from the conduct of several foreign and domestic audits. ITA officials also met with a wide variety of firms currently using the DL to clarify comments and assess the ways in which they were administering their licenses. This knowledge was extremely beneficial to the internal review of the DL procedure conducted by an ITA task force. By analyzing the intent of both the existing regulations and the January proposal, reviewing the results of recent audit activity, and considering the comments we received, the task force was better able to focus on key strengths and weaknesses in the DL procedure. The Department has prepared a new proposed regulation based on the following observations:

.   The DL is the cornerstone of the marketing program for most U.S. firms that export controlled commodities. The DL procedure facilitates billions of dollars in sales each year and involves thousands of intra-company transfers; without it, U.S. firms would be less able to compete effectively in the international marketplace.

.   Operations under DL procedure have changed considerably over the years, as U.S. business has expanded greatly its overseas marketing and production operations, and foreign competition has been increasing.

.   Since the program's inception, effective administration of the process has been dependent on internal corporate controls. Some firms have designed good programs, but have become complacent in carrying them out, and some have control programs that simply need to be improved.

.   The great majority of U.S. exporters will not jeopardize their DL privilege through inadvertent or willful violations of the DL regulations.

.   Once the Department establishes the reliability of DL participants, it is the responsibility of each exporting company to maintain an effective export monitoring program and OEA must audit such programs to ensure that the requirements of the DL procedure are met.

.   There is a need and opportunity to strengthen the DL procedure to ensure adequate controls without weakening the position of U.S. firms in international markets.

. With the recent hiring of additional personnel, OEA is now able to monitor more effectively the compliance of firms and to expand its program of educating the business community on DL requirements. In addition, OEA will be able to perform more thorough pre-license reviews and audits to establish participant reliability.

Based on the industry comments and an internal ITA review, we believe that not all of the requirements proposed in January are absolutely necessary for the building of an effective export control system. The requirements that we now propose will be, we believe, effective in safeguarding the national security while not unduly burdening the business community.

DL Holder Export Control Requirement

The purpose of these current proposals is to eliminate any of the January proposals that could have restricted legitimate economic activity under the DL procedure without contributing to the national security. This new proposal places greater emphasis on self-control to be exercised by DL holders and their foreign consignees, on the reliability of these entities, and on DL holders' internal control programs (which must be acceptable to OEA as a precondition for receiving or renewing a license)O. the internal control program must consist of the following elements:

. Identification of positions in the applicant firm and consignee firms responsible for compliance with the requirements of the DL procedure;

. Systems for assuring compliance with product and country restrictions, including controls over reexports to approved sales territories;

. A process for screening OEMs (original equipment manufacturers) that includes the collection and analysis of the following types of information; the names of the OEM principals, the size of the OEM (e.g., the number of employees), and the sales volume;

. Exporter's internal audit system or program;

. Nuclear end-use/end-user controls;

. An education program for those parties in the applicant firm and consignee firms involved in sales of products under the DL procedure;

. A system for distribution and verification of receipt by consignees of the Table of Denial Orders (Supplement No. 1 to Part 388) and other material necessary to assure compliance; and

. Methodology for screening customers against the Table of Denial Orders.

This approach will substantially reduce the potential for diversion as well as the prospect of inadvertent violations of the procedures and permit OEA to better control what is actually being exported. We have sought throughout the revised proposal to minimize the paperwork burden, retaining only what is essential for effective control.

The approach of the new proposed regulations differs significantly from that of the January proposal. There is reduced emphasis on minimal threshold requirements, such as the number of licenses or transactions, although these remain as general guidelines for which exceptions can be justified. The new approach depends more upon the applicant providing sufficient evidence of the reliability of all parties with respect to the prevention of diversion of goods to proscribed destinations. Toward that end, an applicant will have to demonstrate that it has taken adequate steps, including the institution and execution of an appropriate internal control program, and has adequate experience to assure against improper use or diversion. With this additional evidence of reliability, initial applications and renewals of DLs can and will be reviewed more thoroughly and judged primarily on the demonstrated ability of the parties to comply with the regulatory requirements.

Eligibility Standards

The January proposal to revise experience standards would have required that the applicant has received at least 50 individual validated licenses in the previous year, and have had a minimum one-year written relationship with consignees other than subsidiaries. Public comments noted that these requirements would not improve our control over the process and would not accurately measure applicant/consignee reliability.

The internal task force review concluded that, while the quantitative standards of the proposed criteria are useful, there are other, more effective, factors that could also be used in evaluating applications. As noted above, increased emphasis will be given to evidence of the reliability of the exporter and proposed consignees, the effectiveness of established control mechanisms, and in some cases, the results of a pre-approval audit or interview.

The present proposal of "reasonable expectation" that the DL will replace 25 individual validated licenses is utilized so as not to penalize smaller firms. The new proposal also allows for exceptions to the one-year relationship when there is other evidence of the consignee's reliability.

Customer Reexport Assurances (Certification)

The January proposal would have required distributors to obtain assurances (in the form of written certifications) against unauthorized reexports from their customers in countries not listed in Supplement No. 2 to Part 373 of the Export Administration Regulations. Public comments indicated that carrying out this requirement may present legal problems in some countries as well as a loss of customers due to their unwillingness to undertake extra paperwork when comparable goods were available from alternative sources that did not impose this requirement. The Department task force concluded that the written assurance requirement would cause delays that would negate much of the advantage of the DL, and further concluded that other means are available to seek to have foreign customers comply with the limits on reexports. The new proposal deletes the written assurance requirement and imposes a requirement (currently employed by a number of firms) that the distributor, at a minimum, notify each customer, except those in countries listed in Supplement No. 2 to Part 373, that the goods were received from the U.S. under a special license and that such license precludes unauthorized reexport. Also, customers who are approved consignees on the DL, and agencies of foreign governments, would not be subject to the notification requirement.

Customer Lists

The January proposal would have required that DL holders submit an initial list of actual or anticipated customers, followed by quarterly updates. Comments indicated that the requirement may be contrary to local laws in a number of foreign countries, that independent distributors would rather change sources of supply than reveal the identify of their customers, and that the lists, if they could be compiled, would be so lengthy that providing them would unduly burdensome. the task force concluded that the demonstrated volume of customer names would be so great (a minimum of one million names), and would be ever-changing, with the result that meaningful review could not be accomplished. As a result, other ways were sought to assure that parties who might not be approved to.receive goods under individual validated licenses are not recipients of similar goods under the DL. Thus, it was decided that, for a few selected items on the Commodity Control List, shipment under the DL would be permitted only to customers who have been in fact pre-approved by OEA; this is a practice now administratively employed on applications involving certain of these types of commodities, which have been identified in a new Supplement No. 4. In this way, effective limits on parties and equipment of primary concern can be maintained without burdening either the government or the exporting community excessively. In addition, OEA will review customers during audits of consignee activities. Moreover, DL holders and consignees are encouraged to ask the Office of Export Enforcement about unknown or questionable customers, and will be given guidance in recognizing potential patterns for diversion. A new regulatory section is also being established listing the administrative sanctions that may be imposed on firms that fail to comply with DL requirements; emphasizing strict liability for dealing with denied parties.

Drop Shipments

In the January proposal, the ability of the DL holder to ship directly to a distributor's customer ("drop shipment"), at the request of the distributor, would have been limited to customers in the distributor's own country. Most comments indicated that this restriction would have an extreme adverse effect on most marketing programs and would make the DL unattractive to many current holders. The task force acknowledges that direct shipments from the U.S. may provide increased control because of the requirement for a destination control notice on shipping papers and the ease of auditing within the U.S., while continuing to see a need for more structure to the drop shipment provision. Thus, the new proposal allows continued use of drop shipments, but provides for a more specific definition of allowable drop shipments.

Sales Territory

Another January proposal would have required six sales in each country in a consignee's authorized sales territory. The intent was to assure that territories were realistic and that the consignee had sufficient business activity in each country to be familiar with customers and country procedures to ensure adequate control. It has been determined that it is appropriate to maintain the six-sale requirement, but only for those countries in the distributor's authorized sales territory not listed in Supplement No. 2 to Part 373.

Permissive Reexports

In January, we proposed eliminating the distributors' opportunity to take advantage of a variety of permissive reexport provisions. these options generally were seen as unnecessary in view of broadening of the procedure over the years. Comments indicated that many of the permissive reexport provisions were unnecessary, but that withdrawal of all such provisions would not be equitable. The task force concluded that certain permissive reexport provisions are generally unrelated to DL holders and should be deleted (Ship and Plane Stores, G-NNR, and G-FTZ). The two broadest permissive reexport provisions for DL holders, GLV and GTE, are unnecessary because the same shipments can be made within authorized sales territories under other provisions of the DL. The new proposal deletes inapplicable or unnecessary permissive reexport provisions, but continues other permissive reexports that would be useful to DL holders.

Commodity Descriptions

The January proposal to require more specific product information on the DL application would have required each commodity to be shipped under the license to be listed by sub-paragraph on the Commodity Control List (CCL). Comments pointed out that this would be extremely difficult for DL holders who handle a wide range of products, and would require excessive amendment requests as product lines change. In addition, most commenters noted the difficulty of listing all spare and replacement parts by sub-paragraph.

Because this requirement is considered essential to OEA knowledge of what items are being shipped under the DL, the new proposal continues to require listing of CCL entry and sub-paragraph. The task force agreed that parts to service the exporter's products need not be listed in detail on the application.

Excluded Commodities

The January proposal would have excluded certain commodities from shipment under the DL, except within the countries listed in Supplement No. 2 to Part 373. Comments noted that some commodity descriptions lacked clarity, others caught items that are being phased out of production, and most of the excluded commodities are available elsewhere, thus making U.S. exporters less competitive without restricting availability effectively. The proposed exclusions have been re-reviewed by the task force and by OEA technicians. The result has been a more focused set of proposals that address national security concerns more precisely. The new proposal narrows the list of commodities excluded from shipment on a DL to truly strategic commodities that will be excluded for all destinations.

A few other commodities are being identified in a new Supplement No. 4. These include certain low-volume exports that, by current administrative practice, are not authorized for shipment under a DL unless the applicant lists the customers on the license application. Some of the commodities listed in the new Supplement No. 4 may not be shipped to any destination unless the applicant specifically identifies the commodities on the application, along with a listing of proposed customers for the commodities, and the commodities and customers are approved by OEA. Other commodities in Supplement No. 4 may be shipped to countries listed in Supplement No. 2 under a DL, but cannot be shipped to other destinations unless the commodities and customers are listed and OEA approves them. This action permits shipment to pre-approved customers of commodities that might otherwise have to be excluded from the DL entirely.

Administrative Penalties

The January proposal placed parties to the DL on notice that misuse of the license could result in loss of the privilege. No adverse comments were received and this provision is retained and clarified in the new proposal. These administrative penalties stand in addition to those that may be imposed under the Export Administration Act and Part 387 of the Regulations.

Audits

Another January proposal called for more extensive pre-approval review of DL applications and expanded auditing of existing license holders and consignees. Comments generally supported these actions and frequently suggested that improvements in these areas could decrease the need for some of the other proposals. These proposals have been expanded and clarified.

Administrative Conditions

The Department recognizes that export control programs in other countries may warrant the same treatment as that afforded countries in Supplement No. 2. Such treatment may be made available by administrative action within OEA. Conversely, participation in the DL procedure may be restricted by administrative action within OEA where insufficient protection is afforded against the diversion of controlled commodities.

Validity Period

This new rule proposes to increase the initial validity period of the DL from one year to two years, with a two-year extension, and with subsequent renewal periods of four years. It was considered that this change was justified on the basis of having a more thorough pre-approval license application review process and audits. An ancillary benefit will be a reduced paperwork burden on DL holders.

List of Subjects in 15 CFR Parts 373 and 376

Exports.

Accordingly, the Export Administration Regulations (15 CFR Parts 373 and 376) are proposed to be amended as follows:

PART 373--[AMENDED]

1. Section 373.1 is amended by adding a paragraph (f) reading as

follows:
373.1 Introduction

*   *   *   *   *   *

(f) <u>Compliance</u>. Improper use or failure to comply with the conditions
of any special licensing procedure described in this Part 373 may, in
addition to any enforcement action under Part 387 (see particularly #
387.4), result in the loss or restriction of export privileges under that
licensing procedure, including:

(1) Temporary suspension of privileges under the special license for
the license holder and any or all foreign consignees;

(2) Revocation of the special license;

(3) Deletion of foreign consignees;

(4) Restriction of commodities that may be shipped under the special
license;

(5) Requirement that certain exports or reexports be individually
authorized during an OEA review of the adequacy of procedures by the license
holder or particular consignees;

(6) Restriction of sales by consignees to specific parties; or

(7) Requirement that a license holder provide an audit report to OEA
of selected consignees or overseas operations.

2. In # 373.3, the introductory paragraph, paragraph (b), paragraphs
(c)(1)(i),(c)(1)(iii) and (c)(2), and paragraphs (d)(1),(d)(3)(ii)(D)and (G)
and (d)(3)(iv) are revised; and paragraphs (c)(1)(iv),(c)(4),(5) and
(6),(d)(3)(iii)(A) and (B) are added, reading as follows:

373.3 Distribution License.

A Distribution License procedure is established that authorizes exports
of certain commodities under an international marketing program to
consignees that have been approved in advance as foreign distributors or
users. This procedure is a special privilege reserved for firms with
extensive foreign distribution, thorough knowledge of and experience with
the Export Administration Regulations, and the ability and internal control
mechanisms to assure compliance with the requirements of the license. Thus,
there is no automatic right to participate in the Distribution License
procedure. Participants will be expected to establish eligibility and will
be audited at intervals to assure that the Distribution License is being
used properly. The Distribution License procedure is subject to the
limitations in # 373.1.

(a) *   *   *

(b) <u>Ineligible or restricted commodities</u>. (1) The following
commodities are ineligible for export under the Distribution License
procedure, and must be shipped under an individual validated license of

reexport authorization:

(i)   Commodities related to nuclear weapons, nuclear explosive devices, nuclear testing, the chemical processing of irradiated special nuclear or source material, the production of heavy water, the separation of isotopes of source and special nuclear material, or the fabrication of nuclear reactor fuel containing plutonium (see # 378.3):

(ii)   Commodities listed in Supplement No. 1 to Part 373 (except as authorized by footnote):

(iii)   Electronic, mechanical, or other devices, as described in # 376.13(a), primarily useful for surreptitious interception of wire or oral communications:

(iv)   Commodities listed in a Supplement to Part 377 as being under short supply controls: and

(v)   Aircraft parts and accessories covered by # 390.7.

(2)   Commodities listed in Supplement No. 4 to Part 373 are subject to certain restrictions when exported under a Distribution License.   Certain commodities in this Supplement cannot be exported under a Distribution License to any destination unless the applicant specifically lists the appropriate commodities and identifies the customers (end-users) of approved consignees abroad who will be receiving the commodities.   Other commodities in the Supplement cannot be exported under a Distribution License to a country not listed in Supplement No. 2 to Part 373 unless the applicant lists the commodities and identifies the customers.   When OEA grants permission to export, the applicant and approved foreign consignees will be authorized to ship only those Supplement No. 4 items listed and approved, and only to pre-approved end-users.

(c)   <u>Eligible</u> exporters and <u>consignees.</u>

(1)   *   *   *

(i)   A subsidiary, affiliate, or branch of the U.S. exporter.   The subsidiary, affiliate, or branch must be under the full and active control of the exporter and a majority of any voting stock in the subsidiary, affiliate, or branch must be owned by the exporter, or

(ii) *   *   *

(iii)   An end-user importing the commodities for his/her own use or for use in the production or manufacture of commodities.   For purposes of this section, a foreign party who modifies, but does not change, the essential character of a U.S. commodity, or attaches a U.S. commodity in essentially original form to foreign equipment, is not an end-user and should be considered a distributor under (c)(1)(ii) above.

(2)   Prerequisite volume of business.

(i)   The exporter shall have a reasonable expectation that the Distribution License, if granted will replace at least 25 individual validated export licenses that would otherwise be required.

(ii) The applicant must be able to establish to OEA an ongoing business relationship of at least one year with proposed foreign consignees described in # 373.3(c)(1)(ii) and (iii).

(iii) The one-year relationship may be waived upon suitable evidence of reliability, e.g., if the proposed consignee--

(A) Is approved under another Distribution License;

(B) Has been established as reliable by the Department of Commerce through pre-license checks, verification of information supplied by the applicant, or extensive experience as a consignee under individual validated licenses;

(C) Is an affiliate of another approved foreign consignee and is under the full and active control of the foreign consignee.

(3) *   *   *

(4) Certification of an internal control program. The applicant must be able to establish the existence of an adequate internal control program to assure compliance with all conditions of the Distribution License and the Export Administration Regulations.

(5) Essential elements of an internal control program. The applicant must submit for OEA approval the firm's internal control program to ensure exporter and approved consignee compliance with all conditions of the Distribution License and the Export Administration Regulations. An internal control program shall include, as a minimum, the following:

(i) Identification of positions in the applicant firm and consignee firms responsible for compliance with the requirements of the Distribution License procedure;

(ii) A system for distribution and verification of receipt by consignees of the Table of Denial Orders (Supplement No. 1 to Part 388) and other material necessary to assure compliance;

(iii) Systems for assuring compliance with product and country restrictions, including controls over reexports to approved sales territories;

(iv) An internal audit system or program;

(v) Nuclear end-use/end-user controls;

(vi) An education program for those parties in the applicant firm and consignee firms involved in sales of products under the Distribution License procedure;

(vii) Methodology for screening customers against the Table of Denial Orders; and

(viii)   A process for screening Original Equipment Manufacturers (OEMs) that includes the collection and analysis of the following types of information:

(A)   Names of OEM principals;
(B)   Size of OEM, e.g., number of employees;
(C)   Sales volume;
(D)   Sales territory (including sales to the Soviet Bloc);
(E)   Servicing responsibilities;
(F)   Financial stability of the OEM;
(G)   OEM's reputation in the trading community; and
(H)   OEM's proposed use and disposition of the exported commodities.
(ix)   A records maintenance program.

(6)   Notification of special restrictions. It is the responsibility of the exporter to notify all consignees of any special conditions or restrictions applicable to goods received under a Distribution License.

(d)   <u>Application</u> <u>for</u> <u>Distribution</u> <u>License</u>.   (1)   Prior consultation. The preparation of an initial application for a Distribution License requires a substantial amount of work by the exporter. Therefore, a prospective applicant is required to consult with the Special Licensing Unit of the Office of Export Administration before preparing and submitting an application.

(2)   *   *   *

(3)   *   *   *

(ii) *   *   *

*   *   *   *   *

(D)   List separately on the application, or on an attachment, a description of each type of commodity to be exported, and the appropriate Export Control Commodity Number and sub-paragraph designation from the Commodity Control List (CCL) (Supplement No. 1 to # 399.1) for each. Only commodities included in a CCL entry specifically listed on the application and approved by OEA may be exported under a Distribution License, except that spare or replacement parts for listed commodities may be included without specifying a CCL entry if such parts shipments will not exceed 20% of the value of the total exports under the license during any 12 month period and the applicant lists on the application--"Spare and replacement parts for commodities included in CCL entries." (The listing of the CCL entries by Export Control Commodity Number and sub-paragraph designation will generally constitute a sufficient description ;of the commodities being shipped. However, the exporter is encouraged to include as specific a description as possible in order to speed the processing of the application.) OEA may impose more specific limits on the commodities covered ;by the license. Listing of CCL entries that include items excluded by # 373.3(b) does not permit export or distribution of those excluded items, except with specific approval as indicated in # 373.3(b)(2).

*   *   *   *   *

(G) Leave blank item 9(a), "Quantity," the processing code under item 9(c), and item 9(d), "Unit Price" and "Total Price."

*   *   *   *   *

(iii)*   *   *

(A) Notice restricting reexport. Each Form ITA-6052P submitted by a party other than an end-user as described in # 373.3(c)(1)(iii) shall include a commitment that the commercial invoice for any shipment of commodities received under the Distribution License will include a notice restricting unauthorized reexport. This notice will not be required when the shipment is to a customer in a country listed in Supplement No. 2 to this Part 373. or when the customer is either another approved consignee under the Distribution License or a foreign government agency. The notice shall read as follows:

"These commodities were authorized for export from the United States under a special Distribution License procedure on the condition that they

(B) The ultimate consignee(s) listed in item 7 of the license application must submit written certification on the Form ITA-6052P, or on a separate attachment of at least six sales during the previous year within each country in the assigned sales territory that is not listed in Supplement No. 2 to Part 373. Each time that a particular Distribution License is extended, the consignee must submit written verification of at least six sales per year within those countries.

(iv) Comprehensive narrative statement. (A) A comprehensive narrative statement shall be submitted by the applicant in support of the application. This statement shall describe the applicant's internal control system and distribution methods pertinent to the application.

(B) The statement shall detail the applicant's internal control program, having, as a minimum, the requirements set forth in # 373.3(c)(5).

(C) In addition, the statement shall detail the nature and duration of the business relationship existing between the applicant and each consignee. If the consignee is a subsidiary, affiliate, or branch of the U.S. exporter, the statement shall show clearly that the qualifications set forth in # 373.3(c) are met and shall show the form of ownership or other control exercised by the U.S. exporter. If the U.S. exporter has assigned a sales territory to the consignee that includes a country or countries other than the one in which the consignee is located, the statement shall list the country or countries. For countries not listed in supplement No. 2, the statement shall include a justification for the need to include such countries in the sales territory. (For purposes of this # 373.3, a "sales territory" is defined as a list of specific destinations within Country Groups T&V, excluding Afghanistan and the People's Republic of China, in which the exporter, or his distributor, has a history of sales, or in which sales have been planned during the validity period of the license.) If the consignee is a distributor other than a subsidiary, affiliate, or branch of the U.S. exporter, the statement shall include the terms of the distributorship agreement and a copy of the portion of the written agreement assuring compliance with U.S. Export Administration Regulations as described

in # 373.3(c)(1)(ii) and (iii). If the written agreement assigns a sales
territory to the consignee that includes a country or countries other than
the one in which the consignee is located, a copy of that portion of the
written agreement shall also be included. In addition, the statement shall
list, for each consignee, the volume of business in terms of general
commodity categories involved for the preceding year.

(D) If the government of the country where the consignee is located
restricts the inspection of records by a representative of the U.S.
Government, the narrative statement must be accompanied by a statement from
the consignee describing in full an alternative arrangement that would
permit a review of the consignee's activities adequate to determine whether
or not he/she has complied with the U.S. export control laws and regulations
as required by # 373.3(1)(4). Approved consignees who sell to parties who
subsequently will resell must include in the statement a certification that
they will advise such party of the reexport restrictions on products
received under the procedure.

3. Paragraph (e) # 373.3 is amended by redesignating sub-paragraphs
(1), (2) and (3) as (2) (3) and (4) respectively; by removing the phrase "of
one year" from the end of the new paragraph (e)(2); by adding a sentence to
the end of (e)(2)(v) reading--"The licensee shall assure that each approved
consignee acknowledges receipt of reprints and addenda, and shall maintain
copies of acknowledgments."; and by adding a new (e) (1) and (5) reading as
follows:

373.3 Distribution License.

(e) Action on License Applications.

(1) Pre-approval review. The Distribution License procedure
authorizes multiple export transactions without a review and approval of
each individual transaction by OEA. Thus, before approving such a license,
OEA must be fully satisfied that the persons benefiting from this special
licensing procedure can be relied upon to adhere to the conditions of the
license and the Export Administration Regulations, and that the approval of
the application will not be detrimental to U.S. interests. To permit OEA to
make such judgments, each application will be reviewed by OEA and the Office
of Export Enforcement to establish the reliability of the parties to the
license. Such review may entail an audit of past export transactions,
inspection of documents, and interview in the United States and abroad. If
OEA cannot verify the appropriateness of this special licensing procedure or
establish the reliability of the proposed parties to the license, it may
deny the application or modify it by eliminating persons from the
application or by removing certain commodities or countries included in the
application. However, failure to obtain approval to participate in this
special licensing procedure does not preclude the filing of an application
for an individual validated license or reexport authorization.

(5) Validity period. A new Distribution License will be valid for two
years from the last day of the month in which it is issued, and may be
extended once by amendment for a two-year period. Thereafter, a new
application must be submitted. If approved, it will be valid for four years.

4. Paragraph (f)(2)(ii) of # 373.3 is amended by inserting in the

first sentence after the phrase "reason to know the commodities" the phrase
"will be diverted or reexported to unauthorized destinations or end-users,
or"; and by designating the last sentence of the paragraph as a new
paragraph (f)(3), titled "Rejection."

5. Section 373.3(i) is amended by adding an introductory paragraph and
revising (i)(4) to read as follows:

#373.3 Distribution License.

*   *   *   *   *

(i) <u>Reexports</u>. Unless a distributor meets the qualifications set
forth in this # 373.3(i), no commodities received by an approved consignee
under a Distribution License may be reexported without specific prior
written approval from OEA. The written approval may be included on the
validated Distribution License, a validated Form ITA-6052P, or a validated
Form ITA-699P (See Part 374).

*   *   *   *   *

(4) Permissive reexports. Approved distributors may take advantage of
the permissive reexport provisions of # 374.2 (a)(4),(b),(d),(f),(g) and
(i), and may reexport any commodity that at the time of reexport may be
exported diretly from the United States to the new country of destination
under General License G-DEST. Adequate records of each reexport, including
reference to the applicable provision of # 374.2, must be maintained by the
distributor.

*   *   *   *   *

6. Paragraph (j) of # 373.3 is amended by adding the following five
sentences:

373.3 Distribution License.

*   *   *   *   *

(j)* * * This provision is limited to situations in which the
approved consignee receiving a purchase order requests either the U.S.
license holder or another approved consignee under the same license to ship
directly to the customer of the consignee receiving the order, either in
that consignee's own country or his authorized sales territory. Only an
approved consignee may request the "by order of privilege" under the
Distribution License. Also, this procedure does not apply to reexports by
one distributor consignee to another distributor consignee's customers nor
to exports from the U.S. exporter to a distributor's customers locted
outside countries listed in Supplement No. 2 to this Part 373 if the
commodity involved is included in Supplement No. 4 to this Part 373 (see #
373.3(b)(2)). OEMs not approved as consignees may not invoke the drop
shipment privilege of # 373.3(j). Furthermore, unless spceifically
authorized on the license or subsequently in writing by OEA, the exporter or
consignee may not directly invoice the party receiving the commodities under
the "by order of privilege."

7. Paragraph (1) of # 373.3 is amended by adding a paragraph (4)(i), reading as follows:

373.3 Distribution License

*   *   *   *   *

(1) Records.

*   *   *   *   *

(4) Inspection of records.

(i) The records of both U.S. exporters and approved consignees will be audited by OEA at suitable intervals. As part of the audit procedure, a consignee may be required on occasion to submit to OEA a listing of all sales under this license during the previous month.

*   *   *   *   *

8. The following entries are added/revised in Supplement No. 1 to Part 373, "Commodities Excluded from Certain Special License Procedures," each with a footnote reading "Excluded from the Distribution License procedure only."--entry 1355 is added between 3336 and 1357; an additional entry 1565 is added following the present two entries numbered 1565; and an entry 1584 is added between 1570 and 1585, reading as follows:

PART 373--SPECIAL LICENSING PROCEDURES

*   *   *   *   *

Supplement No. 1--Commodities Excluded From Certain Special Licensing Procedure

*   *   *   *   *

1355 Crystal pullers: computerized, or that are rechargeable without opening;

Molecular beam epitaxial equipment;

Electron beam systems for mask-making or semiconductor wafer or device processing;

Electron beam, ion beam, or x-ray equipment for projection image transfer.

Digitally controlled equipment specially designed for, testing digital microcircuits, and assemblies thereof, capable of test rates of 40 megahertz or greater.

*   *   *   *   *

1565 Specialized processing units that have an "equivalent multiply rate" in excess of 2 million (product) operations per second.

*   *   *   *   *

1584 Cathode ray oscilloscopes having amplifier bandwidths greater
than 350 MHz;

Oscilloscopes having cathode-ray tubes incorporating microchannel plate
electron multipliers capable of operating at frequencies greater than 1000
MHz;

Digital oscilloscopes with sequential sampling of the input signal at
an interval of less than 2 nanoseconds.

*   *   *   *   *

9. A Supplement No. 4 to Part 373 is added, reading as follows:

PART 373--SPECIAL LICENSING PROCEDURES

*   *   *   *   *

Supplement No. 4--Special Distribution License Restrictions for Certain
Commodities Included in the Commodity Control List

The following commodities are subject to certain special restrictions,
as specified in the applicable footnote (see # 373.3(b)(2)).

1355A[1]: Plasma-enhanced or photo-enhanced chemical reactor equipment as
defined in subparagraph (b)(1)(iii)(c);

Equipment designed for ion implantation, or for ion-enhanced or photo-
enhanced diffusion, as defined in subparagraph (b)(1)(vii);

Photo-optical or non-photo-optical step and repeat or partial field
equipment for transfer of the image onto the wafer, as defined in paragraph
(b)(2)(ix);

Projection image transfer for processing slices (wafers) of 4 inches or
greater in diameter.

Digitally controlled equipment specially designed for testing
microcircuits, and assemblies thereof, capable of performing functional
(truth table) testing at a pattern rate greater than 20 MHz.

1370A[2]: Machine tools for generating opticalf quality surfaces,
specially designed components and accessories therefor, and specially
designed software.

1532A[2]: Linear measuring machines, except optical comparators, with two
or more axes having a range in any axis greater than 200mm and an accuracy
(including any compensation) less (finer) than 0.0008mm per any 300mm
segment of travel, as defined in paragraph (b);

Angular measuring systems having an accuracy equal to or less than 1
second of arc, except optical instruments, such as auto-collimators, using
collimated light to detect angular displacements of a mirror, as defined in

paragraph (c).

458B[2]: Photographic equipment: aerial camera film having extended sensitivity and/or high resolution or high temperature processing, as defined in paragraphs (b),(c),(d) and (e).

1733A[2]: Base materials, non-composite ceramic materials, ceramic-ceramic composite materials and precursor materials for the manufacture of high-temperature fine technical ceramic products: precursor materials polycarbosilanes and polydiorganosilanes (for producing silicon carbide), as defined in paragraph (d)(1); Polysilazanes (for producing silicon nitride), as defined in paragraph (d)(2);

Polycarbosilazanes (for producing ceramics with silicon, carbon and nitrogen components), as defined in paragraph (d)(3).

1746[2]: Polymeric substances and manufactures thereof; aromatic polyamides, as defined in paragraph (d).

4755B[2]: Silicone fluids and resins: silicone diffusion pump fluids having the capacity for producing ultimate pressures of less than 10--Torr, as defined in paragraph (a).

1757A[2]: Semiconductor materials: silicone, gallium, gallium III/V compounds, gallium phosphide, indium, indium compounds, heteroepitaxial materials, elemental Cd and Te, CdTe compounds, SiH_4, $SiClH_3$, $SiCl_4$, $SiCl_3H$ and $SiCl_2H_2$, single crystal sapphire, B_2O_3, germanium, resist materials sensitive to X-rays, electron or ion beams, or specified for dry development, single crystal forms of bismuth germanium oxide, lithium niobate, lithium tantalate and/or alfuminum phosphate.

PART 376--[AMENDED]

10. Section 376.10 is amended by adding paragraphs (a)(4)(xxv) and (xxvi), reading as follows:

376.10   Electronic computers and related equipment.

(a) Digital computers.

*   *   *   *   *

(4) Definitions of terms.

*   *   *   *   *

(xxv) "Equivalent multiply rate" is defined as the maximum number of multiplication operations that can be performed per second, neglecting setup or pipeline filling operations. This rate is based on the maximum rate achievable fully utilizing all hardware architectural features (including multiple or staged (pipelined) arithmetic units); assuming optimal operand lengths of 16 bits or greater and optimal operand locations in the "most immediate memory"; and ignoring initialization, interrupts, and data reordering times:

(A) If the basic multiplication operation includes multiple simultaneous multiplications either because of complicated computational arithmetic operations (complex multiplication, convolution, recursive filtering) or parallel pipelining, the "equivalent multiple rate" is the basic multiply rate times the number of multiplies that can be performed simultaneously;

(B) If multiple arithmetic units are used within a single processing unit, the "equivalent multiply rate" is the "equivalent multiply rate" of one unit multiplied by the number of units;

(C) If multiple processing units of the same or different types (e.g., array processor, image enhancement processor) are contained in a system, the "equivalent multiply rate" is the sum of the "equivalent multiply rates" of each of the processing units.

(xxvi) "Most immediate memory" is defined as the portion of "main memory" most directly accessible by the central processing unit:

(A) For single level "main memories," the "most immediate memory" is the internal memory:

(B) For hierarchical "main memories," the "most immediate memory" is:

(1) The cache memory,

(2) The instruction stack, or

(3) The data stack.

*   *   *   *   *

Authority: Secs. 203, 206, Pub. L. 95-223, Title II, 91 Stat. 1623, 1628 (50 U.S.C. 1702, 1704), Executive Order No. 12470 of March 30, 1984 (49) FR 13099, April 3, 1984.

William T. Archey,

Acting Assistant Secretary Trade Administration.

(FR Doc. 84-24126 Filed 9-10-84; 1:00 pm)

Billing Code 3510-DT-M

Appendix C

Federal Register, Vol. 50, No. 51, Friday, March 15, 1985

DEPARTMENT OF COMMERCE
International Trade Administration
15 CFR Part 391

[Docket No. 50222-5022]

Addition of "Foreign Availability Procedures and Criteria"
to the Export Administration Regulations

AGENCY: Office of Export
Administration, International Trade
Administration; Commerce

ACTION: Proposed rule with request for comments

SUMMARY: The Department of Commerce was required by the Export
Administration Act to initiate and review claims of foreign
availability on all items controlled for national security reasons.
The proposed regulations set out the procedure for initiating foreign
availability claims and the criteria by which such claims shall be
assessed and reviewed. The Department's program of foreign
availability assessment is intended to lead to elimination of export
controls that are ineffective in achieving the national security
objectives of the export control system.

DATE: Comments must be received by May 14, 1985.

ADDRESS: Written comments (six copies) should be sent to: Betty Ferrell,
Exporter Assistance Division, Office of Export Administration, U.S.
Department of Commerce, P.O. Box 273, Washington, D.C. 20044.

FOR FURTHER INFORMATION CONTACT: Robert Rarog, Foreign Availability
Assessment Division, Telephone: (202)377-4890.

SUPPLEMENTARY INFORMATION:

BACKGROUND:

A foreign availability assessment capability was mandated as a function
of the Department of Commerce by the Export Administration Act of 1979.
Accordingly, Commerce established a Foreign Availability Assessment Division
to implement this function. This division will provide timely, technically
sound, and objective assessments of foreign availability for the purpose of
determining appropriate levels of export controls.

The proposed regulations define procedures and criteria to address
foreign availability for commodities and technical data controlled for
national security purposes. The Department intends to issue separate

regulations to assess claims for items controlled for foreign policy
purposes because the basic purposes of national security and off foreign
policy based controls are different.

Foreign availability exists for items controlled for national security
purposes when "comparable" foreign commodities or technical data are
available in "sufficient" quantities to the proscribed countries to satisfy
their needs so that U.S. exports of such items would not make a significant
contribution to such countries' military potential. In determining
comparability of foreign commodities and technical data, the following
factors will be considered: (a) End uses, (b) similarity of design or
resolution of technical problems, and (c) similarity of performance and
reliability characteristics. Availability of such items to the proscribed
countries must not be effectively restricted by international agreements or
foreign law. Additional information for this comparison shall related to
parts and component availability, production data, capacity, costs, export
history to proscribed country destinations, and any other information
pertinent to the objectives and effectiveness of national security controls.

The primary objective of foreign availability assessment is to
determine levels of export controls for commodities and technical data that
are both effective and consistent with national security concerns. License
approval and decontrol on foreign availability grounds are clearly part of
this process but will be made only when such actions would not permit
exports that could contribute in any significant way to the military
potential of a country or combination of countries to which national
security export controls are directed.

Foreign availability assessment requires information on foreign items
that is both detailed and reliable. Since such data may be used to modify
controls imposed for national security reasons, it should be broader in
scope and more detailed than the material often collected by U.S. firms on
their foreign competitors in the ordinary course of business.   The
Department of Commerce views participation by industry in data collection as
an element of a successful foreign availability program. While the
Department will use every means available government-wide to gather the type
of reliable information required on foreign commodities and technical data,
one of the best potential sources of such information will be the U.S.
business community and its representatives overseas.

The proposed regulations present minimum standards for industry
submission of foreign availability claims. Supporting data in the form of
test results, marketing or other relevant data will, however, greatly assist
in timely and complete assessments. Information should be detailed, product
specific and, whenever possible, subject to verification. Unsubstantiated
assertions will not, of themselves, be accepted as proof of foreign
availability. A submission need only be accompanied by the best available
evidence, but the Department may refuse to process a submission it if
appears that no reasonable attempt has been made to supply substantiating
evidence or that the claim is otherwise totally lacking in substance.

The foreign availability program is intended to play a major role in
the level of export controls that are maintained. Industry is therefore
urged to submit comments on the substance of the proposed regulations.

Rulemaking Requirements and Invitation to Comment

In connection with various rulemaking requirements, the Office of Export Administration has determine that:

1. Since this regulation involves a foreign affairs function, the provisions of the Administration Procedure Act, 5 U.S. C. 553, requiring a notice of proposed rulemaking, an opportunity for public participation, and a delay in effective date are inapplicable. Nevertheless, to help ascertain the economic impact of the regulation upon the general public, the regulation is being issued in proposed form and public comment is being solicited.

2. This proposed rule contains a new collection of information requirement under the Paperwork Reduction Act of 1980, 44 U.S.C. 3501 et seq. This new collection of information requirement has been submitted to the Office of Management and Budget (OMB) for review under Section 3504(h) of the Paperwork Reduction Act of 1980.

3. The Regulatory Flexibility Act does not apply to this proposed rule because it is not a rule within the meaning of Section 601(2) of the Act. Accordingly, no initial Regulatory Flexibility Analysis has been prepared.

4. Because this proposed rule is being issued with respect to a foreign affairs function, it is not subject to Executive Order No. 12291 (46 FR 13193, February 19, 1981), "Federal Regulation."

The period of submission of comments will close May 14, 1985.

All comments received before the close of the comment period will be considered by the Department in the development of final regulations. While comments received after the end of the comment period will be considered if possible, their consideration cannot be assured. Public comments will become a matter of public record.

Comments that are accompanied by a request that the information be treated confidentially because of its business proprietary nature or for any other reason will be accepted on the conditions described below.

Public comments on these proposed regulations will be a matter of public record and will be available for public inspection and copying. In the interest of accuracy and completeness, comments in written form are preferred. If oral comments are received, they must be followed by written memoranda, which will also be a matter of public record and will be available for public review and copying. Communications from agencies of the United States Government of foreign governments will not be made available for public inspection. The public record concerning these regulations will be maintained in the International Trade Administration Freedom of Information Records Inspection Facility, Room 4104, U.S. Department of Commerce, 14th Street and Pennsylvania Avenue, NW., Washington, D.C. 20230.

Records in this facility, including written public comments and memoranda summarizing the substance of oral communications, may be inspected and copied in accordance with regulations published in Part 4 of Title 15 of the Code of Federal Regulations. Information about the inspection and copying of records at the facility may be obtained from Particia L. Mánn, International Trade Administration Freedom of Information Officer, at the above address or by calling (202)377-3031.

The Office of Export Administration (OEA) is especially interested in receiving comments on the business and economic effects of the proposed regulations. Because providing such comments may involve the disclosure of proprietary business information, OEA will accept comments on a confidential basis.

Persons may request confidential treatment for their comments involving proprietary information on paperwork burden, sales, or any other aspects of the business or economic impact of the proposed regulations. The request must include a full statement of the reasons why confidential treatment should be granted. The business or financial information for which confidential treatment is requested should be submitted to OEA on sheets of paper separate from any non-confidential information submitted. The top of each page should be marked with the term "CONFIDENTIAL BUSINESS INFORMATION." OEA will either accept the submission in confidence or, if the submission fails to meet the standards for confidential treatment, will return it. A non-confidential summary must accompany each submission of confidential information. The summary be made available for public inspection.

Information accepted by OEA as privileged under subsections (b)(3) or (4) of the Freedom of Information Act (5 U.S.C., Section 552 (b)(3) and (4) will be kept confidential and will not be available for public inspection, except according to law.

List of Subjects in 15 CFR Part 391

Exports, Foreign availability, Science, and Technology, Technical advisory committees.

Accordingly, the Export Administration Regulations (15 CFR Parts 368-399) are proposed to be amended by adding a Part 391, to read as follows:

PART 391 - FOREIGN AVAILABILITY PROCEDURES AND CRITERIA

Sec.

391.1	Definitions.
391.2	Foreign availability claims.
391.3	Criteria for determination.
391.4	Procedures.
391.5	Appeals.

Authority: secs. 203, 206, Pub. I. 95-223, Title II, 91 Stat. 1626, 1628 (50 U.S.C. 1702, 1704), E.O. 12470 of March 30, 1984 (49 13099, April 3, 1984).

391.1 Definitions.

(a) **Available in fact.** As used in this Part 391, "available in fact" means that a non-U.S. origin item may be obtained by the proscribed countries.

(b) **Proscribed countries.** As used in this Part 391 "proscribed countries" means Country Groups Q, W, and Y (as defined in Part 385).

These countries are: The USSR, Albania, Bulgaria, Czechoslovakia, the German Democratic Republic (including East Berlin), Hungary, Laos, the Mongolian People's Republic, Poland and Romania. Country Group Z (North Korea, Vietnam, Kampuchea, and Cuba) is not included since these countries are subject to a virtual embargo notwithstanding any foreign availability.

(c) **Foreign availability.** "Foreign availability" for a national security controlled item exists when the Secretary of Commerce determines that a non-U.S. origin item of comparable quality is available in fact to proscribed countries in quantities sufficient to satisfy their needs so that U.S. exports of such an item would not make a significant contribution to the military potential of such countries.

(d) **Foreign availability submission.** A "foreign Availability Submission" (FAS) is a written claim submitted by an applicant requesting a foreign availability assessment in accordance with the requirements contained in section 391.3 (b)(1).

(e) **Item.** An "item" as used in Part 391 may be a commodity or technical data.

(f) **Non-U.S. origin.** A commodity or technical data is of "non-U.S. origin" when it is not subject to U.S. export or re-export controls.

391.2 Foreign availability claims.

(a) **General requirements.** Foreign availability claims must be submitted in writing and must refer to specific items controlled for national security purposes (reasons for control are noted in each Commodity Control list entry of Supplement No. 1 # 399.1).

(b) **Applications.** A formal determination by the Department of Commerce of foreign availability may serve as grounds for license approval or decontrol.

(1) **Validated License Approval.** A claim of foreign availability may be made in connection with an application for a validated license or a request for re-export authorization for exports to any destination (except Country Group Z). A foreign availability claim consists of a Foreign Availability Submission (FAS) which shall become part of the appropriate license application. An assessment of foreign availability, however, will be made only on items in applications that have been denied on national security grounds. A FAS may be submitted at the time an export license application or request for re-export authorization is filed, or at any time up to thirty (30) days after the date appearing on a denial. A FAS should contain at least the following elements:

Name of sources outside the U.S. and their overseas business addresses.

Product names and model designations of both the U.S. commodities or technical data and their non-U.S. commodities or technical data and their non-U.S. origin counterparts.

Available technical information, including known performance attributes and quality considerations needed for comparison of U.S. and non-U.S. origin commodities or technical data.

Information on production and demand, including quantities of known trade in such commodities to proscribed countries.

Unsupported claims may be returned to the applicant without action.

Information on sources of foreign availability provided in the FAS will be reviewed in conjunction with any other pertinent information available to the Department of Commerce. Such information may include data received from other sources, including the Department of Defense and other appropriate governmental agencies. A detailed description of foreign availability sources, including any supporting data available to the applicant, will greatly assist in a timely and complete assessment. Such supporting data may include such items as foreign manufacturers' catalogs, brochures, operation or maintenance manuals, articles from reputable trade publications, photographs, and other credible data. Foreign availability assessment criteria outlined in # 391.3 of this part should be considered when assembling data in support of a FAS.

(2) Decontrol. (i) Claims based on foreign availability may be submitted for the purpose of removing commodities or technical data from national security controls. The Foreign Availability Assessment Division, in consultation with the Department of Defense and other appropriate Government agencies, has responsibility for reviewing and consolidating claims for action to determine appropriate levels of control.

(ii) Claims should include the same information as that listed in paragraph (b)(1) above, including information for all known foreign producers. Foreign availability assessment criteria outlined in # 391.3 of this part should be considered when assembling data to support a claim of an FAS.

(iii) Any person, including a trade association, or the Department of Commerce's Technical Advisory Committees, may submit a foreign availability claim. The Department may also begin a foreign availability assessment on its own initiative to determine whether national security controls should be maintained on specific items.

(iv) Claims must be addressed to: Foreign Availability Assessment Division, Office of Export Administration, Room 2606 U.S. Department of Commerce, 14th & Pennsylvania Ave., NW Washington, D.C. 20230.

 # 391.3 Criteria for determination.

(a) **Non-U.S. origin.** Only information pertaining to non-U.S. origin commodities or technical data (as defined in # 391.1) will be considered in supporting of foreign availability claims.

(b) **Availability in fact.** Only non-U.S. origin commodities or technical data that are available in fact to the proscribed countries will be considered in establishing foreign availability.

(c) **Standards of comparison for commodities.** All of the following tests must be met in determining the comparability and quantitative sufficiency of U.S. and non-U.S. origin commodities:

(1) Comparable Quality. U.S. and non-U.S. origin commodities must be substantially similar in: (i) Function; (ii) technological approach; (iii) performance thresholds; and (iv) maintainability and service life when such attributes are relevant to the purposes for which controls were placed on that commodity.

(2) Sufficient quantity. For all submissions, comparable non-U.S. origin commodities must be available in fact to the proscribed countries in quantities sufficient to satisfy their needs so that U.S. exports would not make a significant contribution to the military potential of such countries.

(d) **Standards of comparison for technical data.** Non-U.S. origin technical data submitted as evidence of foreign availability must meet the following standards of comparison as to comparable quality:

(1) Non-U.S. origin technical data is or can be used or adapted for use in ways and with results similar to those of its U.S. counterparts;

(2) End products of the use of non-U.S. origin technical data are substantially similar to end products resulting from the use of its U.S. counterparts.

(e) **Evidence.** The Department of Commerce may consider evidence from any source in determining the existence of foreign availability. A claim of foreign availability for an item supported by reliable evidence shall be accepted unless contradicted by other reliable evidence available to the Department. To the extent consistent with the national security and foreign policy interests of the United States and with the production of confidential business information, the Department of Commerce will inform the claimant of evidence contradicting the representations and supporting evidence where such evidence is the basis for a negative determination of foreign availability. The Department of Commerce will normally rely upon its own and other governmental sources for evidence bearing on the needs of proscribed countries and whether the denial of a license or continuation of controls would be ineffective in achieving the national security purposes of the controls.

 # 391.4 Procedures.

(a) **Claims associated with license applications.** Assessments of foreign availability for items included in a validated license application (or request for reexport authorization) will be initiated only when all the following conditions are met: (1) A license denial based only on national security grounds has been forwarded to the applicant, and (2) an FAS is received no later than 30 days from the date on the license denial. If a FAS has been submitted prior to the license denial, the applicant will be notified that an assessment of foreign availability has been initiated at the time of license denial. If no FAS was submitted, the applicant will be informed that a foreign availability assessment will be initiated upon the Department's receipt of a timely and appropriate FAS. The Department of Commerce will seek to complete its evaluation of the claim within 90 days. Except as provided immediately below, if a positive determination is made, a validated license will be forwarded to the applicant; if a positive determination is not made, a negative foreign availability determination notice informing the applicant, to the extent consistent with the U.S. national security and foreign policy interests, of the reasons for denial will be forwarded. Despite a positive determination of foreign availability, the Secretary of Commerce, in consultation with the Secretary of Defense, may determine that approval of a validated license would be detrimental to national security. In such cases, no approval will occur, and the applicant will be so informed.

In cases where a positive determination of foreign availability has been made and a validated license issued, the Foreign Availability Assessment Division will decide whether to initiate a foreign availability assessment to determine whether national security controls should be maintained on such items.

(b) **Decontrol submissions.** The Foreign Availability Assessment Division will collect and evaluate all foreign availability information for decontrol purposes and initiate appropriate assessments. Such assessments will refer to generic equipment categories or characteristics or will propose changes to the Commodity Control List. Standards outlined in # 391.3 shall be used to make the assessments. When appropriate, preliminary findings will be forwarded to the Department of Defense, other relevant U.S. Government agencies, and/or the Department of Commerce's Technical Advisory Committees for review and comment. Except as provided below, in cases where the Department of Commerce determines the existence of foreign availability, action to decontrol the relevant commodities or technical data will be taken and notice of such action will be published in the **Federal Register.** Negative foreign availability determinations shall also be published in the **Federal Register.** Information used to arrive at final determinations may come from any source, Government or non-Government, deemed appropriate by the Department of Commerce. In cases where a decontrol submission consists of a TAC certification, the Department will seek to complete its evaluation within 90 days. Despite positive foreign availability determinations, the President may determine that decontrol would be detrimental to the national security. In such cases, no decontrol will occur. Where such a determination has been made, the Department will publish that determination in the **Federal Register** with a concise statement of its basis and the estimated economic impact of the decision. In addition, negotiations will be initiated to eliminate sources of foreign availability on such items.

When the Department of Commerce determines that conditions under which a positive determination of foreign availability were made have changed so as to cast doubt on the continued existence of foreign availability, a review of the original decontrol action may be undertaken. If foreign availability is determined no longer to exist, controls may be re-imposed. Appropriate notice will be published in the Federal Register.

391. 5 Appeals.

Appeals of negative foreign availability determinations must be received by the Office of the Assistant Secretary for Trade Administration. International Trade Administration, 14th Street and Pennsylvania Ave., NW, Room 3898B, U.S. Department of Commerce, Washington, D.C. 20230 no later than 45 days after the date appearing on the negative foreign availability assessment notice. A determination to deny a license or continue controls notwithstanding foreign availability shall not be subject to appeal. Appeals with be conducted according to standards and procedures.

Appendix D

PUBLIC LAW 98-365 - July 17, 1984

Public Law 98-365
98th Congress

An Act

To establish a system to promote the use of land remote-sensing
satellite data, and for other purposes.

*Be it enacted by the Senate and House of Representatives of the United
States of America in Congress Assembled, That this Act may be cited as the
"Land Remote-Sensing Commercialization Act of 1984".*

TITLE I - DECLARATION OF FINDINGS, PURPOSES,

AND POLICIES

FINDINGS

SEC. 101. The Congress finds and declares that -

(1) the continuous civilian collection and utilization of land remote-
sensing data from space are of major benefit in managing the Earth's natural
resources and in planning and conducting many other activities of economic
importance;

(2) The Federal Government's experimental Landsat system has
established the United States as the world leader in land remote-sensing
technology;

(3) the national interest of the United States lies in maintaining
international leadership in civil remote sensing and in broadly promoting
the beneficial use of remote-sensing data;

(4) land remote sensing by the Government or private parties of the
United States affects international commitments and policies and national
security concerns of the United States;

(5) the broadest and most beneficial use of land remote-sensing data
will result from maintaining a policy of nondiscriminatory access to data;

(6) competitive, market-driven private sector involvement in land
remote sensing is in the national interest of the United States;

(7) use of land remote-sensing data has been inhibited by slow market
development and by the lack of assurance of data continuity;

(8) the private sector, and in particular the "value-added" industry,

is best suited to develop land remote-sensing data markets;

(9) there is doubt that the private sector alone can currently develop
a total land remote-sensing system because of the high risk and large
capital expenditure involved;

(10) cooperation between the Federal Government and private industry
can help assure both data continuity and United States leadership;

(11) the time is now appropriate to initiate such cooperation with
phased transition to a fully commercial system;

(12) such cooperation should be structured to involve the minimum
practicable amount of support and regulation by the Federal Government and
the maximum practicable amount of competition by the private sector, while
assuring continuous availability to the Federal Government of land remote-
sensing data;

(13) certain Government oversight must be maintained to assure that
private sector activities are in the national interest and that the
international commitments and policies of the United States are honored; and

(14) there is no compelling reason to commercialize meteorological
satellites at this time.

PURPOSES

Sect. 102. The purposes of this Act are to -

(1) guide the Federal Government in achieving proper involvement of
the private sector by providing a framework for phased commercialization of
land remote sensing and by assuring continuous data availability to the
Federal Government;

(2) maintain the United States worldwide leadership in civil remote
sensing, preserve its national security, and fulfill its international
obligations;

(3) minimize the duration and amount of further Federal investment
necessary to assure data continuity while achieving commercialization of
civil land remote sensing;

(4) provide for a comprehensive civilian program of research,
development, and demonstration to enhance both the United States
capabilities for remote sensing from space and the application and
utilization of such capabilities; and

(5) prohibit commercialization of meteorological satellites at this
time.

POLICIES

SEC. 103. (a) It shall be the policy of the United States to preserve
its right to acquire and disseminate unenhanced remote-sensing data.

(b) It shall be the policy of the United States that civilian

unenhanced remote-sensing data be made available to all potential users on a
nondiscriminatory basis and in a manner consistent with applicable antitrust
laws.

(c) It shall be the policy of the United States both the commercialize
those remote-sensing space systems that properly lend themselves to private
sector operation and to avoid competition by the Government with such
commercial operations, while continuing to preserve out national security,
to honor our international obligations, and to retain in the Government
those remote-sensing functions that are essentially of a public service
nature.

DEFINITIONS

SEC. 104 For purposes of this Act:

(1) The term "Landsat system" means Landsats 1, 2, 3, 4 and 5, and any
related ground equipment, systems, and facilities, and any successor civil
land remote-sensing space systems operated by the United States Government
prior to the commencement of the six-year period described in title III.

(2) The term "Secretary" means the Secretary of Commerce.

(3)(A) The term "nondiscriminatory basis" means without preference,
bias, or any other special arrangement (except on the basis of national
security concerns pursuant to section 607) regarding delivery, format,
financing, or technical considerations which would favor one buyer or class
or buyers over another.

(B) The sale of data is made on a nondiscriminatory basis only if (i)
any offer to sell or deliver data is published in advance in such manner as
will ensure that the offer is equally available to all prospective buyers;
(ii) the system operator has not established or changed any price, policy,
procedure, or other term or condition in a manner which gives one buyer or
class of buyer de facto favored access to data; (iii) the system operator
does not make unenhanced data available to any purchaser on an exclusive
basis; and (iv) in a case where a system operator offers volume discounts,
such discounts are no greater than the demonstrable reductions in the cost
of volume sales. The sale of data on a nondiscriminatory basis does not
preclude the system operator from offering discounts are consistent with the
provisions of this paragraph.

(C) The sale of data on a nondiscriminatory basis does not require
(i) that a system operator disclose names of buyers or their purchases; (ii)
that a system operator maintain all, or any particular subset of, data in a
working inventory; or (iii) that a system operator expend equal effort in
developing all segments of a market.

(4) The term "unenhanced data" means unprocessed or minimally
processed signals or film products collected from civil remote-sensing space
systems. Such minimal processing may include rectification of distortions,
registration with respect to features of the Earth, and calibration of
spectral response. Such minimal processing does not include conclusions,
manipulations, or calculations derived from such signals or film products or

combination of the signals or film products with other data or information.
(5) The term "system operator" means a contractor under title II or title III or a license holder under title IV.

TITLE II - OPERATION AND DATA MARKETING OF LANDSAT

SYSTEM

OPERATION

SEC. 201. (a) The Secretary shall be responsible for -

(1) the Landsat system, including the orbit, operation, and disposition of Landsats 1, 2, 3, 4, and 5; and

(2) provision of data to foreign ground stations under the terms of agreements between the United States Government and national that operate such ground stations which are in force on the date of commencement of the contract awarded pursuant to this title.

(b) The provisions of this section shall not affect the Secretary's authority to contract for the operation of part or all of the Landsat system, so long as the United States Government retains -

(1) ownership of such system;

(2) ownership of the unenhanced data; and

(3) authority to make decisions concerning operation of the system

CONTRACT FOR MARKETING OF UNENHANCED DATA

SEC. 202. (a) In accordance with the requirements of this title, the Secretary, by means of a competitive process and to the extent provided in advance by appropriation Acts, shall contract with a United States private sector party (as defined by the Secretary) for the marketing of unenhanced data collected by the Landsat system. Any such contract -

(1) shall provide that the contractor set the prices of unenhanced data;

(2) may provide for financial arrangements between the Secretary and the contractor including fees for operating the system, payments by the contractor as an initial fee or as a percentage of sales receipts, or other such considerations;

(3) shall provide that the contractor will offer to sell and deliver unenhanced data to all potential buyers on a nondiscriminatory basis;

(4) shall provide that the contractor pay to the United States Government the full purchase price of any unenhanced data that the contractor elects to utilize for purposes other than sale;

(5) shall be entered into by the Secretary only if the Secretary has determined that such contract is likely to result in net cost savings for the United States Government; and

(6) may be rewarded competitively after the practical demise of the space segment of the Landsat system, as determined by the Secretary.

(b) Any contract authorized by subsection (a) may specify that the contractor use, and, at his own expense, maintain, repair, or modify, such elements of the Landsat system as the contractor finds necessary for commercial operations.

(c) Any decision or proposed decision by the Secretary to enter into any such contract shall be transmitted to the Committee on Commerce, Science, and Transportation of the Senate and the Committee on Science and Technology of the House of Representatives for their review. No such decision or proposed decision shall be implemented unless (A) a period of thirty calendar days has passed after the receipt by each such committee of such transmittal, or (B) each such committee before the expiration of such period has agreed to transmit and has transmitted to the Secretary written notice to the effect that such committee has no objection to the decision or proposed decision. As part of the transmittal, the Secretary shall include information on the terms of the contract described in subsection (a).

(d) In defining "United States private sector party" for purposes of this Act, the Secretary may take into account the citizenship of key personnel, location of assets, foreign ownership, control, influence, and other such factors.

CONDITIONS OF COMPETITION FOR CONTRACT

SEC. 203. (a) The Secretary shall, as part of the advertisement for the competition for the contract authorized by section 202, identify and publish the international obligations, national security concerns (with appropriate protection of sensitive information), domestic legal considerations, and any other standards or conditions which a private contractor shall be required to meet.

(b) In selecting a contractor under this title, the Secretary shall consider -
(1) ability to market aggressively unenhanced data;

(2) the best overall financial return to the Government, including the potential cost savings to the Government that are likely to result from the contract;

(3) ability to meet the obligations, concerns, considerations, standards, and conditions identified under subsection (a);

(4) technical competence, including the ability to assure continuous and timely delivery of data from the Landsat system;

(5) ability to effect a smooth transition with the contractor selected under title III; and

(6) such other factors as the Secretary deems appropriate and relevant.

(c) If, as a result of the competitive process required by section 202(a), the Secretary receives no proposal which is acceptable under the provisions of this title, the Secretary shall so certify and fully report such finding to the Congress. As soon as practicable but not later than thirty days after so certifying and reporting, the Secretary shall reopen the competitive process. The period for the subsequent competitive process shall not exceed one hundred and twenty days. If, after such subsequent competitive process, the Secretary receives no proposal which is acceptable under the provisions of this title, the Secretary shall so certify and fully report such finding to the Congress. In the event that no acceptable proposal is received, the Secretary shall continue to market data from the Landsat system.

(d) A contract awarded under section 202 may, in the discretion of the Secretary, be combined with the contract required by title III, pursuant to section 304(b).

SALE OF DATA

SEC. 204. (a) After the date of the commencement of the contract described in section 202(a), the contractor shall be entitled to revenues from sales of copies of data from the Landsat system, subject to the conditions specified in sections 601 and 602.

(b) The contractor may continue to market data previously generated by the Landsat system after the demise of the space segment of that system.

FOREIGN GROUND STATIONS

SEC. 205. (a) The contract under this title shall provide that the contractor shall act as the agent of the Secretary by continuing to supply unenhanced data to foreign ground stations for the life, and according to the terms, of those agreements between the United States Government and such foreign ground stations that are in force on the date of the commencement of the contract.

(b) Upon the expiration of such agreements, or in the case of foreign ground stations that have no agreement with the United States on the data of commencement of the contract, the contract shall provide -

(1) that unenhanced data from the Landsat system shall be made available to foreign ground stations only by the contractor; and

(2) that such data shall be made available on a nondiscriminatory basis.

TITLE III - PROVISION OF DATA CONTINUITY AFTER THE

LANDSAT SYSTEM

PURPOSES AND DEFINITION

SEC. 301. (a) It is the purpose of this title -

(1) to provide, in an orderly manner and with minimal risk, for a transition from Government operation to private, commercial operation of civil land remote-sensing systems; and

(2) to provide data continuity for six years after the practical demise of the space segment of the Landsat system.

(b) For purposes of this title, the term "data continuity" means the continued availability of unenhanced data -

(1) including data which are from the point of view of a data user

(A) functionally equivalent to the multispectral data generated by the Landsat 1 and 2 satellites; and

(B) compatible with such data and with equipment used to receive and process such data; and

(2) at an annual volume at least equal to the Federal usage during fiscal year d1983.

(c) Data continuity may be provided using whatever technologies are available.

DATA CONTINUITY AND AVAILABILITY

SEC. 302. The Secretary shall solicit proposals from United States private sector parties (as defined by the Secretary pursuant to section 202) for a contract for the development and operation of a remote-sensing space system capable of providing data continuity for a period of six years and for marketing unenhanced data in accordance with the provisions of sections 601 and 602. Such proposals, at a minimum, shall specify -

(1) the quantities and qualities of unenhanced data expected from the system;

(2) the projected date upon which operations could begin;

(3) the number of satellites to be constructed and their expected lifetimes;

(4) any need for Federal funding to develop the system;

(5) any percentage of sales receipts or other returns offered to the Federal Government;

(6) plans for expanding the market for land remote-sensing data;
and

(7) the proposed procedures for meeting the national security
concerns and international obligations of the United States in
accordance with section 607.

AWARDING OF THE CONTRACT

SEC. 303. (a)(1) In accordance with the requirements of this title, the
Secretary shall evaluate the proposals described in section 302 and, by
means of a competitive process and to the extent provided in advance by
appropriation Acts, shall contract with the United States private sector
party for the capability of providing data continuity for a period of six
years and for marketing unenhanced data.

(2) Before commencing space operations the contractor shall obtain a
license under title IV.

(b) As part of the evaluation described in subsection (a), the
Secretary shall analyze the expected outcome of each proposal in terms of -

(1) the net cost to the Federal Government of developing the
recommended system;

(2) the technical competence and financial condition of the
contractor;

(3) the availability of such data after the expected termination
of the Landsat system;

(4) the quantities and qualities of data to be generated by the
recommended system;

(5) the contractor's ability to supplement the requirement for
data continuity by adding, at the contractor's expense, remote-sensing
capabilities which maintain United States leadership in remote sensing;

(6) the potential to expand the market for data;

(7) expected returns to the Federal Government based on any
percentage of data sales or other such financial consideration offered
to the Federal Government in accordance with section 305;

(8) the commercial viability of the proposal;

(9) the proposed procedures for satisfying the national security
concerns and international obligations of the United States;

(10) the contractor's ability to effect a smooth transition with
any contractor selected under title II; and

(11) such other factors as the Secretary deems appropriate and
relevant.

(c) Any decision or proposed decision by the Secretary to enter into any such contract shall be transmitted to the Committee on Commerce, Science, and Transportation of the Senate and the Committee on Science and Technology of the House of Representatives for their review. No such decision or proposed decision shall be implemented unless (1) a period of thirty calendar days has passed after the receipt by each such committee of such transmittal, or (2) each such committee before the expiration of such period has agreed to transmit and has transmitted to the Secretary written notice to the effect that such committee has no objection to the decision or proposed decision. As part of the transmittal, the Secretary shall include the information specified in subsection (a).

(d) If, as a result of the competitive process required by this section, the Secretary receives no proposal which is acceptable under the provisions of this title, the Secretary shall so certify and fully report such finding to the Congress. As soon as practicable but not later than thirty days after so certifying and reporting, the Secretary shall reopen the competitive process. The period for the subsequent competitive process shall not exceed one hundred and eighty days. ·If, after such subsequent competitive process, the Secretary receives no proposal which is acceptable under the provisions of this title, the Secretary shall so certify and fully report such finding to the Congress. Not earlier than ninety days after such certification and report, the Secretary may assure data continuity by procurement and operation by the Federal Government of the necessary systems, to the extent provided in advance by appropriation Acts.

TERMS OF CONTRACT

SEC. 304. (a) Any contract entered into pursuant to this title -

(1) shall be entered into as soon as practicable, allowing for the competitive procurement process required by this title;

(2) shall, in accordance with criteria determined and published by the Secretary, reasonable assure data continuity for period of six years, beginning as soon as practicable in order to minimize any interruption of data availability;

(3) shall provide that the contractor will offer to sell and deliver unenhanced data to all potential buyers on a nondiscriminatory basis;

(4) shall not provide a guarantee of data purchases from the contractor by the Federal Government;

(5) may provide that the contractor utilize, on a space-available basis, a civilian United States Government satellite or vehicle as a platform for a civil land remote-sensing space system, if -

(A) the contractor agrees to reimburse the Government immediately for all related costs incurred with respect to such utilization, including a reasonable and proportionate share of fixed, platform, data transmission, and launch costs; and

(B) such utilization would not interfered with or otherwise compromise intended civilian Government missions, as determined by the agency responsible for the civilian platform; and

(6) may provide financial support by the United States Government, for a portion of the capital costs required to provide data continuity for a period of six years, in the form of loans, loan guarantees, or payments pursuant to section 305 of the Federal Property and Administrative Services Act of 1949 (41 U.S.C. 255).

(b)(1) Without regard to whether any contract entered into under this title is combined with a contract under title II, the Secretary shall promptly determine whether the contract entered into under this title reasonably effectuates the purposes and policies of title II. Such determination shall be submitted to the President and the Congress, together with a full statement of the basis for such determination.

(2) If the Secretary determines that such contract does not reasonably effectuate the requirements of title II, the Secretary shall promptly carry out the provisions of such title to the extent provided in advance in appropriations Acts.

MARKETING

SEC. 305. (a) In order to promote aggressive marketing of land remote-sensing data, any contract entered into pursuant to this title may provide that the percentage of sales paid by the contractor to the Federal Government shall decrease according to stipulated increases in sales levels.

(b) After the six-year period described in section 304(a)(2), the contractor may continue to sell data. If licensed under title IV, the contractor may continue to operate a civil remote-sensing space system.

REPORT

SEC. 306. Two years after the date of the commencement of the six-year period described in section 304(a)(2), the Secretary shall report to the President and to the Congress on the progress of the transition to fully private financing, ownership, and operation of remote-sensing space systems, together with any recommendations for actions, including actions necessary to ensure United States leadership in civilian land remote sensing from space.

TERMINATION OF AUTHORITY

SEC. 307. The authority granted to the Secretary by this title shall terminate ten years after the date of enactment of this Act.

TITLE IV - LICENSING OF PRIVATE REMOTE-SENSING

SPACE SYSTEMS

GENERAL AUTHORITY

SEC. 401. (a)(1) In consultation with order appropriate Federal agencies, the Secretary is authorized to license private sector parties to operate private remote-sensing space systems for such period as the Secretary may specify and in accordance with the provisions of this title. (2) In the case of a private space system that is used for remote sensing and other purposes, the authority of the Secretary under this title shall be limited only to the remote-sensing operations of such space system.

(b) No license shall be granted by the Secretary unless the Secretary determines in writing that the applicant will comply with the requirements of this Act, any regulations issued pursuant to this Act, and any applicable international obligations and national security concerns of the Untied States.

(c) The Secretary shall review any application and make a determination thereon within one hundred and twenty days of the receipt of such application. If final action has not occurred within such time, the Secretary shall inform the applicant of any pending issues and of actions required to resolve them.

(d) The Secretary shall not deny such license in order to protect any existing license from competition.

CONDITIONS FOR OPERATION

SEC. 402. (a) No person who is subject to the jurisdiction or control of the Untied States may, directly or through any subsidiary or affiliate, operate any private remote-sensing space system without a license pursuant to section 401.

(b) Any license issued pursuant to this title shall specify, at minimum, that the licensee shall comply with all of the requirements of this Act and shall -

(1) operate the system in such manner as to preserve and promote the national security of the Untied States and to observe and implement the international obligations of the United States in accordance with section 607;

(2) make unenhanced data available to all potential users on a nondiscriminatory basis;

(3) upon termination of operations under the license, make disposition of any satellites in space in a manner satisfactory to the President;

(4) promptly make available all unenhanced data which the Secretary may request pursuant to section 602;

(5) furnish the Secretary with complete orbit and data collection characteristics of the system, obtain advance approval of any intended deviation from such characteristics, and inform the Secretary immediately of any unintended deviation;

(6) notify the Secretary of any agreement the licensee intends to enter with a foreign nation, entity, or consortium involving foreign nations or entities;

(7) permit the inspection by the Secretary of the licensee's equipment, facilities, and financial records;

(8) surrender the license and terminate operations upon notification by the Secretary pursuant to section 403(a)(1); and

(9)(A) notify the Secretary of any "value added" activities (as defined by the Secretary by regulation) that will be conducted by the licensee or by a subsidiary or affiliate; and

(B) if such activities are to be conducted, provide the Secretary with a plan for compliance with the provisions of this Act concerning nondiscriminatory access.

ADMINISTRATION AUTHORITY OF THE SECRETARY

SEC. 403. (a.) In order to carry out the responsibilities specified in this title, the Secretary may -

(1) grant, terminate, modify, condition, transfer, or suspend licenses under this title, and upon notification of the licensee may terminate licensed operations on an immediate basis, if the Secretary determines that the licensee has substantially failed to comply with any provision of this Act, with any regulation issued under this Act, with any terms, conditions, or restrictions of such license, or with any international obligations or national security concerns of the United States;

(2) inspect the equipment, facilities, or financial records of any licensee under this title;

(3) provide penalties for noncompliance with the requirements of licenses or regulations issued under this title, including civil penalties not to exceed $10,000 (each day of operation in violation of such licenses or regulations constituting a separate violation);

(4) compromise, modify, or remit any such civil penalty;

(5) issue subpenas for any materials, documents, or records, or for the attendance and testimony of witnesses for the purpose of conducting a hearing under this section;

(6) seize any object, record, or report where there is probably cause to believe that such object, record, or report was used, is being used, or is likely to be used in violation of this Act or the requirements of a license or regulation issued thereunder; and

(7) make investigations and inquiries and administer to or take from any person an oath, affirmation, or affidavit concerning any matter relating to the enforcement of this Act.

(b) Any applicant or licensee who makes a timely request for review of an adverse action pursuant to subsection (a)(1), (a)(3), or (a)(6) shall be entitled to adjudication by the Secretary on the record after an opportunity for an agency hearing with respect to such adverse action. Any final action by the Secretary under this subsection shall be subject to judicial review under chapter 7 of title 5, United States Code.

REGULATORY AUTHORITY OF THE SECRETARY

SEC. 404. The Secretary may issue regulations to carry out the provisions of this title. Such regulations shall be promulgated only after public notice and comment in accordance with the provisions of section 553 of title 5, United States Code.

AGENCY ACTIVITIES

SEC. 405 (a) A private sector party may apply for a license to operate a private remote-sensing space system which utilizes, on a space-available basis, a civilian Untied States Government satellite or vehicle as a platform for such system. The Secretary, pursuant to the authorities of this title, may license such system if it meets all conditions of this title and -

(1) the system operator agrees to reimburse the Government immediately for all related costs incurred with respect to such utilization, including a reasonable and proportionate share of fixed, platform, data transmission, and launch costs; and

(2) such utilization would not interfere with or otherwise compromise intended civilian Government missions, as determined by the agency responsible for such civilian platform.

(b) The Secretary may offer assistance to private sector parties in finding appropriate opportunities for such utilization.

(c) To the extent provided in advance by appropriation Acts, any Federal agency may enter into agreements for such utilization if such agreements are consistent with such agency's mission and statutory authority, and if such remote-sensing space system is licensed by the Secretary before commencing operation.

(d) The provisions of this section do not apply to activities carried out under title V.

(e)   Nothing in this title shall affect the authority of the Federal
Communications Commission pursuant to the Communications Act of 1934, as
amended (47 U.S.C. 151 et seq.).

TERMINATION

SEC. 406.   If, five years after the expiration of the six-year period
described in section 304(a)(2), no private sector party has been licensed
and continued in operation under the provisions of this title, the authority
of this title shall terminate.

TITLE V - RESEARCH AND DEVELOPMENT

CONTINUED FEDERAL RESEARCH AND DEVELOPMENT

SEC. 501.   (a)(1) The Administrator of the National Aeronautics and
Space Administration is directed to continue and to enhance such
Administration's programs of remote-sensing research and development.

(2)   The administrator is authorized and encouraged to -

(A) conduct experimental space remote-sensing programs (including
applications demonstration programs and basic research at
universities);

(B) develop remote-sensing technologies and techniques, including
those needed for monitoring the Earth and its environment; and

(C) conduct such research and development in cooperation with
other Federal agencies and with public and private research entities
(including private industry, universities, State and local governments,
foreign governments, and international organizations) and to enter into
arrangements (including joint ventures) which will foster such
cooperation.

(b)(1) The Secretary is directed to conduct a continuing program of -

(A) research in applications of remote-sensing;

(B) monitoring of the Earth and its environment; and

(C) development of technology for such monitoring.

(2)   Such program may include support of basic research at universities
and demonstrations of applications.

(3)   The Secretary is authorized and encouraged to conduct such
research, monitoring, and development in cooperation with other Federal
agencies and with public and private research entities (including private
industry, universities, State and local governments, foreign governments,
and international organizations) and to enter into arrangements (including
joint ventures) which will foster such cooperation.

(c)(1) In order to enhance the United States ability to manage and utilize its renewable and nonrenewable resources, the Secretary of Agriculture and the Secretary of the Interior are authorized and encouraged to conduct programs of research and development in the applications of remote sensing using funds appropriated for such purposes.

(2) Such programs may include basic research at universities, demonstrations of applications, and cooperative activities involving other Government agencies, private sector parties, and foreign and international organizations.

(d) Other Federal agencies are authorized and encouraged to conduct research and development on the use of remote sensing in fulfillment of their authorized missions, using funds appropriated for such purposes.

(e) The Secretary and the Administrator of the National Aeronautics and Space Administration shall, within one year after the date of enactment of this Act and biennially thereafter, jointly develop and transmit to the Congress a report which includes (1) a unified national plan for remote-sensing research and development applied to the Earth and its atmosphere; (2) a compilation of progress in the relevant ongoing research and development activities of the Federal agencies; and (3) an assessment of the state of our knowledge of the Earth and its atmosphere, the needs for additional research (including research related to operational Federal remote-sensing space programs), and opportunities available for further progress.

USE OF EXPERIMENTAL DATA

SEC. 502. Date gathered in Federal experimental remote-sensing space programs may be used in related research and development programs funded by the Federal Government (including applications programs) and cooperative research programs, but not for commercial uses or in competition with private sector activities, except pursuant to section 503.

SALE OF EXPERIMENTAL DATA

SEC. 503. Data gathered in Federal experimental remote-sensing space programs may be sold en bloc through a competitive process (consistent with national security interests and international obligations of the United States and in accordance with section 607) to any United States entity which will market the data on a nondiscriminatory basis.

TITLE VI - GENERAL PROVISIONS

NONDISCRIMINATORY DATA AVAILABILITY

SEC. 601. (a) Any unenhanced data generated by any system operator under the provisions of this Act shall be made available to all users on a nondiscriminatory basis in accordance with the requirements of this Act.

(b) Any system operator shall make publicly available the prices, policies, procedures, and other terms and conditions (but, in accordance with section 104(3)(C), not necessarily the names of buyers or their purchases) upon which the operator will sell such data.

ARCHIVING OF DATA

SEC. 602. (a) It is in the public interest for the United States Government -

(1) to maintain an archive of land remote-sensing data for historical, scientific, and technical purposes, including long-term global environmental monitoring;

(2) to control the content and scope of the archive; and

(3) to assure the quality, integrity, and continuity of the archive.

(b) The Secretary shall provide for long-term storage, maintenance, and upgrading of a basic, global, land remote-sensing data set (hereinafter referred to as the "basic data set") and shall follow reasonable archival practices to assure proper storage and preservation of the basic data set and timely access for parties requesting data. The basic data set which the Secretary assembles in the Government archive shall remain distinct from any inventory of data which a system operator may maintain for sales and for other purposes.

(c) In determining the initial content of, or in upgrading, the basic data set, the Secretary shall -

(1) use as a baseline the data archived on the date of enactment of this Act;

(2) take into account future technical and scientific developments and needs;

(3) consult with and seek the advice of users and producers of remote-sensing data and data products;

(4) consider the need for data which may be duplicative in terms of geographical coverage but which differ in terms of season, spectral bands, resolution, or other relevant factors;

(5) include, as the Secretary considers appropriate, unenhanced data generated either by the Landsat system, pursuant to title III, or by licensees under title IV;

(6) include, as the Secretary considers appropriate, data collected by foreign ground stations or by foreign remote-sensing space systems; and

(7) ensure that the content of the archive is developed in accordance with section 607.

(d) Subject to the availability of appropriations, the Secretary shall request data needed for the basic data set and pay to the providing system operator reasonable costs for reproduction and transmission. A system operator shall promptly make requested data available in a form suitable for processing for archiving.

(e) Any system operator shall have the exclusive right to sell all data that the operator provides to the Untied States remote-sensing data archive for a period to be determined by the Secretary but not to exceed ten year from the date the data are sensed. In the case of data generated from the Landsat system prior to the implementation of the contract described in section 202(a), any contractor selected pursuant to section 202 shall have the exclusive right to market such data on behalf of the United States Government for the duration of such contract. A system operator may relinquish the exclusive right and consent to distribution from the archive before the period of exclusive right has expired by terminating the offer to sell particular data.

(f) After the expiration of such exclusive right to sell, or after relinquishment of such right, the data provided to the United States remote-sensing data archive shall be in the public domain and shall be made available to requesting parties by the Secretary at prices reflecting reasonable costs of reproduction and transmittal.

(g) In carrying out the functions of this section, the Secretary shall, to the extent practicable and as provided in advance by appropriation Acts, use existing Government facilities.

NONREPRODUCTION

SEC. 603. Unenhanced data distributed by any system operator under the provisions of this Act may be sold on the condition that such data will not be reproduced or disseminated by the purchaser.

REIMBURSEMENT FOR ASSISTANCE

SEC. 604. The administrator of the National Aeronautics and Space Administration, the Secretary of Defense and the head of other Federal agencies may provide assistance to system operators under the provisions of this Act. Substantial assistance shall be reimbursed by the operator, except as otherwise provided by law.

ACQUISITION OF EQUIPMENT

SEC. 605. The Secretary may, by means of a competitive process, allow a licensee under title IV or any other private party to buy, lease, or otherwise acquire the use of equipment from the Landsat system, when such equipment is no longer needed for the operation of such system or for the sale of data from such system. Officials of other Federal civilian agencies are authorized and encouraged to cooperate with the Secretary in carrying out the provisions of this section.

RADIO FREQUENCY ALLOCATION

SEC. 606. (a) Within thirty days after the date of enactment of this Act, the President (or the President's delegee, if any, with authority over the assignment of frequencies to radio stations or classes of radio stations operated by the United States) shall make available for nongovernmental use spectrum presently allocated to Government use, for use by United States Landsat and commercial remote-sensing space systems. The spectrum to be so made available shall conform to any applicable international radio or wire treaty or convention or regulations annexed thereto. Within ninety days thereafter, the Federal Communications Commission shall utilize appropriate procedures to authorize the use of such spectrum for nongovernmental use. Nothing in this section shall preclude the ability of the Commission to allocate additional spectrum to commercial land remote-sensing space satellite system use.

(b) To the extent required by the Communications Act of 1934, as amended (47 U.S.C. 151 et seq.), an application shall be filed with the Federal Communications Commission for any radio facilities involved with the commercial remote-sensing space system.

(c) It is the intent of Congress that the Federal Communications Commission complete the radio licensing process under the Communications Act of 1934, as amended (47 U.S.C. 151 et seq.), upon the application of any private sector party or consortium operator of any commercial land remote-sensing space system subject to this Act, within one hundred and twenty days of the receipt of an application for such licensing. If final action has not occurred within one hundred and twenty days of the receipt of such an application, the Federal Communications Commission shall inform the applicant of any pending issues and of actions required to resolve them.

(d) Authority shall not be required from the Federal Communications Commission for the development and construction of any United States land remote-sensing space system (or component thereof), other than radio transmitting facilities or components, while any licensing determination is being made.

(e) Frequency allocations made pursuant to this section by the Federal Communications Commission shall be consistent with international obligations and with the public interest.

CONSULTATION

SEC. 607. (a) The Secretary shall consult with the Secretary of Defense on all matters under this Act affecting national security. The Secretary of Defense shall be responsible for determining those conditions, consistent with this Act, necessary to meet national security concerns of the United States and for notifying the Secretary promptly of such conditions.

(b)(1) The Secretary shall consult with the Secretary of State on all matters under this Act affecting international obligations. The Secretary of State shall be responsible for determining those conditions, consistent with this Act, necessary to meet international obligations and policies of

the United States and for notifying the Secretary promptly of such
conditions.

(2) Appropriate Federal agencies are authorized and encouraged to
provide remote-sensing data technology, and training to developing nations
as a component of programs of international aid.

(3) The Secretary of State shall promptly report to the Secretary any
instances outside the United States of discriminatory distribution of data.

(c) If, as a result of technical modifications imposed on a system
operator on the basis of national security concerns, the Secretary, in
consultation with the Secretary of Defense or with other Federal agencies,
determines that additional costs will be incurred by the system operator, or
that past development costs (including the cost of capital) will not be
recovered by the system operator, the Secretary may require the agency aor
agencies requesting such technical modifications to reimburse the system
operator for such additional or development costs, but not for anticipated
profits. Reimbursements may cover costs associated with required changes in
system performance, but not costs ordinarily associated with doing business
abroad.

AMENDMENT TO NATIONAL AERONAUTICS AND SPACE ADMINISTRATION AUTHORIZATION, 1983

SEC. 608. Subsection (a) of section 201 of the National Aeronautics
and Space Administration Authorization Act, 1983 (Public Law 97-324; 96
Stat. 1601) is amended to read as follows:

"(a) The Secretary of Commerce is authorized to plan and provide for
the management and operation of civil remote-sensing space systems, which
may include the Landsat 4 and 5 satellites and associated ground system
equipment transferred from the National Aeronautics and Space
Administration; to provide for user fees; and to plan for the transfer of
the operation of civil remote-sensing space systems to the private sector
when in the national interest".

AUTHORIZATION OF APPROPRIATIONS

SEC. 609. (a) There are authorized to be appropriated to the Secretary
$75,000,000 for fiscal year 1985 for the purpose of carrying out the
provisions of this Act. Such sums shall remain available until expended,
but shall not become available until the time periods specified in sections
202(c) and 303(c) have expired.

(b) The authorization provided for under subsection (a) shall be in
addition to moneys authorized pursuant to title II of the National
Aeronautics and Space Administration Authorization Act, 1983.

TITLE VII - PROHIBITION OF COMMERCIALIZATON OF

WEATHER SATELLITES

PROHIBITION

SEC. 701. Neither the President nor any other official of the
Government shall make any effort to lease, sell, or transfer to the private
sector, commercialize, or in any way dismantle any portion of the weather
satellite systems operated by the Department of Commerce or any successor
agency.

SEC. 702. Regardless of any change in circumstances subsequent to the
enactment of this Act, even if such change makes it appear to be in the
national interest to commercialize weather satellites, neither the President
nor any official shall take any action prohibited by section 701 unless this
title has first been repeated.

Approved July 17, 1984.

LEGISLATIVE HISTORY - H.R. 5155:

HOUSE REPORT No. 98-647 (Comm. on Science and Technology).
SENATE REPORT No. 98-458 (Comm. on Commerce, Science, and Transportation).
CONGRESSIONAL, RECORD, Vol. 130 (1984):
          Apr. 9, considered and passed House.
          June 8, considered and passed Senate, amended
          June 28, House concurred in Senate amendment with an amendment.
          June 29, Senate concurred in House amendment.

WEEKLY COMPILATION OF PRESIDENTIAL DOCUMENTS, Vol. 20, No. 29 (1984):
          July 17, Presidential Statement.

Appendix E

Federal Register / Vol. 52, No. 132 / Friday, July 10, 1987 / Rules and Regulations

DEPARTMENT OF COMMERCE

NATIONAL OCEANIC AND ATMOSPHERIC ADMINISTRATION
15 CFR Part 960
[Docket No. 51191-7064]

Licensing of Private Remote-Sensing Space Systems

AGENCY: National Oceanic and Atmospheric Administration, commerce.

ACTION: Final rule.

SUMMARY: NOAA is establishing procedures to license operators of private remote-sensing space systems in the United States under Title IV of the Land Remote-Sensing Commercialization Act of 1984, Pub. L. 98-365, 15 U.S.C. 4201 *et set.* (the Act). A Notice of Proposed Rulemaking (NPR) was published on March 24, 1986 (51 FR 9971). Twelve persons commented on the NPR, primarily on two issues: The jurisdictional scope of the regulations and the First Amendment rights of the press.

NOAA has responded to the comments and believes that the Final Regulations will facilitate licensing and thereby aid the agency in carrying out its responsibility to develop and promote private sector-owned remote-sensing systems while adequately protecting the basic U.S. interests articulated by the Act: National security, international obligations, including the supervision required by Article VI of the Outer Space Treaty, and ensuring access to unenhanced data on a nondiscriminatory basis.

EFFECTIVE DATE: This rule is effective August 10, 1987.

FOR FURTHER INFORMATION CONTACT: Peggy Hardwood, NOAA, National Environmental Satellite, Data, and Information Service, FB-4, Room 2051, Washington, DC 20233, (301) 763-4522; or call John Milholland, NOAA, Office of General Counsel at (202) 673-5200.

SUPPLEMENTARY INFORMATION: Title IV of the Act requires that any person subject to the jurisdiction or control of the United States who directly or indirectly operates a private remote-sensing space system must obtain a license from the Secretary of Commerce. The authority to issue this license has been delegated to the Administrator of the National Oceanic and Atmospheric Administration (NOAA) and redelegated to the Assistant Administrator for Environmental Satellite, Data, and Information Services.

NOAA believes that further refinement of the Act's detailed licensing criteria by regulation generally is not necessary or useful. As a result, the NPR proposed primarily procedural requirements and public comments were limited. Comments addressed principally two of the four issues on which NOAA specifically solicited comments in the NPR: The jurisdictional scope of the regulations, and the effect of national security and foreign policy concerns on First Amendment rights. These two issues are discussed first.

1.   Jurisdictional Scope of the Regulations

     Section 960.2 of the proposed regulations provides guidance on when the remote-sensing operations of a non U.S. entity will have sufficient connections with the United States to subject the entity to U.S. jurisdiction or control for licensing purposes. This section balances the interest in ensuring that foreign companies compete with U.S. firms on an equal basis against that of imposing extra-territorial applications of U.S. law which could discourage foreign operators from dealing with U.S. companies.

     Comment: During the initial comment period, NOAA received comments from the U.S. State Department, EOSAT Corporation, the National Research Council, SPOT Image Corporation, Messerschmitt-Boelkow-Blohm, GmbH (MBB), and the European Space Agency (ESA) on this issue. As a result of later consultations with the Departments of Defense of State, NOAA received additional comments on this issue from the Department of State. The State Department suggested that the United States should license any operator of a remote sensing space system who chooses to use a U.S. launch vehicle or space platform. It did not address the extent to which additional connections should provide the basis for licensing. The three nonOU.S. launch vehicle or space platform. It did not address the extent to which additional connections should provide the basis for licensing. The three non-U.S. commentators all supported NOAA's pragmatic approach, whereby licensing is not dependent solely on the use of a U.S. launch vehicle (e.g. Example 1), but objected to the potential jurisdictional reach over foreign operators particularly those operators whose only connection with the United States would be in maintaining a data acquisition, and processing and/or data distribution facility in the United States. They argued that jurisdiction should be limited to cases where the operator's "space segment is carried on the registry of the United States" or where "the primary spacecraft command and control center" is located in the United States. (Comments of MBB, p. 14-15; see also SPOT Image, p. 4-5, and ESA, p. 3). The National Research Council supported this view.

     EOSAT, a U.S. corporation, urged NOAA to amend # 960.2 and specify that operation in the U.S. of either a command and data acquisition center or a small retail distribution outlet would subject the operator to U.S. licensing requirements at least where the operator is "sufficiently active in the U.S. remote sensing data market to have a significant competitive impact on that market, and upon U.S. companies (who are automatically subject to regulation under the Act)" (EOSAT comments, p. 3)

     Response: NOAA reaffirms a basic premise of its scheme that jurisdiction under the Act pertains to operators of remote-sensing systems rather than the systems themselves and, for that reason, disagrees that registration of the spacecraft carrying a space system should be the controlling factor for purposes of licensing. NOAA agrees that the locus of operational control of the system should be a major factor in determining jurisdiction but believes that other ground operations which the operator or its affiliates conduct in the United States to support its remote-sensing operations may also be relevant. Under the approach suggested by the foreign commentators, they would have to obtain a license if they flew any space system on a U.S. launched spacecraft or the U.S. portion of the space station since both would be carried on the U.S. registry. Under the regulations, additional U.S. connections would be examined. (See Example 1 with which all commentators agree.)

NOAA has deleted proposed Example 3 which indicated that any operator of a remote-sensing system would have to obtain a license if it maintained both a processing and a distributing facility in the U.S. NOAA may still require a license in these circumstances, but in some cases to do so might be inappropriate. NOAA will retain the flexibility to make determinations on a case-by-case basis.

NOAA's approach is consistent with section 402(a) of the Act which precludes any person "subject to the jurisdiction or control of the United States" from operating any private remote-sensing space system without a license either "directly or through any subsidiary or affiliate". Clearly, this section anticipates the licensing of some operators doing business in the United States even if that business does not include the direct operation of the space system. There is no reason to distinguish between a U.S. data marketing company that forms a foreign subsidiary to launch and operate a space system and is subject to U.S. licensing requirements and a foreign company which forms a U.S. marketing subsidiary. In either case the U.S. undeniably has jurisdiction over an entity which is providing necessary support to an affiliated operator of a private remote-sensing space system. NOAA is sensitive to the practical effects of trying to assert its authority too aggressively, for example inducing companies to carry out their marketing activities offshore, and this is one reason for taking a case-by-case approach.

Comment: A related issue was raised by SPOT Image which pointed out that NOAA's licensing authority is limited to private remote-sensing space systems. It suggested that a public system be defined as "* * * any legal entity in which the majority of voting control is owned by one or more foreign governments or intergovernmental organizations or agencies thereof." The State Department, on the other hand, opposed any definition that might preclude licensing certain public foreign entities because of the difficulty in distinguishing when they are public, semi-public, or private.

Response: NOAA appreciates the Department of State's concern but wants to make clear that it has no intention of trying to license truly public, government remote-sensing systems and has amended the definition of "person" in # 960.3 accordingly. However, the commentators' suggested definition, which would apply only to foreign governmental systems and depends solely on voting control, is too narrow a criterion in view of the wide variety of potential public/private relationships. For licensing purposes, NOAA considers the Centre Nationale d'Etudes Spaciale, the government operator of the SPOT satellite system, to be a public entity.

2.   The First Amendment and National Security Concerns

Comment: "Joint Media Parties" (Radio-Television News Directors Association (RTNDA), American Society of Newspaper Editors, National Broadcasting Company, Society of Professional Journalists/Sigma Delta Chi, and Turner Broadcasting System), the American Newspaper Publishers Association (ANPA), and the Reporters Committee for Freedom of the Press have commented on behalf of the news media that NOAA should be more explicit in recognizing that any licensing restrictions it may impose must comport with First Amendment standards. The RTNDA was the most active, commenting initially on May 23, 1985, on the Proposed Regulations, on September 11, 1986, on NOAA's response to Representative Bill Nelson's inquiry concerning the RTNDA's position, and on February 11, 1987, on comments provided by the Department of State and Defense advocating that NOAA retain the case by case approach taken in the Proposed Regulations. The commentators objected because NOAA retain the case by case approach taken in the Proposed Regulations. The commentators objected because NOAA did not attempt to define more specifically the meaning of the terms "national security" and "international obligations" which occur throughout the Act. The RTNDA concluded that the regulations were unconstitutionally vague "because they would authorize NOAA to impose impermissible prior restraints and content-based regulations on the press." The RTNDA went on to say that this lack of specificity might have a chilling effect on media interest and/or investment in this new technology and suggested that NOAA's posture is overly regulatory and insufficiently sensitive to development of the remote-sensing industry. However, no commentator attempted to define these terms; rather the RTNDA formulated a standard for the judicial review of agency decisions to be included in this Preamble, and a related standard for # 960.11 of the regulations to be cross referenced in ## 960.9, 960.12, and 960.14. (The RTNDA also suggested similar language for the legislative history of revisions to the Act).

Response: NOAA recognizes that is licensing authority is subject to all Constitutional and statutory safeguards and is committed to exercising this authority with full regard for the First Amendment rights of all applicants and licensees including the press. The Act requires NOAA to consult with the Departments of Defense and State on all matters affecting national security and foreign policy interests respectively. In response to NOAA's request for consultation on these regulations, both Departments have stated that they will not require NOAA to impose any restriction on remote-sensing activities that is not essential for national security purposes or to meet international obligations.

Nothing in these regulations is intended to place any limits on access to images that would not be placed on such access here on Earth. No provision in these rules, or any action implementing the Land Remote-Sensing Commercialization Act of 1984, is intended to detract in any way from the First Amendment rights of any person including any organization which engages in news gathering and dissemination. National security, foreign policy, and international considerations will not be invoked as a basis for taking any action adverse to the interests of licenses, applicants, users unless the remedy is necessary and effective under existing judicial standards.

Where the RTNDA disagrees with the Department of State and Defense is in determining what standards apply. In the RTNDA's view, "Since restrictions would in most cases be designed to prevent journalists from publishing certain information, those restrictions - whether in the form of application denials, license conditions or license sanctions such as suspension or termination - would function as prior restraints."

The agencies disagree. In certain situations, a restriction might be imposed on dissemination of images that would amount to a prior restraint and such a restriction would be subject to review in accordance with the applicable Constitutional standards for such cases. In many cases, however, a restriction may simply be a denial of access to information, for example to photograph a defense installation, a type of restriction already in effect. (See 18 U.S.C. 795, 976.). This action would be reviewed under a different standard but, under any standard, the restrictions imposed would have to be necessary and effective in accomplishing the intended purpose. Relevant factors could include the state of the art of remote-sensing at the time of an application, particularly that of unlicensed foreign operators and the feasibility of protecting sensitive areas. These factors can only be determined in the context of an individual application. Consequently, the regulations provide for pre-application consultation and encourage discussion of the issues in a meaningful way at the earliest possible time. NOAA is committed to fostering commercial use of remote-sensing to the maximum extent possible while still protecting vital national security interests.

Comment: The RTNDA expressed concern that # 960.12(d)(1) might allow the Departments of Defense or State to insert terms and conditions into a license without any express standard to ensure that these would be constitutional.

It suggested a modification requiring that NOAA independently review conditions proposed by either agency according to the review standards proposed by the RTNDA.

Response: NOAA does not have independent authority to determine whether national security or foreign policy conditions are justified. Section 607 of the Act states that the Secretaries of Defense and State "shall be responsible for determining those conditions, consistent with the Act, necessary to meet * * *"national security concerns and international obligations. Any such conditions are reviewable in accordance with the appropriate judicial standard as discussed earlier and # 960.9 has been amended to require explicitly that the determining Secretary fully document the basis for the determination.

Comment: The Proposed Regulations should be amended to ensure that an adequate record exists for any licensing action adverse to an applicant or licensee.

Response: The Proposed Regulations recognize in several sections the necessity of an adequate record for any action. Sections 960.9, 960.11, 960.12(d)(1), and 960.14 have been amended to incorporate additional suggestions of commentators.

3.   Other Issues

Comment: The media commentators requested clarification that the Act's
nondiscriminatory access requirements will not hinder news gathering
organizations from publishing images gathered by remote-sensing before
making the data available to other purchasers, particularly competitors.

Response: Under section 104(3) of the Act, which defines the
boundaries of nondiscriminatory access, a licensed organization could
collect data from the system, screen it for newsworth items, and publish the
unenhanced data without violating the Act.   Section 104(3) of the Act, which
defines the boundaries of nondiscriminatory access, a licensed organization
could collect data from the system, screen it for newsworthy items, and
publish the unenhanced data without violating the Act.   Section 104(3)
explicitly states that a licensee need not make all its data publicly
available, but it is obliged to distribute only those scenes it saves for
its own actual use or for sale.   It simply must make available whatever data
it intends to use, or to offer for sale to one buyer, on equal terms to all
prospective buyers.   Where licensees use the data for general publication,
which by definition will make it equally available to anyone willing to buy
a newspaper or tune in a television, this distribution, coupled with a
nondiscriminatory offer of sale of the data within a reasonable time of
publication, complies with the requirement.

However, in most cases, a news organization does not publish unenhanced
data but must specifically process it to get imagery that will be meaningful
to the public.   This processing constitutes a "value-added activity" and
under section 402(b)(9) of the Act any licensed operator intending to engage
in such activities must provide a plan to ensure nondiscriminatory access to
the unenhanced data. Therefore, NOAA has added a new subsection to #
960.11(b) confirming that, where the purpose of a value-added activity is to
provide an image for widespread publication, the plan need only establish
that the unenhanced data will be made available on a nondiscriminatory basis
to all buyers at the time the image or other value-added product is
published or as promptly as reasonably possible thereafter.

Comment: EOSAT suggested that NOAA's definition of "unenhanced data" in
960.3 should refer to unprocessed or minimally processed signals and
minimally processed film products derived from such signals but should not
include film products *per se*.   EOSAT also suggested that the definition
should exclude from the concept of minimal processing any manipulations that
are not "substantial" and "irreversible" and proposed adding the following
examples of minimal processing: "contrast adjustments, geographic resampling
(for map projections and geocoded products) and spatial sharpening of data
through combination of signals collected by the licensee and having
differing spatial resolution."

EOSAT generally endorsed NOAA's interdependent definition of "value-
added activity" but suggested that this concept should refer to changes that
are "irreversible" as well as "substantial" to be consistent with the
concept of minimal processing and to sharpen to distinction between the two.

Another commentator, MBB, felt that EOSAT's suggestion with respect to
film products could "adversely affect both value adders and other remote
sensing operators" because space based remote-sensing by photographic means

"Could be adopted as a remote-sensing technique by a private remote-sensing technique by a private remote-sensing operator [and] not all film products are necessarily derived from signals."

Comment: NOAA agrees that including "irreversible" and "substantial" changes in both definitions is useful and will ensure that changes such as a simple change of format will not frustrate the purpose of section 601 of the Act.

NOAA agrees with MBB that private operators could adopt photography as a space based remote-sensing technique and, therefore, does not accept the suggestion that film will never be used as a primary medium.

NOAA also disagrees that the specific examples suggested would clarify the distinction between unenhanced and value-added data products. After reviewing a discussion provided by EOSAT in connection with its Purchase Agreement NOAA concluded that the terms "contrast adjustments" and "spatial sharpening" still must be qualified by the terms, "substantial and irreversible."

Comment: The term "substantially failed to comply" should be more clearly defined.

Response: NOAA agrees and has incorporated commentators' definition in #960-14.

Comment: The only "plans" which an applicant need provide with respect to providing nondiscriminatory access to data (#960.12) should be those required by #960.6(f) for operators also engaged in value-added activities.

Response: NOAA agrees and has cross-referenced ## 960.12 and 960.6 as requested.

Comment: The citizenship information specified by ## 960.2 and 960.6 is confusing and possibly unnecessary.

Response: NOAA agrees and has modified these sections as requested.

Comment: An officer of a corporate general partner should be able to sign an application if authorized.

Response: NOAA agrees. See #960.5(b).

Comment: The 120 days period within which the Administrator must act on an application for a license should start with the receipt of the application and should not be extended by the 21 days allocated by # 960.9 to determine whether the application is complete. *Response*: The 120 day period begins to run upon receipt of a complete application. If the application contains all the necessary information at the time it is first received, the 120 days begins to run at this time. However, if it is incomplete, the time does not begin until the necessary information is received.

Comment: Section 9601.11 is too burdensome in requiring operators engaged in value-added activities to provide a plan for ensuring nondiscriminatory access.

Response: The Act does not require such a plan for value-added products, but only for unenhanced data. Section 960.11 has been amended to clarify this point.

Comment: One commentator has indicated that the regulations may not adequately address the issue of classified information. Although privileges can be claimed to protect such information during the course of any administrative or judicial proceeding, this commentator suggested that is unclear what the impact of a successful claim of privileges would be upon the conduct and outcome of such proceedings.

Response: In light of this uncertainty NOAA intends to explore with the commentator ways of clarifying what the consequences of a successful claim of privilege would be.

The technology of remote sensing from space is developing rapidly. These regulations have been drafted in general terms to accommodate this development to the maximum extent possible. NOAA will periodically review the regulations to ensure that they do not inadvertently inhibit new commercial opportunities.

Other Actions Associated With Rulemaking

A.   *Classification Under Executive Order 12291*

NOAA has concluded that these regulations are not major because they will not result in:

(1) An annual effect on the economy of $100 million or more;

(2) A major increase in costs or prices for consumers, individual industries, Federal, state or local government agencies, or geographical regions; or

(3) Significant adverse effects on competition, employment, investment, productivity, innovation or on the ability of United States-based enterprises to compete with foreign based enterprises in domestic or export markets.

The regulations establish the procedures for licensing in accordance with the criteria established by the Act. The regulations will not result in the direct, or major indirect economic or environmental effect. They are intended to promote the U.S. space remote-sensing industry by facilitating the licensing process and by ensuring that foreign companies competing with U.S. companies in the remote-sensing market do so on an equal basis to the maximum extent practicable.

B.   Regulatory Flexibility Act (5, U.S.C. 601 et seq.)

This rule is essentially procedural and establishes a process intended to minimize any adverse impact on any entity - large or small - which may need a license to operate a remote-sensing space system. Because of the large size and cost of space remote-sensing projects, small businesses are unlikely to be able to amass the capital necessary to enter the field. The only involvement of small business concerns is likely to be as contractors or subcontractors who do not require a license. The General Counsel of the Department of Commerce has, therefore, certified that this regulation will not have a significant economic impact on a substantial number of small entities.

C.   Paperwork Reduction Act of 1960 (Pub. L. 96-511)

The information requirements for these regulations have been reviewed by the Office of Management and Budget. The control number is 0648-0174.

D.   National Environmental Policy Act

Publication of this rule does not constitute a major federal action significantly affecting the quality of the human environment. Therefore, an environmental impact statement is not required.

List of Subjects in 15 CFR Part 960

Scientific equipment, Space transportation and exploration.

Dated: July 6, 1987.

Thomas N. Pyke, Jr.

Assistant Administrator for Environmental Satellite, Data and Information Services.

Accordingly, a new Part 960 of Title 15 of the Code of Federal Regulations is added to subchapter D as follows:

PART 960 - LICENSING OF PRIVATE REMOTE-SENSING SPACE SYSTEMS

Subpart A - General

Sec.

960.1   Purpose.
960.2   Scope.
960.3   Definitions.

Subpart B - Application Process

960.4	Pre-application consultation.
960.5	General.
960.6	Information to be submitted with application.
960.7	Amendment, withdrawal, and termination of an application.
960.8	Confidentiality of information.
960.9	Review procedures.
960.10	Timely approval or denial of application and issuance of license.
960.11	Criteria for approval or denial.
960.12	Contents of license.

Subpart C - Enforcement Procedures

960-13	General.
960.14	License sanctions.
960.15	Civil penalties.
960.16	Seizure.

Authority: 15 U.S.C. 4244.

Subpart A - General

960.1   Purpose.

These regulations establish the minimum practicable procedures and
informational requirements to license and supervise the operation of a
private remote-sensing space system under Title IV of the Land Remote-
Sensing Commercialization Act of 1984 (The Act). They are intended to
facilitate the policy of the Act by encouraging development of private
sector-owned remote-sensing space systems and promote of commercialization
of land remote-sensing systems in the United States while complying with the
requirements of the Act, including:

(a) To preserve and promote the national security of the United States;

(b) To ensure that data from private operational remote-sensing space
systems will be sold on a nondiscriminatory basis; and

(c) To fulfill the international obligations of the United States.

To the extent there is a tension between the policy of promoting the
commercial use of remote-sensing systems and the policies of promoting
national security interests as determined by the Secretary of Defense or
international obligations as determined by the Secretary of State, the
Secretary of Commerce may, in his or her discretion, undertake reasonable
efforts to satisfactorily resolve the matter in favor of commercialization.

960.2   Scope.

The Act and these regulations apply to any person subject to the
jurisdiction or control of the United States who operates a private remote-

sensing space system either directly or through an affiliate or subsidiary. For the purposes of these regulations, a person, affiliate, or subsidiary is subject to the jurisdiction or control of the United States if such person is:

(a) An individual who is a citizen of the United States;

(b) A corporation, partnership, association or other entity organized or existing under the laws of the United States or any state, territory or possession thereof; or

(c) Any other private space system operator having substantial connections with the Untied States or deriving substantial benefits from U.S. law that support its international remote-sensing operations. Relevant connections include using a U.S. launch vehicle and/or platform, operating a spacecraft command and/or data acquisition station in the U.S., and processing the data at and/or marketing it from facilities within the U.S. The following examples are intended to illustrate the application of this paragraph.

Example 1. A non-U.S. corporation launches an operational remote-sensing space system using a U.S. operated launch vehicle and/or a platform launched from U.S. territory. The company operates no spacecraft command ground station in the U.S. although it has technicians and supervisors present in the U.S. to ensure integration of this foreign-built satellite or space system with the launch vehicle. The company acquires data directly from the space system and processes and distributes it from facilities outside the U.S., although it advertises the availability of data and/or information in U.S. publications.

The company is not subject to U.S. jurisdiction or control and requires no license for its remote-sensing activities.

Example 2. A company's operation is the same as in Example 1 expect that it acquires, processes and distributes the data to U.S. and foreign customers from one or more facilities with the U.S.

The company is subject to U.S. jurisdiction or control and requires a license.

Where ground activities in the U.S. are less extensive than those described above, such as mere operation of a data acquisition facility or a small retail distribution outlet for U.S. customers, the Administrator will decide on an individual basis whether the operator is subject to U.S. jurisdiction or control for purposes to Title IV. In such cases, the use of a U.S. launch vehicle and/or platform may be significant although such use alone is not a sufficient connection.

Interested persons with questions may request a formal, binding opinion from the Administrator concerning the application of these regulations to their operation. Informal opinions by agencies should not be relied upon.

960.3   Definitions.

For purposes of these regulations, the following terms have the following meanings:

Act means the Land Remote-Sensing Commercialization Act of 1984 (Pub. L. 98-365, 15 U.S.C. 4201 *et seq.*);

Administrator means the administrator of NOAA, or his designee;

affiliate means any person: (a) Which owns or controls more than 5% interest in the applicant or licensee, or b) which is under common ownership or control with the applicant or licensee;

Application means any written request submitted under this part for: (a) Issuance of a license for the operation of a private remote-sensing space system; (b) transfer or renewal of any such license; of (c) an amendment to any such license as a result of a substantial change in any of the specified terms and conditions of the license;

Basic data set means data collected by any licensed private remote-sensing space system that (a) has been selected to be maintained by the United States Government in a public archive, and (b) shall remain distinct from any inventory of data that a system operator may maintain for sales and for other purposes. Section 602 of the Act.

Appendix F

Department of Defense Directive

SUBJECT: International Transfers of Technology, Goods, Services, and Munitions

References: (a) Public Law 96-72, "The Export Administration Act of 1979," as amended (50 U.S.C. 2401 et seq.)
   (b) Public Law 94-329, "The Arms Export Control Act," as amended (22 U.S.C. 2751 et seq.)
   (c) National Security Decision Directive Number 5, "Conventional Arms Transfer Policy," July 8, 1981
   (d) through (q), see enclosure 1

A. PURPOSE

This Directive:

1. Implements relevant portions of references (a) through (c) by establishing policy, assigning responsibilities, and prescribing procedures for international transfer of defense-related technology, goods, services, and munitions.

2. Establishes the DoD International Technology Transfer (IT^2) Panel and Subpanels, whose charters are at enclosure 2.

3. Cancels DoD Directive 2030.4, DoD Directive 5030.28, and the Secretary of Defense Memorandum of December 29, 1983 (references (d), (e), and (f)).

B. APPLICABILITY AND SCOPE

1. This Directive applies to the Office of the Secretary of Defense, the Organization of the Joint Chiefs of Staff (OJCS), the Military Departments, and the Defense Agencies (hereafter referred to collectively as "DoD Components").

2. This Directive applies to all technology transfer mechanisms and shall be implemented through such processes as strategic trade licensing, munitions licensing, security assistance, and DoD research, development, and acquisition activities.

3. The policies, procedures, and responsibilities contained in NDP-1 and DoD Directive 5230.11 (references (g) and (h)) concerning disclosures of classified military information are not affected by this Directive.

C. DEFINITIONS

The terms used in this Directive are defined in enclosure 3.

D.   <u>POLICY</u>

It shall be DoD policy to treat defense-related technology as a valuable, limited national security resource, to be husbanded and invested in pursuit of national security objectives. Consistent with this policy and in recognition of the importance of international trade to a strong U.S. defense industrial base, the Department of Defense shall apply export controls in a way that minimally interferes with the conduct of legitimate trade and scientific endeavor. Accordingly, DoD Components shall:

1.   Manage transfers of technology, goods, services, and munitions consistent with U.S. foreign policy and national security objectives.

2.   Control the export of technology, goods, services, and munitions that contribute to the military potential of any country or combination of countries that could prove detrimental to U.S. security interests.

3.   Limit the transfer to any country or international organization of advanced design and manufacturing know-how regarding technology, goods, services, and munitions to those transfers that support specific national security or foreign policy objectives.

4.   Facilitate the sharing of military technology only with allies and other nations that cooperate effectively in safeguarding technology, goods, services, and munitions from transfer to nations whose interests are inimical to the United States.

5.   Give special attention to rapidly emerging and changing technologies to protect against the possibility that militarily useful technology might be conveyed to potential adversaries before adequate safeguards can be implemented.

6.   Seek, through improved international cooperation, to strengthen foreign procedures for protecting sensitive and defense-related technology.

7.   Strive, before transferring valuable defense-related technology, to ensure that such technology is shared reciprocally.

E.   <u>PROCEDURES</u>

1.   In all technology transfer cases referred for review, the DoD Components concerned shall:

a.   Consider proposed transfers of technology, goods, services, and munitions on a case-by-case basis.

b.   Conduct policy reviews, technical evaluations, operational and military mission impact assessments, and intelligence assessments of proposed transfers.

c.   Ensure that transfers of technology, goods, services, and munitions:

(1) Are consistent with U.S. national security and foreign policy objectives.

(2) Do not constitute an unreasonable risk to U.S. security in the degree to which they reduce technological lead-time.

(3) Receive positive consideration when such transfers will result in tangible and direct benefits to the defense objectives of the United States and its allies or to the defense industrial base. Such benefits should be at least equivalent to the value of the technology transferred.

d. Make sensitive transfers conditional upon agreements with allied and other nations that restrict the transfer of technology, goods, services, and munitions that harm or may harm the security of the United States and the security of U.S. allies and other friendly nations.

e. Oppose transfers of sensitive technology, goods, services, and munitions through multinational organizations in which potential adversaries participate.

f. Assess whether recipient nations:

(1) Restrict their transfer or export of U.S. technology, goods, services, and munitions to other nations who use, or may use, such technology, goods, services, and munitions against the best interests of the United States.

(2) Secure written U.S. Government agreement before reexporting U.S. technology, goods, services, and munitions.

(3) Maintain control over U.S. technology, goods, services, and munitions.

(4) Report promptly and fully to the U.S. Government any known or suspected transfers of U.S. technology, goods, services, and munitions that do not have U.S. Government approval.

(5) Transfer non-U.S. critical technology, goods, services, and munitions harmful to U.S. security.

g. Assess annually the total effect of transfers of technology, goods, services, and munitions on U.S. security, regardless of the transfer mechanisms involved.

h. Support approved DoD programs designed to inform government, Congress, industry, academia, and the public on the dangers of the loss of Western technological leadership.

2. In strategic trade cases, the DoD Components concerned shall:

a. Assess whether proposed transfers of technology and goods through actual or potential military use could threaten U.S. security, regardless of the stated end use or end user of such technology and goods.

b.   Ensure that potential transfers of technology and goods are assessed with a primary consideration to control of critical technology as described by Pub. L. 96-72 and the "DoD Militarily Critical Technologies List" (references (a) and (i)).

c.   Disapprove exceptions to the Coordinating Committee of the Consultative Group (COCOM) lists that are disadvantageous to the security of the United States and its allies.

d.   Support North Atlantic Treaty Organization (NATO) efforts to control technology and goods.

e.   Provide support to, and cooperate with, non-COCOM countries to control the transfer of militarily relevant technology and goods to the Warsaw Pact nations.

f.   Assess whether recipient nations support U.S. objectives in COCOM and the COCOM embargo.

3.   In munitions licensing cases, the DoD Components concerned shall:

a.   Give favorable consideration to transfers of services and munitions to U.S. allies and friendly nations that are intended to achieve specific U.S. defense objectives.

b.   Ensure that transfers of munitions and services involving critical technology receive special scrutiny, taking into account the importance of arms cooperation with NATO and other close friendly nations and allies, potential third-party transfers, and the protection of advanced military operational capabilities and associated technology.

c.   Ensure that decisions on munitions license applications that involve or may lead to the disclosure of classified military information are in compliance with NDP-1 and DoD Directive 5230.11 (references (g) and (h)).

4.   The DoD Components concerned shall submit unresolved technology security cases and issues to the appropriate DoD IT^2 Subpanel for resolution.

5.   Two subcommittee reports to the DoD Steering Committee on National Security and Technology Transfer (references (j) and (k), when approved, may provide additional procedural guidance affecting publications and technology monitoring.

F.   <u>COORDINATING COMMITTEE OF THE CONSULTATIVE GROUP (COCOM)</u>

1.   COCOM, founded in 1949, is an informal multinational organization made up of the NATO nations (except Iceland and Spain) and Japan. COCOM'S mission is to maintain a uniform export control system among its member nations in order to protect Western security.

2.   DoD Components concerned with strategic trade policy shall seek to strengthen COCOM by:

a.   Promoting the development of a professional secretariat.

b.   Promoting the tightening of the strategic control list.

c.   Encouraging enforcement of COCOM controls.

d.   Promoting a threshold on the COCOM list beyond which technology and goods cannot be transferred to potential adversaries.

e.   Promoting broader membership of free-world nations in COCOM and associate agreements with COCOM for advanced, industrialized nations.

f.   Promoting the establishment of a military committee to consider strategic issues related to the control programs.

g.   Providing full-time DoD policy representation to COCOM.

h.   Supporting and promoting other measures that strengthen the COCOM organization and function and that support U.S. objectives.

G.   RESPONSIBILITIES

1.   The Under Secretary of Defense for Policy (USD(P)) shall:

a.   Develop, coordinate, and issue policies relating to technology transfer control in accordance with DoD Directive 5111.1 (reference (1)).

b.   Prepare technology transfer control and enforcement policy guidance and coordinate overall application of DoD policy.

c.   Represent the Department of Defense in interagency, national, and international forums concerning policy for technology transfer control and enforcement matters.

d.   For technology transfer policy matters, serve as DoD point of contact for foreign governments, international agencies, other federal agencies, interagency groups, industry, and DoD Components.

e.   Act as the DoD receiving point for all strategic trade, COCOM, and munitions license cases.

f.   Conduct policy reviews on technology, goods, services, and munitions transfer cases.

g.   Prepare the coordinated DoD position for strategic trade, COCOM, and munitions license cases. If the projected recommendation differs from recommendations of the DoD Components concerned, advise the DoD Components of the recommendation and supporting rationale in sufficient time to permit submission of the issue to the DoD IT^2 Subpanel A before issuing the position.

h.   Issue coordinated DoD recommendations on strategic trade, COCOM, and munitions transfer cases to the Commerce and State Departments.

      i.   Develop and maintain comprehensive reference data bases on technology, goods, services, and munitions transfer matters that are accessible to all DoD Components.

      j.   Provide to DoD Components a weekly update of the disposition of significant transfer cases.

      k.   Provide executive direction of the DoD IT^2 Panel in accordance with enclosure 2.

      l.   Develop, review, and negotiate international

      m.   Assess, with the support of the Director, Defense Intelligence Agency (DIA), and the Chairman, National Disclosure Policy Committee, recipient nations':

      (1) Laws, regulations, and internal operating procedures to determine their ability to enforce technology security and control provisions of applicable U.S. export license stipulations, specific cooperative program agreements with the U.S. Government, COCOM embargoes, and other industrial and government agreements.

      (2) Reliability in maintaining control over technology, goods, services, and munitions that originate in the United States and whose transfer to other nations may be against the best interests of the United States.

      (3) Reliability in securing prior written U.S. Government approval before exporting technology, goods, services, and munitions originating in the United States to other nations.

      (4) Reliability and promptness in reporting known or suspected transfers of U.S. technology, goods, services, and munitions that were not approved by the U.S. Government.

      (5) Support of U.S. objectives in COCOM and the COCOM embargo.

      (6) Cooperation and support for the principle of sharing technology of comparable value with the United States.

      (7) Reliability in preventing transfer to potential adversaries of non-U.S. critical technology, goods, services, and munitions harmful to the U.S. security.

      n.   Request the Under Secretary of Defense for Research and Engineering (USDR&E) to provide technical advisors and consultants necessary to support development of DoD technology transfer policy.

      o.   Assess annually the total effect of technology, goods, services, and munitions transfers on the security of the United States, regardless of the transfer mechanism involved.

      p.   Support the U.S. intelligence and enforcement communities in their efforts to halt or control the flow of technology, goods, services, and munitions to potential adversaries.

q.   Establish, through the appropriate DoD IT[2] Subpanel, working groups and task forces to develop ways and means to protect technology from exploitation by potential adversaries.

2.   The <u>Under Secretary of Defense for Research and Engineering</u> shall:

a.   Manage overall DoD technical and acquisition efforts related to technology, goods, services, and munitions transfer it accordance with DoD Directive 5129.1 (reference (o)).

b.   Oversee implementation of DoD technology transfer policy for all research, development, and acquisition matters.

c.   For research, development, and acquisition matters, act as DoD point of contact with industry, other federal agencies, interagency groups, DoD Components, academia, and appropriate international forums.

d.   Coordinate the technical review of strategic trade, COCOM, and munitions cases and establish the DoD technical positions, with supporting rationales, regarding the proposed transfer of technology, goods, services, and munitions.

e.   Develop and administer programs to identify and define lists of militarily critical technologies that should be controlled for export, including necessary guidelines.

f.   Manage technical efforts in support of DoD participation in and implementation of studies and analyses of COCOM, U.S. export controls, and related technology, goods, services, and munitions transfer matters.

g.   Develop the DoD technical portion for the "DoD Militarily Critical Technologies List" (reference (1)) revisions and COCOM negotiations.

h.   Provide technical advisors and consultants as needed to support the USD(P) in the development of DoD technology transfer policy.

i.   Provide technical support of DoD views in interagency, national, and international forums of technology, goods, services, and munitions transfer matters.

j.   Provide technical support for USD(P) assessments of the foreign availability of technology, goods, services, and munitions.

k.   Develop, review, and negotiate international agreements in accordance with this Directive, DoD Directive 5530.3, and DoD Instruction 2050.1 (references (m) and (n)).

1.   Develop and maintain a comprehensive technical data base for technology, goods, services, and munitions transfer cases.

m.   Participate on the DoD IT[2] Panel and Subpanels in accordance with enclosure 2.

n.   Support the U.S. intelligence and enforcement communities in their efforts to halt or control the flow of technology, technical data, goods, services, and munitions to potential adversaries.

o.   For technology transfer research cases:

(1)   Serve as the receiving point in the Department of Defense.
(2)   Obtain a policy position from the USD(P).

(3)   Conduct reviews and prepare coordinated DoD recommendations, with supporting rationales.

(4)   Advise DoD Components if the projected recommendation differs from their recommendations and provide an opportunity for the DoD Components to submit the issue to the DoD IT^2 Subpanel B before issuing a DoD position. If a case is appealed, within 15 days the case shall be decided and all interested parties notified or the case shall be referred to the Deputy Secretary of Defense or Secretary of Defense for a final decision.

(5)   Issue, after the appeal process is completed, the coordinated DoD recommendation.

3.   The <u>Assistant Secretary of Defense (International Security Policy)</u> (ASD(ISP)) shall:

a.   Monitor compliance with this Directive through the Deputy Assistant Secretary of Defense (International Economic, Trade, and Security Policy) (DASD(IETSP)).

b.   Chair the DoD IT^2 Panel and participate on the DoD IT^2 Subpanels in accordance with enclosure 2.

4.   The <u>Chairman of the Joint Chiefs of Staff</u> shall:

a.   Conduct and provide operational and military mission impact assessments on technology, goods, services, and munitions transfer issues, as requested.

b.   Provide operational expertise and military judgment in interagency, national, and international forums on technology, goods, services, and munitions transfer matters.

c.   Participate on the DoD IT^2 Panel and Subpanels in accordance with enclosure 2.

5.   The <u>Director, Defense Intelligence Agency</u>, shall:

a.   Formulate DoD coordinated intelligence assessments concerning the types and numbers of illegal transfer of technology, goods, services, and munitions and the associated transfer mechanisms.

b.   Designate a point of contact to represent the DIA on technology, goods, services, and munitions transfer matters.

c. Conduct and provide intelligence reviews on technology, goods, services, and munitions transfer cases.

e. Conduct end-user checks on the declared ultimate consignee on technology, goods, services, and munitions transfer cases.

f. Provide intelligence expertise in interagency, national, and international forums on technology, goods, services, and munitions transfer matters.

g. Provide intelligence concerning the total effect of transfers of technology, goods, services, and munitions on U.S. security.

h. Participate on the DoD IT^2 Panel and Subpanels in accordance with enclosure 2.

i. Assist in identifying and assessing critical technology.

6. The Heads of DoD Components shall:

a. Designate a point of contact in their respective Component for technology, goods, services, and munitions transfer matters.

b. Conduct assessments of proposed technology, goods, services, and munitions transfer cases as required and provide coordinated positions.

c. Assist in identifying and assessing critical technology and in supporting DoD participation in export control list reviews.

d. Participate on the DoD IT^2 Panel and Subpanels in accordance with enclosure 2.

e. Consistent with this Directive, DoD Directive 5530.3, and DoD Instruction 2050.1 (references (m) and (n), coordinate the development and negotiation of international agreements pertaining to technology, goods, services, and munitions transfers.

f. Assure the calculation of nonrecurring cost recoupment charges in accordance with DoD Directive 2140.2 (reference (p)).

H. **EFFECTIVE DATE AND IMPLEMENTATION**

This Directive is effective immediately. Forward two copies of implementing documents to the Assistant Secretary of Defense (International Security Policy) within 120 days.

Caspar W. Weinberger
Secretary of Defense

Enclosure - 3
1. References
2. DoD International Technology Transfer (IT^2) Panel and Subpanels
3. Definitions

Index

About the Author

MANLEY RUTHERFORD IRWIN is Professor of Economics at the University of New Hampshire. The author of numerous books and articles that address issues of U.S. telecommunications and public policy, he has served as consultant to the Federal Communications Commission, the Office of Telecommunications Planning, and the President's Task Force on Communications Policy.